Birds and Birding in Wyoming's Bighorn Mountains Region

Jacqueline L. Canterbury
Department of Biology
Sheridan College
Sheridan, WY 82801

Paul A. Johnsgard
School of Biological Sciences
University of Nebraska–Lincoln
Lincoln, NE 68588

and

Helen F. Downing
(1917–2010)

Zea Books
Lincoln, Nebraska 2013

Text copyright © 2013 J. L. Canterbury & P. A. Johnsgard
Drawings copyright © 2013 P. A. Johnsgard

ISBN 978-1-60962-040-0 paperback
ISBN 978-1-60962-041-7 ebook

Set in Chaparral Pro types.
Design and composition by Paul Royster.

Zea Books are published by the University of Nebraska–Lincoln Libraries

Electronic (pdf) edition available online at
http://digitalcommons.unl.edu/zeabook/

Print edition can be ordered from Lulu.com, at
http://www.lulu.com/spotlight/unllib

Dedication

The first edition of this book was dedicated to and prepared specifically for the more than 100 observers who contributed their information over a twenty-five year period. The second edition is dedicated to the memory of Helen Downing, who graciously allowed J. L. Canterbury and P. A. Johnsgard to update and expand it.

Abstract

The Bighorn Mountains consist of a relatively well-isolated north-south mountain range in north-central Wyoming that had their origins during the early Cenozoic era, 50-65 million years ago. The present-day Bighorn range is more than 100 miles in length and has a maximum elevation of 13,167 feet (Cloud Peak), only slightly less than the highest peak in Wyoming (Gannett Peak, at 13,804 feet). The mountains are flanked to the west by the Bighorn River basin, and to the east by the Powder River basin, both of which support only semi-desert vegetation dominated by sagebrush. Elevations of the Powder River basin near the Montana border and the Bighorn River near Worland are below 3,700 feet, and annual precipitation at Worland averages less than ten inches annually. The nearly 10,000-foot range of regional elevations and associated climate variations have produced a wide variation of terrestrial vegetation types. The mountains are still largely covered with native grasslands and mostly coniferous forest vegetation, the latter ranging from juniper scrub at low altitudes through ponderosa and lodgepole pines at middle elevations, to subalpine fir, Engelmann spruce and limber pine transitional to alpine tundra, which begins at 9,800–11,400 feet. Most of the still-forested areas lie within the 1.1 million-acre Bighorn National Forest.

We defined the Bighorn region as encompassing or about 6,800 square miles (latilong blocks 4 and 5), and determined that at least 327 bird species have been reliably reported from the region, plus 15 species of hypothetical status. This compared with a total of 427 species reported for all of Wyoming as of 2010 (Faulkner, 2010). Breeding within the region has been confirmed for 190 species. Among the breeders, 77 species have breeding ranges that were classified as to having an either clearly eastern-oriented or western-oriented affinity in North America. Of these, 55 (71 percent) were judged to be western-oriented and 22 (29 percent) eastern-oriented, indicating that the strongest zoogeographic affinities of Bighorn region birds are with western North America.

Species descriptions indicate relative abundance, breeding status by latilong, locality/date records for rarer species, and other relevant information. Many regional birding areas are described and mapped, and results of recent regional breeding bird surveys and seasonal bird counts are summarized. Line drawings illustrate representatives of each of the 53 avian families documented for the region, and there are more than 60 literature citations.

Table of Contents

Preface 11
Foreword to the 1st Edition (1990) 12
Acknowledgments for the 1st Edition (1990) 12
Seasonal Abundance and Distributional Terminology . 13
Molt, Plumage, and Age Terminology 14
Foreword to the 2nd Edition (2013) 14
Acknowledgments for the 2nd Edition (2013) 16

Part I. The Bighorn Mountains of Wyoming

Physiography and Vegetation Zones in the Bighorn
    Mountains 19
Bird Distribution in the Bighorn Mountains 23
Geology and Biogeography of the Bighorn Mountains . 27
Notes on Regional Birding 34
Birding Areas by Vegetation Type 35
Suggested Birding Locations and Site Descriptions . . 36
Birding Loops
    Sheridan and South Sheridan Loop 37
    North Sheridan Loop 41
    Dayton Loop 45
    Story Loop 48
    Buffalo Loop 53
Birding in the Bighorn Mountains Roadless Areas . . . 56
Suggested Roadless-Area Birding Trails 57
Birding by Car in the Bighorn Mountains 59

Part II. Annotated List of Regional Birds

Family Anatidae: Waterfowl 64
Family Phasianidae: Partridges, Grouse & Pheasants . . 75
Family Gaviidae: Loons 79
Family Podicipedidae: Grebes 81
Family Phalacrocoracidae: Cormorants 84

Family Pelecanidae: Pelicans	85
Family Ardeidae: Bitterns & Herons	86
Family Threskiornithidae: Ibises	90
Family Cathartidae: American Vultures	92
Family Pandionidae: Ospreys	94
Family Accipitridae: Hawks & Eagles	96
Family Rallidae: Rails & Coots	102
Family Gruidae: Cranes	104
Family Charadriidae: Plovers	106
Family Recurvirostridae: Stilts and Avocets	109
Family Scolopacidae: Sandpipers & Snipes	111
Family Laridae: Gulls & Terns	119
Family Stercorariidae: Jaegers	123
Family Columbidae: Pigeons & Doves	125
Family Cuculidae: Cuckoos	127
Family Tytonidae: Barn Owls	129
Family Strigidae: Typical Owls	130
Family Caprimulgidae: Poorwills & Nighthawks	134
Family Apodidae: Swifts	136
Family Trochilidae: Hummingbirds	138
Family Alcedinidae: Kingfishers	140
Family Picidae: Woodpeckers	141
Family Falconidae: Falcons	146
Family Tyrannidae: American Flycatchers	149
Family Laniidae: Shrikes	154
Family Vireonidae: Vireos	156
Family Corvidae: Crows, Jays & Magpies	158
Family Alaudidae: Larks	162
Family Hirundinidae: Swallows	164
Family Paridae: Titmice & Chickadees	168
Family Sittidae: Nuthatches	170
Family Certhiidae: Creepers	172
Family Troglodytidae: Wrens	174
Family Polioptilidae: Gnatcatchers	177
Family Cinclidae: Dippers	179
Family Regulidae: Kinglets	181

Contents

    Family Turdidae: Thrushes 183
    Family Mimidae: Mockingbirds & Relatives 188
    Family Sturnidae: Starlings 190
    Family Motacillidae: Pipits 191
    Family Bombycillidae: Waxwings 193
    Family Calcariidae: Longspurs and Snow Buntings . . . 195
    Family Parulidae: American Warblers 197
    Family Emberizidae: Towhees & Sparrows 205
    Family Cardinalidae: Cardinals & Grosbeaks 215
    Family Icteridae: Blackbirds, Orioles & Bobolink . . . 219
    Family Fringillidae: Northern Finches 224
    Family Passeridae: Old World Sparrows 230
    Hypothetical and Questionable Species 231

Appendix
    Tables 1–3: Regional North American Breeding Bird
        Surveys (BBS) 233
    Table 4: Christmas Bird Counts (CBC) for Story/Big
        Horn, Sheridan, Buffalo, Wyo. 241

    References 242
    Index to Species 247
    About the Authors 251

List of Maps
    Major Birding Locations of North Central Wyoming . . 28
    Sheridan and South Sheridan Loop 39
    North Sheridan Loop 42
    Dayton Loop 46
    Story Loop 49
    Story, Wyoming 52
    Buffalo Loop 54

Preface

Helen Davidson Downing was born in Montgomery, Alabama, in 1917. Before she started school, the Davidson family moved to Monett, a small town in southwest Missouri where her father worked for the St. Louis & San Francisco ("Frisco") Railroad. Helen graduated from Monett High School in 1935, and during World War II attended air-traffic control school where she met her future husband, Darrel Downing. Helen worked in air traffic control as a weather specialist during the war and for a few years after. Helen and Darrel married in Kansas City, Missouri in 1947 and a short time later they moved to Laramie, Wyoming, Darrel's new air traffic control duty station. Their daughter, Ariel, was born in Laramie. The family later moved to Sheridan, Wyoming. Helen worked occasionally in air traffic control, and had jobs in local businesses and as registrar at Sheridan College, the local community college.

Helen's interest in birding began in Sheridan around 1960 and after retirement she spent innumerable hours studying birds in the Sheridan area and around north central Wyoming. She loved to carefully observe birds and record their habits. Her many reports are known for their thoroughness and meticulous detail. Helen was co-author on the 1982 book *Wyoming Avian Atlas*, which was updated and incorporated into the *Wyoming Bird and Mammal Atlas* published in 1992 by the Wyoming Game and Fish Department. The Department continually updates this monumental work and the later editions (1992, 2004, 2012) are titled *Atlas of Birds, Mammals, Amphibians, and Reptiles in Wyoming*. She was editor and contributor to the 1990 book *Birds of North Central Wyoming and the Bighorn National Forest, 1966-1990*. Helen also served as a regional editor for the American Birding Association's journal *American Birds*.

Helen Downing passed away on February 20, 2010, and now rests in the Sheridan Municipal Cemetery, near a row of tall pine trees, from which the birds can be heard singing in the early mornings.

Contributed by Ariel Downing

More information on Helen Downing's birding records can be found at the Sheridan County Fulmer Public Library in the Wyoming Room: http://www.sheridanwyolibrary.org

Foreword to the 1st Edition (1990)

Development of the Project. The late Platt H. Hall and the late Jesse T. (Tom) Kessinger were the pioneer birders. Platt and Tom searched out "best birding spots" and laid a good foundation for those who followed. They began keeping written records of bird observations in 1966: Hall from 1966 to mid-1977 and Kessinger from 1966 to mid-1972. The editor kept written records from 1970 to the present (1990). The collection of observations from other birders was begun by the editor in 1970, and the unpublished manuscript was called "Sheridan Area Birds". Names of the observers who contributed to this project are not listed here, to eliminate the possibility of inadvertently omitting someone. The species accounts have been taken strictly from the record of bird observations compiled by the editor. Supporting evidence is available to substantiate all entries. Please give proper credit if any of the information herein is used in another publication. Publishing of these data was made possible entirely by private funds and is a non-profit project.

Area Covered. The associated map shows the area from which reports have been received. This is roughly from the Wyoming-Montana border on the north to the southern city limits of Buffalo and from the Powder River on the east to the western boundary of the Bighorn National Forest.

The Seasons. The seasonal division used by *American Birds* is used here: Spring: March to May; Summer: June & July; Fall: August to November; Winter: December to February.

Abbreviations. BLM = Bureau of Land Management; C. G. = Camp Ground; L4 & 5 = Latilongs 4 & 5; F. R. = Forest Service Road; P. G. = Picnic Ground; REA = Rural Electrification Association; R. S. = U. S. Forest Service Ranger Station; USF&W = U. S. Fish & Wildlife Service; USFS = U. S. Forest Service, Tongue District; U. W. = University of Wyoming; WG&F = Wyoming Game & Fish Department, District 3; V. A. = Veterans Administration.

Acknowledgments for the 1st Edition (1990)

Special credit To Michael Humphris for word processor instruction, for creating the graphics, for reviewing the manuscript, and for help in distribution of the publication; to Melinda Biehl for proofreading the entire manuscript; to Dr. Kenneth L. Diem for advice on taxonomic order; to Ariel Downing for providing manuscript procedure; to Harold Golden and Carol and Charles Orr for Bighorn National Forest information; to Geoffrey Lear for researching production costs; to Pete Widener for reviewing the raptor section; to Bob Williams for reviewing the game bird section; to Roger Wilson for creating the map of the area; and to Dr. Phillip Wright for counseling and support for the project.

Seasonal Abundance and Distributional Terminology

The following terms used to describe relative regional abundance:

Abundant — common species that are always seen and notable for their large numbers
Common — always or almost always encountered on every outing
Fairly common — usually encountered in small numbers, but sometimes in large numbers in favored situations.
Uncommon — not usually encountered unless a special search is made, and even then in only small numbers.
Rare — more than 10 regional records but generally not expected
Extremely rare — fewer than 10 records

The following terms used to describe seasonal occurrence:

Transient — A seasonal migrant
Resident — Present throughout the year
Summer resident — Breeding in summer is known or likely
Summer visitant — Breeding in summer is unknown or unlikely
Winter visitant — A species that typically arrives in fall and departs in spring

Latilong: A latilong (abbreviated "L") is the area bounded on all sides by a single degree of latitude and longitude, sometimes called a "degree block." L4 & L5 respectively refer to latilongs 4 and 5 (as in the *Atlas of Birds, Mammals, Reptiles and Amphibians in Wyoming*), counting left to right from top left corner of state; Latilong 4 lies to the west of 107 degrees W. Longitude (approximately the longitude of Story); Latilong 5 is located to the east. The latilong concept is useful in distributional studies because these rectangular one-degree blocks are nearly uniform in size at Wyoming's latitude, and populations can thereby be easily mapped in a grid-like manner. In Wyoming, latilong blocks are approximately 50 x 70 miles in length; the two latilongs included within this book's coverage represent approximately 6.800 square miles, or about seven percent of Wyoming's total 97,809 square-mile area.

Molt, Plumage, and Age Terminology

Molt and plumage cycles differ greatly among species and strongly affect the appearance of birds. With a few exceptions, the plumages of females and immature birds are inconspicuous and are less variable between species than are the breeding plumages of males. Those species having single annual adult molts show little or no seasonal change in plumage, except for any caused by fading or feather wear. Species having only annual molts and year-around adult ("definitive") plumages are nearly always monogamous, often with long-term pair bonds.

Those species with two molts per year usually show marked seasonal plumage change, at least in one sex. The term "basic plumage" refers to the feather appearance of birds among such species molting after the breeding-season (this dull plumage is often called the "eclipse plumage" in male ducks), while the term "alternate plumage" (often called the nuptial plumage) refers to courtship and breeding-season feathering in these species. Species with two molts annually and in which the males have distinctive nuptial plumages are often non-monogamous, or may be monogamous but establish or reestablish pair bonds every year.

"Dependent young" refers to those still in the nest ("nestlings"), or mobile young (chicks, ducklings, colts, etc.) still being cared for by the adult(s). Confirmation of breeding is the record of an active nest or of dependent young. Many very young birds have distinctive "juvenile plumages" in which they first gain the power of flight, or "fledge." This "fledging period" may vary among species from less than 10 days to more than 100 days. Newly fledged and still-dependent birds are called "fledglings," and later are called juveniles while they retain their initial coat of contour feathers. When several years are required to attain maturity, intermediate "immature" or "sub-adult" plumage stages may also be recognized.

Foreword to the 2nd Edition (2013)

This new edition was jointly undertaken in 2009 by Jacqueline Canterbury and Paul Johnsgard, with the permission of Ariel Downing. We believed that an updated account would be useful to people interested in learning more about the birds of this ornithologically interesting east-west transition region, which lies between the Black Hills, which are mostly eastern in their bird fauna, and the Rocky Mountains, in which the birds are predominantly western oriented.

Jacqueline Canterbury has provided descriptions of the vegetation zones and bird distributions in the Bighorn area. She also provided notes on regional birding loops, described birding locations and site descriptions, and helped design the associated maps. She also assumed the major role in updating regional records and describing recent changes in regional species presence and abundance, with special attention directed toward the sandhill crane.

Paul Johnsgard updated and expanded the species accounts and the avian taxonomy, and provided an account of the zoogeographic significance and other ecological aspects of the bird life of the Bighorn Mountains. Space did not allow for detailed species descriptions beyond their status and distributions, but brief summaries of habits and ecology have been provided by Johnsgard for all regularly occurring species. Additional life history information for all the Rocky Mountains and Great Plains regularly breeding species can be found elsewhere (Johnsgard (2009a, 2009b).

Species nomenclature and overall taxonomy have been updated to confirm with recent (2013) usage of the American Ornithologists' Union (A.O.U.). Only those records obtained since Helen Downing's 1990 summary that are deemed of significance have been cited in this new edition; these sources include Faulkner (2010), Orabona *et al.* (2010), eBird, Christmas Counts, Breeding Bird Surveys, personal observations and others. Since the 1990 edition, several new species have been added to the regional list, partly as a result of taxonomic changes by the A.O.U. as to accepted species limits. The graph-like summaries of weekly occurrences included in the first edition were considered to be of limited current value in the light of recent global warming trends, and have been excluded, and replaced by summaries of monthly records for migrant species. Average spring arrival dates reported by Helen Downing for the period 1966–1988 are also provided; because of recent climate changes they probably should be adjusted earlier by as much as two weeks.

The present edition includes a total of 327 documented species, of which 56 are considered as extremely rare. Another 15 species for which evidence of occurrence is still inadequate are considered as hypothetical. The region thus supports about 250 species that range from abundant to rare. For the entire state of Wyoming, Faulkner (2010) accepted 427 species (including 243 breeders), as well as 27 more inadequately documented species,.

We have also summarized 1990–2009 Christmas Bird Count data for the three locations (Sheridan, Big Horn–Story, and Buffalo), and North American Migration Counts (Spring Bird Counts) for Johnson County, 1984–2001, and Sheridan County, 2009–2012. The latter counts are patterned much like the Audubon Christmas Bird Counts in that a day is spent counting birds in a specified area, keeping track of hours and miles in travel, and-or during feeder-watching. However, the area observed for a single count includes an entire county, rather than being limited to a circumscribed count circle as required in Christmas Counts. The Spring Bird Counts are made on the second Saturday in May, to coincide with the period of maximum spring migration.

Breeding Bird Surveys have been summarized for six regional locations having diverse plant and bird communities, and population trends data have been summarized for many species where these data are statistically significant. For this edition we have more clearly defined the geographic limits of data-inclusion as extending from 106–108 degrees W. longitude, and from 44–45 degrees N. latitude, encompassing latilongs 4 & 5, as defined in the *Atlas of Birds, Mammals, Reptiles and Amphibians in Wyoming* (Orabona *et al.*, 2010). The study area thus includes all of Sheridan County and parts of Big Horn, Johnson and Washakie counties.

Except for a drawing of a Red Crossbill, which was done by Jeanne Konkel for the cover of the earlier edition, the line drawings illustrating family representatives were done by Johnsgard. Miscellaneous and eBird records for rare species have been summarized through spring, 2013, and late information was added until the manuscript was finished in the summer of 2013.

Acknowledgments for the 2nd Edition (2013)

The participation of hundreds of people in performing Breeding Bird Surveys, Christmas Bird Counts and Spring Migration Counts allowed for the accumulation of the long-term regional population data presented here. Deane Bjerke provided summaries of data from the Buffalo Spring Count, and Charlie Gibson provided summaries of data for the Sheridan Spring Count. Many individuals helped Jackie Canterbury in her birding trips, locality surveys, and data collection, including Jean Daly and Rob Davidson. The support of the local Audubon Society at all stages is highly appreciated. Vistara Parham and Jenny Williams have allowed many people to view the birds at their feeders. Others who provided helpful information included Douglas Faulkner, Matt Fraker, and Andrea Orabona. Persons interested in becoming involved in learning more about regional birds, and enjoying those of the

Acknowledgments for the 2ⁿᵈ Edition

Bighorn region should contact both the local Audubon chapter and Jackie Canterbury at jackie.canterbury@gmail.com in Sheridan, Wyoming.

Rob Davidson provided help with driving to local sites, and his knowledge of the Bighorn Mountains was invaluable. Roger Wilson provided the original regional map and outlined the new birding route maps. Many thanks to Wolfgang Schwartz who produced the final birding maps. Don Brewer, BLM Buffalo Field Office, provided valuable information on raptors. Jean Daly provided morale support and local knowledge. Ken and Barbara Shuster have allowed Jackie to bird on the grounds of the Bradford Brinton in cooperation with Science Kids and the leadership of Sarah Mentock. The assistance of Dr. D. Knight in helping to update vegetational information is greatly appreciated. The editing and book design were done by Prof. Paul Royster, Coordinator of Scholarly Communications, University Libraries, University of Nebraska-Lincoln, who also arranged for the hard-copy version to be published by Lulu Enterprises. We appreciate and gratefully acknowledge the generous support of and use of the facilities of Sheridan College and the University of Nebraska–Lincoln.

Part I
The Bighorn Mountains of Wyoming

Physiography and Vegetation Zones in the Bighorn Mountains

by Jacqueline L. Canterbury

Physiography

The Bighorn Mountains were named for the regional abundance of bighorn sheep (Urbanek, 1988). This mountain range of north-central Wyoming reaches a maximum of 13,167 feet between the Powder River Basin to the east and the Bighorn Basin to the west. The range is 120 miles long and about 30 miles wide (Hoffman and Alexander, 1976). The Pryor Mountains sit to the northwest, and the Owl Creek range to the southwest. The Owl Creek range is the only upland connection between the Bighorns and the Rocky Mountains to the west. There are precipitation differences associated with elevational differences and airflow patterns producing a more arid pattern on the western slope. These differences have a direct effect on both vegetation and bird life (Despain, 1973).

Vegetation Zones

Vegetation zones are altitudinally distributed in the Bighorn Mountains, as they are elsewhere in the Rocky Mountains. The dominant tree assemblages of the Bighorn Mountains at higher elevations are lodgepole pine (*Pinus contorta*) and Engelmann spruce-subalpine fir (*Picea engelmanni–Abies lasiocarpa*). Ponderosa pine (*Pinus ponderosa*), trembling aspen (*Populus tremuloides*), limber pine (*Pinus flexilis*), and Douglas-fir (*Psuedotsuga menziesii*) are more common at low-elevations, but are less common in general. At higher elevations from about 8,200 feet to 9,500 feet subalpine fir and Engelmann spruce are typical. These are interspersed with subalpine meadows.

At intermediate altitude from 7,000 to 9,500 feet, lodgepole pine forms a nearly continuous forest. At still lower elevations from 6,500 to 7,500 feet, Douglas-fir forests occur commonly between the lodgepole forest higher up and the ponderosa pine woodlands below. Ponderosa pine forest occurs in the eastern Bighorn foothills from about 4,300 feet to 6,100 feet. However, on the drier western slope ponderosa pine is replaced by a juniper–sagebrush community. Additionally, in arid foothill areas mountain-mahogany is common on rocky soils. On north facing slopes of canyons on the western slope, Douglas-fir forms a closed canopy (Meyer *et al.*, 2003).

In the Bighorns, low elevation grasslands and shrublands transition into escarpments and mountain foothills that are crowned by mountains. The foothills grade into coniferous forests, the latter found primarily in the mountains where temperature, moisture, and nutrients are more favorable. Scattered throughout the forest landscapes are meadows and aspen groves, finally terminated by alpine tundra above treeline. The dramatic changes in elevation have resulted in the evolution of several climate-based biological zones. Birds have evolved and adapted to utilize the resources in these specific environmentally adapted communities of plants and associated animals, so it is important to describe them if one is to understand their local distribution and abundance patterns. The major Bighorn Mountain landscapes and their associated birds are as follows:

Riparian: Riparian (riverine) landscapes represent transitional areas from rivers and streams to the adjacent lands, and provide some of the most biologically productive environments for birds. Though riparian areas represent only about one percent of the western region, they are known to have a remarkably high value for wildlife, especially birds (Montgomery, 1996; Knopf *et al.*, 1988). The high level of biodiversity in riparian habitats is related to its structural diversity that provides for roosting, nesting, and other cover (Slater, 2006). Rosenberg (2004) estimated that about 50 percent of breeding birds in Wyoming are tied to water in some way, preferring riparian habitats and wetlands. The major drainages and associated riparian wetlands, such as the Powder and Bighorn rivers are wooded with a mix of plains cottonwood (*Populus deltoides*), boxelder (*Acer negundo*), and peach-leaf willow (*Salix amygdaloides*). On the western slope of the Bighorn range, narrowleaf cottonwood (*Populus angustifolia*) rather than plains cottonwood is common (Faulkner, 2010).

Marshes, Wetlands, Reservoirs, and Lakes: These habitats represent areas where water is present most or all of the time. Water provides many excellent attributes attractive to birds. Marshes are shallow wetlands with vegetation such as emergent cattails, rushes and sedges that often provide important nesting cover and food sources for birds. Deeper and larger wetlands often contain submerged aquatic plants that are important foods for aquatic birds as well as other species. There are several reservoirs that are normally deep, but some, such as the locally notable Moore's Reservoir, provide vegetation similar to that of typical wetlands. As long as the reservoirs do not fluctuate excessively in water depth, they are good places to attract birds. There are many alpine lakes distributed throughout the higher altitudes of the Bighorn Mountains that have been created by glaciers. These areas are usually not particularly attractive to birds. On the other hand, a lower altitude lake such as Lake DeSmet is probably one of the most important lakes in the region in its attraction to birds.

Meadow: Meadows are dominated by grasses, sedges, and forbs and comprise much of the non-forested portion of the landscape. Forbs become increasingly important in the Bighorn Mountains, and because of this mixture of non-woody vegetation, these mountain grasslands are referred to as meadows. These meadows are widespread and extend over large areas of the Bighorn National Forest. Collectively lupine (*Lupinus sericeus*) and balsamroot (*Balsmorhiza saggitaria*) are two dominant forbs that provide a wonderful spring floral display across the meadows.

Alpine Tundra: The alpine tundra zone includes vegetation that is above treeline. Plants in this environment grow close to the ground where they are more sheltered from climatic extremes. The treeless mountaintops are home to perennial forbs, sedges, shrubs, and grasses such as bluegrass (*Poa alpina*), wheatgrass (*Agropyron latiglume*), and fescue (*Festuca* spp.) Few birds breed in this extreme habitat, and those that do are typically very specialized for breeding during the short summer seasons, tolerating high winds, low humidity, and great fluctuations in daily temperatures (Meyers *et al.*, 2003). The most typical breeding bird of the alpine tundra is the American Pipit. Other species such as the White-crowned Sparrow, Horned Lark, and possibly the Black Rosy-Finch breed locally in this zone.

Subalpine Forest: Forests cover about 62 percent of the Bighorn National Forest (USDA Forest Service, 1994). Owing to altitudinal changes in precipitation, temperatures, wind effects, and substrates, there are marked patterns of altitudinal zonation in the forest. For example, starting at

8,500 feet up to the alpine, subalpine fir and Engelmann spruce are the dominant species. Engelmann spruce and fir in the subalpine can survive to a very old age – up to 500 years for spruce and 200 years for fir (Meyers *et al.*, 2003). Limber pine often extends from the subalpine zone to the lower elevation ponderosa pine zone (States and States, 2004). The best example of this spruce-fir forest type is in the northern part of the Bighorn Mountains.

Middle Elevation Forest: The most common tree species and the most common forest type at middle elevations (7,545 to 9,000 feet) is the lodgepole pine. This forest type comprise about 33 percent of the Bighorn National Forest land area. Lodgepole pines are usually relatively short-lived because they are replaced by other slower-growing but more shade-tolerant trees. However, individual trees as old as 500 years have been found in areas too dry to support spruce-fir forests (Meyers *et al.*, 2003).

Low Elevation Montane Forest: The forest zone immediately below the middle elevation forest is typically below about 7,500 feet and is dominated by ponderosa pine, but it also includes species such as Douglas-fir and limber pine. The seed-caching strategy of the Clark's Nutcracker to provide winter foods is largely responsible for the dissemination of limber pine seeds (Knight, 1994). The most extensive ponderosa pine forests are found on the more mesic eastern slopes of the Bighorn Mountains that comprise 12 percent of the Bighorn National Forest land area (Meyers *et al.*, 2003).

Juniper Woodland: Rocky Mountain juniper (*Juniperus scopulorum*) occurs in the dry lower western foothills of the Bighorn range and in the Bighorn Canyon area, where it occurs from about 3,600-6200 feet (Knight, 1994; Despain, 1973). Besides providing thick cover, the juniper berries provide an important winter food source for a variety of birds and mammals. The waxwings and solitaires forage largely on juniper during this period. Some stands of juniper, such as those in the Shell Canyon Natural Research Area, attract remarkably large numbers of solitaires in winter.

Aspen: Trembling aspen (*Populus tremuloides*) groves are surprisingly uncommon in the Bighorn National Forest, and occupy only one percent of the forest lands (Meyers *et al.*, 2003). Aspen occurs most typically in wet ravines and valley bottoms (Knight, 1994). Larger and older aspen trees are important for cavity-nesting birds because woodpeckers drill in their soft wood, providing homes for them and other cavity nesters, such as bluebirds, chickadees, and small owls. The aspen buds and catkins are seasonally important for many birds.

Sagebrush: Eight ecologically diverse species of sagebrush (*Artemisia* spp.) are adapted to the intermountain basins of Wyoming (Knight, 1994). These species of *Artemisia* occur in a patchwork and can form sagebrush islands within the arid grasslands. Various species of sagebrush can be found from the low elevation grasslands to the high alpine, but the largest stands are outside the limits of the national forest (Meyers *et al.*, 2003). Mountain big sagebrush (*Artemisia tridentata*) is the common regional species. Several birds are closely associated with sagebrush including the Greater Sage-Grouse, Sage Sparrow, Sage Thrasher, Brewer's Sparrow, and Green-tailed Towhee. Another important food source for large mammals that is often associated with sagebrush is curleaf mountain mahogany (*Cercocarpus ledifolius*) which is most common on the foothills outside the national forest boundary.

Bird Distribution in the Bighorn Mountains

by Jacqueline L. Canterbury

Like plants, bird distributions in the Bighorn Mountains vary altitudinally. Three species in the genus *Leucosticte* occur in the alpine regions. The geographically limited Black Rosy-Finch has been reported in the Bighorn Mountains during the breeding season. The Gray-Crowned Rosy-Finch is a common visitor in winter, especially near the towns of Big Horn and Buffalo. Hundreds of Gray-Crowned Rosy-Finches occupy feeders on Red Grade Road in winter. These alpine dwellers are nomadic, and can be expected at different elevations during their life cycle.

In the subalpine spruce-fir zone just below timberline there is habitat for a variety of birds, including the variably nomadic Red and White-Winged Crossbills. Red Crossbills were found at lower elevations in large numbers in 2012-13, possibly due to diminished cone crops in their more northern range. Although generally rare, a group of 200 White-winged Crossbills were observed near Dayton in July of 1984 (Downing, 1990). Both these species are dependent upon large cone crops so their movements are variable (C. Benkman pers. comm.).

Ruby-crowned Kinglets are often heard in early spring in the forest. Scott (1993) has suggested that the Ruby-crowned Kinglet may be the most frequent breeder of the region's coniferous forests. The Swainson's Thrush is a denizen of moist forests, and uses the spruce-fir zone for nesting. The Hermit Thrush uses similar coniferous forest habitats, but is more abundant at higher elevations. Both can often be found along the Dayton Gulch Road in the northern Bighorns. Dayton Gulch is also a good place for the Yellow-rumped (Audubon's) Warbler, which breeds abundantly in coniferous forests. The Boreal Owl is much rarer, and was only recently confirmed to breed in the spruce-fir zone of the Bighorns (Faulkner, 2010). Mountain Chickadees and Brown Creepers also breed in this forest zone, and the Cassin's Finch can often be seen at higher elevations during the breeding season.

Among the non-passerine birds that are often associated with the mid-elevation coniferous forests, typically dominated by lodgepole pine, are such non-passerines as the Sharp-shinned and Cooper's hawks. This forest also supports passerines such as the Dark-eyed Junco, Pine Siskin, Mountain Chickadee, American Robin, Ruby-crowned Kinglet, and Yellow-rumped Warbler (Hanni et al., 2009). The Dark-eyed Junco has an interesting clinal distribution, being found at lower elevations in winter, and at higher elevation during the breeding season.

The lower elevation ponderosa pine forests contain a suite of species that differ from the montane forests of Douglas-fir. Paulin (1999) found that ponderosa pine communities had higher avian species diversity, as compared to Douglas-fir communities. Diem and Zeveloff (1980) identified 113 bird species in ponderosa pine forests. More mature pine forests provide sites for woodpeckers that excavate holes in trees and provide nest sites for Black-capped and Mountain chickadees and Mountain Bluebirds. The Red-headed Woodpecker is found in the eastern Powder River near Arvada, and has been seen in Sheridan along Swaim Road. Lewis's Woodpecker is sometimes found in Tongue River Canyon and has been reported from the burn area on Red Grade Road, and previously at Ash Creek. The White-breasted, Red-breasted, and Pygmy nuthatches have all been recorded from Story at 5,079 feet to 9,000 feet (Downing, 1990), and are associated with older mature pine forests. Ovenbirds can be found during summer in the ponderosa pine forests near Story. Clark's Nutcracker uses many coniferous habitats during its life cycle, but in the Bighorns it preferentially uses limber pines, its primary source of foods during the winter season. However, in winter it can also be found in ponderosa stands at lower elevation (Faulkner, 2010). One of the several recently described subspecies of Red Crossbills is specialized to forage specifically on ponderosa pine seeds (Benkman, 1999). Among the non-passerine birds that are often associated with the low-elevation montane coniferous forests dominated by Douglas-fir, are such species as the Ruffed and Dusky grouse, and owls including the Eastern Screech-owl, Boreal Owl, Northern Pygmy-Owl and Northern Saw-whet Owl.

Although the juniper woodlands comprises only a small percentage of the state's land area, over 100 bird species have been documented in this vegetation type (Rosenberg, 2004). The juniper woodlands of the Bighorn Basin support a distinct suite of birds because of the abundant berries and high insect diversity. Though extremely rare, an Ash-throated Flycatcher was recorded on Wolf Creek in July of 1982. Other species supported by the juniper woodlands are the Western Scrub-Jay, which has been rarely reported, the Pinyon Jay, which has been described as an erratic but common resident, and the Blue-gray Gnatcatcher, which is a rare spring vagrant (Hanni et al., 2009). In the Bighorn Basin, birders are also likely to see the Chipping Sparrow, Brewer's Sparrow, Lark Sparrow, Black-billed Magpie, Mountain Bluebird, Western Scrub-Jay, Violet-Green Swallow, and Green-tailed Towhee.

Nearly 90 species of birds use aspen woodlands in Wyoming (Rosenberg, 2004). Aspen stands provide nesting habitat for cavity-nesting birds that in turn provide secondary nest cavities for a number of species. The excavating action of the Red-naped Sapsucker and various woodpeckers on aspens attracts nesting Northern Saw-Whet Owls, Mountain and Black-capped Chickadees, Tree Swallows, and Mountain Bluebirds. Aspen communities have a diverse understory of shrubs, forbs, and grasses that provide important niches for ground-nesting species such as the Dark-eyed Junco and many grassland sparrows. The Warbling Vireo and the Western Wood-Pewee can be found in the forest canopy, while MacGillivray's Warbler uses the shrubby understory. Sharp-shinned and Cooper's hawks also use aspen stands (Faulkner, 2010).

The central Great Plains grasslands extend westward into Wyoming, where the forested eastern flank of the Bighorn Mountains transitions to the mixed-grass prairies of the plains. Prairie birds include the Horned Lark, which nests in native grasslands from the Great Plains to alpine meadows high above timberline, the Long-billed Curlew and Upland Sandpiper. The Dickcissel occupies the western extreme of their core range in the central Great Plains grasslands. The grassland community also supports the Lark Bunting, Lark Sparrow, Horned Lark, Western Meadowlark, Vesper Sparrow, and Sharp-tailed Grouse. The Western Meadowlark was the most common species of the Breeding Bird Survey in Arvada, Wyarno, Tensleep, and Worland and the second most common species in Dayton (Tables 2 and 4).

The sagebrush ecosystem, botanically referred to as the shrub-steppe, is widespread in the Bighorn Mountains. It has been said metaphorically by writer Greta Erlich (1986) that pronghorns (*Antilocapra americana*) have sagebrush in their blood and distance in their eye. She has also suggested that distance is the blurring of foreground and background, and this can be sensed by all who spend time in sage country.

The Greater Sage-Grouse is the classic "landscape species" of the sagebrush habitat, because it relies on large blocks of plant communities that occur in a mosaic across the sage landscape. Home range sizes vary and needs of these birds seem to be tied to the quality and quantity of sagebrush. Greater Sage-Grouse have disappeared from almost half of their range during historic times (Knick and Connelly, 2011). Providing an adequate land matrix will allow for the survival of this species and other sage-adapted species. The Sage Thrasher, Sage Sparrow and the Brewer's Sparrow are also sage-obligates, and dependent upon the existence of sagebrush habitat, as are the Horned Lark and the Lark Sparrow. Other vertebrate sage obligates include the pygmy rabbit (*Brachilagus idahoensis*), sagebrush vole (*Lemmnicus curtatus*), and sagebrush lizard (*Scloperus graciosus*). Travel south from Sheridan to Buffalo and onto Kumor Road, and also around the Powder River to see the sage habitats and sage-adapted species.

Water is one of the rarest and most important environmental attributes for birds and other organisms. In fact, in Wyoming, nearly 30 percent (68) of the 246 known breeding birds use riparian areas for various purposes (Rosenberg, 2004). Species that can be found at lower elevation riparian habitats in the Bighorn Mountains can be a mix of eastern and western species, and also include some very wide-ranging species such as the Yellow Warbler and Warbling Vireo. They also include some western species such as the Lazuli Bunting and Bullock's Oriole and uncommon eastern species such as the Indigo Bunting and the Baltimore Oriole. There is no firm evidence yet of the Baltimore Oriole breeding in Wyoming (Faulkner, 2010). Other eastern species that extend westward along riparian systems include the Yellow-billed Cuckoo and Red-headed Woodpecker, both of which have been observed in Sheridan. The widespread Sandhill Crane breeds in riparian areas such as on river valleys, marshes, and wet meadows, where birds feed on small vertebrates and invertebrates. Their numbers have been increasing in the Bighorn area since the 1980s. Characteristic riparian species also include the Yellow-breasted Chat, Tree Swallow, and Song Sparrow.

Typical species of the higher elevation montane riparian forests are the Calliope and Broad-tailed hummingbirds. Both hummingbirds select willow-dominated riparian areas in the breeding season, and can be seen around Story and Piney Creek. They also frequent the wildflower meadows along mountain streams. Flycatchers, such as the Willow and Cordilleran, frequent the cool, montane stream environments that are rich in insects, and can be found at Tongue River Canyon near Dayton. The American Dipper can be observed in swift, clear, streams of all major mountain ranges, as it plunges below the water surface in search of stream-bottom insects.

Rosenberg (2004) estimated that over 20 percent of Wyoming's birds use wetlands during breeding. That number increases substantially if one additionally considers feeding, wintering, and migratory stopover habitat. Deep, open water provides habitat for dabbling and diving ducks, loons, gulls, pelicans, and cormorants. Good places to see many of these species are at Moore's Reservoir, South Dam Pond, and Healy Reservoir near Buffalo. The Moore's Reservoir, near Lake DeSmet, provides nesting habitat for Pied-billed Grebes, Virginia Rails, Soras, American Coots, Canada Geese, and a variety of ducks, and it also offers habitats attractive to a number of migrant species (Downing, 1990).

Geology and Biogeography of the Bighorn Mountains

by Paul A. Johnsgard

The Bighorn Mountains lie majestically perched along the north-central edge of Wyoming, roughly halfway between the Black Hills of South Dakota to the east, and the Absaroka and Wind River ranges of the Rocky Mountains to the west. In their physiography the Bighorns generally resemble both the Black Hills and the Rocky Mountains, consisting of Precambrian granite cores partly covered by more recent sedimentary rocks (Darton, 1906; Fenneman, 1931).

The uplift of the Rocky Mountain region began in the late Mesozoic era about 100 million years ago. The major mountain-building phase of these mountains, as well as the Bighorns and Black Hills (the Laramide oreogeny) occurred during the early parts of the Cenozoic era (the so-called "Age of Mammals") from 65–50 million years ago. In the Bighorn region, compression of the earth's crust caused the entire region to bow upwards, the birth of the Bighorn range. Resulting stress ruptures of the earth's crust forced old sedimentary rocks over the tops and sides of deeper and variously older layers (thrust faults), on both the eastern and western slopes of the emerging Bighorn range. This process is evident along U.S. Hwy. 14 at Shell Canyon on the western slope, where Paleozoic sandstone 550 million years old lies directly over 2.9 billion-year-old granite derived directly from Precambian magma, and consists of some of the oldest rocks on earth. A thrust fault is also visible at Five Springs Canyon on U.S. Hwy. 14A, where the western

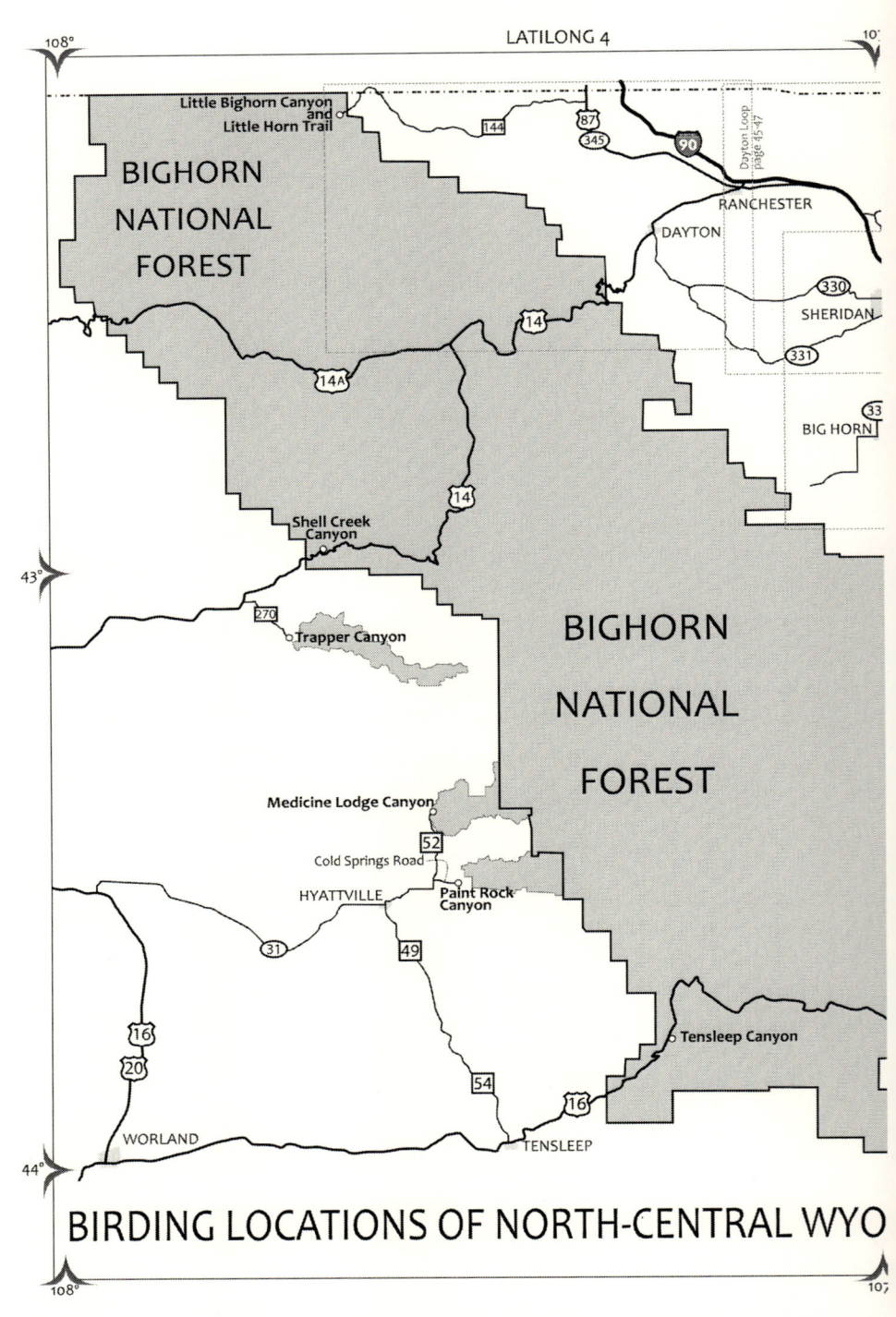

Map 1. Major Birding Locations of North Central Wyoming. Map by Wolfgang Schwartz

LATILONG 5

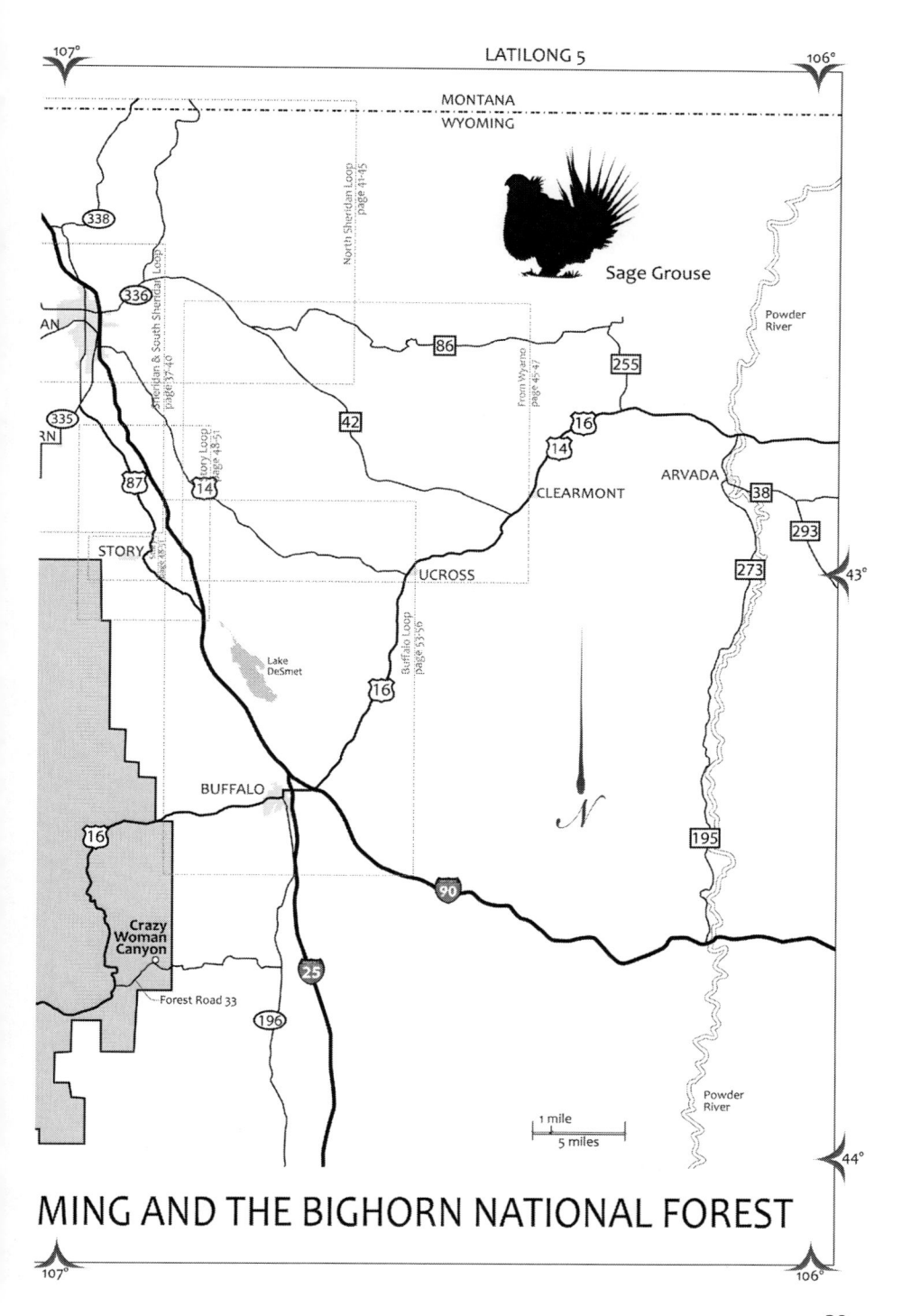

MONTANA
WYOMING

Sage Grouse

North Sheridan Loop page 41-45

Sheridan & South Sheridan Loop page 37-40

From Wyarno page 45-47

Story Loop page 48-51

Buffalo Loop page 53-56

338
336
335
87
86
42
14
255
16
14
38
293
273
195
16
90
25
196

Powder River

ARVADA
CLEARMONT
UCROSS
STORY
Lake DeSmet
BUFFALO
Crazy Woman Canyon
Forest Road 33

43°
44°
107°
106°

1 mile
5 miles

Powder River

MING AND THE BIGHORN NATIONAL FOREST

29

edge of the emerging Bighorn range was forced west into the Bighorn Basin, depositing older Mesozoic (Triassic and Jurassic) sediments over more recent Mesozoic (Cretaceous) shales (Lageson & Spearing, 1988).

By about 30 million years ago (mid-Oligocene epoch) the Bighorn range was formed, and extended roughly 50 miles along a southeast to northwest axis. It is bounded by two relatively flat plateaus now ranging in elevation from about less than 4,000 feet to the east (Powder River Basin) and west (Bighorn Basin) of the present-day range. Two north-flowing rivers (the Powder River and Bighorn River) now drain these arid rain-shadow regions. At the eastern edge of the region near Greybull the Bighorn River now descends to an elevation of under 3,700 feet at the western edge of the study area, as does the Powder River near the Montana border.

During the early Cenozoic era the gradually rising Bighorn Mountains were associated with an increasingly cooler and drier climate, and a replacement of subtropical vegetation with temperate deciduous forests and grasslands. Further continental cooling occurred during the Miocene epoch (5–24 million years ago), with the northern (boreal) coniferous forest starting to replace the deciduous forest. By about 9-10 million years ago the Rockies had reached their present height, and alpine vegetation began to form on mountaintops (Dorn, 1977). The present-day Bighorn range is more than 100 miles in length and has a maximum elevation of 13,187 feet (Cloud Peak), a few hundred feet below the highest peak in Wyoming (Gannett Peak, at 13,804 feet).

During the Pleistocene epoch (2,000,000–10,000 years ago) continental glaciation was widespread and affected all the higher elevations of Wyoming. In the Bighorn Mountains there are many nearly vertical ice-carved canyons (cirques) up to 1,500 feet high, where glaciers carved out sheer-walled granite basins, often leaving alpine lakes at their bases. As none of these now-vanished glaciers reached below 6,500 feet, the lower ends of the associated canyons have retained their pre-glacial and more angular forms (Fenneman, 1931).

The well-forested eastern slopes of the Bighorn Mountains benefit from spring precipitation originating in the Great Plains, while the western slopes lie in the rain shadow of Wyoming's more western ranges. Grasslands are thus more prevalent on the western slopes, and cover about one-third of the 1.1 million-acre Bighorn National Forest (Hurd, 1961). Coniferous forests cover about 80 percent of the region's ancient granite substrates, and are mostly comprised of lodgepole pine, with Engelmann spruce and subalpine fir occurring at high altitudes (Despain, 1973). Forests also cover about 50 percent of the region's sedimentary (limestone and sandstone & shale) substrates. In lower and progressively drier elevations juniper and ponderosa pines predominate. At medium elevations the forests are largely of Douglas-fir. Alpine tundra occurs above about 9,700 feet (3,050 meters) (Despain, 1973).

Botanically, the Bighorn Mountains are second only to the Tetons among Wyoming ranges in terms of their number of rare or endemic plants (Knight, 1994). Plant endemics include at least 12 species or varieties of forbs (Heidel, 2011). There are no endemic species of birds or mammals yet formally identified in the Bighorns, but an endemic race of the northern pocket gopher (*Thomomys talpoides caryi*) does occur there. Other known or likely Bighorn endemic races include the Bighorn snowshoe hare (*Lepus americanus seclusus*), Bighorn pika (*Ochotona princeps obscura*), and still-undescribed forms of the red squirrel (*Tamiasciurus hudsonicus*), marten (*Martes americana*), red-backed vole (*Clethrionomys gapperi*), water vole (*Microtus richardsoni*), spotted frog (*Rana luteiventris*) and wood frog (*Rana sylvatica*) (Beauvais, 2001).

In contrast to the Bighorns, the Black Hills of adjacent western South Dakota rise only to a maximum of 7,242 feet, or well below alpine altitudes. The flora of the Black Hills is essentially like that of the Rocky Mountain flora. However, there are echoes of the eastern deciduous flora as well. These include such typical eastern trees as ironwood (*Ostrya virginiana*) and bur oak (*Quercus macrocarpa*), and shrubs such as the beaked hazelnut (*Corylus cornuta*) and honeysuckle (*Lonicera dioca*) (Dorn, 1977). Wide valleys and canyons include many eastern tree and shrub species, and on north-facing slopes of steep slopes white spruce, paper birch and trembling aspen occur (Pettingill & Whitney, 1965). A variant of the white spruce ("Black Hills spruce") is endemic in the Black Hills. At least two endemic races of mammals also occur there, the Black Hills forms of the red-backed vole (*Clethrionomys gapperi brevicaudus*) and red squirrel (*Tamiasciurus hudsonicua dakotensis*). The Bighorns and Black Hills are ecologically isolated by the 90-mile-wide and arid Powder River basin, and have had little opportunity for biological contacts since early post-glacial times.

Because of their great elevational range, many of the peaks of the Bighorn and Wyoming's Rockies support alpine tundra, whereas the Black Hills region not only has no tundra. The Black Hills also lack such important high montane trees as subalpine fir and Engelmann spruce, and the mid-montane conifer Douglas-fir. Ponderosa pines are the historic dominant coniferous trees over much of the Black Hills, although in addition to the effects of heavy previous lumbering, this important forest component is now being devastated by bark beetles. Lodgepole pine is limited to a single stand of about 150 acres, and limber pine is confined to a stand of only about five acres (Froiland, 1990; Larson and Johnson, 1999). Lodgepole pine has long been the dominant tree over vast areas of the Wyoming Rockies, but its range and abundance are quickly declining throughout the Rocky Mountains, largely as a result of bark beetle infestations.

Compared with the Black Hills, the Bighorns lack such eastern species as the bur oak (*Quercus macrocarpa*), eastern hop hornbeam (*Ostrya virginiana*), paper birch (*Betula papyrifera*) and white spruce (Despain 1973). Altogether, the Black Hills flora has a lower degree of coniferous tree diversity than do the Bighorns and the Wyoming Rocky Mountains. Such botanical diversity differences probably effect the range of available foraging and breeding niches for conifer-dependent birds such as the seed-dependent finches.

Because they have well-developed subalpine and alpine zones, the Bighorn Mountains can support tundra-breeding American Pipits and Black Rosy-finches, but at least currently not White-tailed Ptarmigans. In the subalpine zone, the Pine Grosbeak is a breeder in the Bighorns and Rockies, but in the Black Hills breeding evidence is still undocumented (Tallman, Swanson and Palmer, 2002). Likewise the Boreal Owl is a subalpine breeder in the Bighorns and Rockies, but is absent from the Black Hills. In the mid-level coniferous forests of the Bighorns and Rockies, Dusky Grouse are common breeders, but they were extirpated from the Black Hills by the late 1800s, as also was the Peregrine Falcon. Among mammals, the alpine-adapted pika (*Ochotona princeps*) is present in the Bighorns, but not in the Black Hills.

Sandhill Cranes nest in the lower mountain meadows of the Rockies and, at least as of the last few decades, the Bighorns, but there are no nesting records for the Black Hills. Likewise, Calliope Hummingbirds and Broad-tailed Hummingbirds breed in mountain meadows and riparian corridors from the Bighorns west over much of Wyoming. No hummingbirds currently nest in the Black Hills, although the Broad-tailed nested there formerly. The same pattern of a Bighorns presence by widespread Wyoming nesters, but an absence of Black Hills nesting, is also true of the western-oriented and conifer-nesting Williamson's Sapsucker, Olive-sided Flycatcher, Hammond's Flycatcher, Mountain Chickadee, Pine Grosbeak, and White-winged Crossbill. Of these, only the Olive-sided Flycatcher might possibly be a very rare nester in the Black Hills (Peterson, 1995; Tallman, Palmer and Swanson, 2002).

Among montane mammals, the pika, snowshoe hare (*Lepus americanus*), water vole (*Microtus richardsoni*) and montane vole (*Microtus montanus*) all occur in the Bighorns but have not reached the Black Hills, whereas the red squirrel (*Tamiascirurus hudsonicus*) occurs in both. Curiously, the northern flying squirrel (*Glaucomys sabrinus*) occurs in the mountains of northwestern Wyoming and the Black Hills, but not in the Bighorns (Clark and Stromberg, 1987). The white-winged race of the Dark-eyed Junco (*J. h. aikeni*) is endemic to the Black Hills, as is a local race of the red-bellied snake (*Storeria occipitomaculatus pahasapae*).

The boreal forest-nesting Red-breasted Nuthatch, Orange-crowned Warbler, Golden-crowned and Ruby-crowned kinglets, Red Crossbill, Pine Siskin and Evening Grosbeak all breed from the Rockies east through both the Bighorns and Black Hills, as well as across all of Canada northwardly. The Lincoln's and White-crowned Sparrows also have similar boreal forest breeding distributions that include the Bighorns, but do not breed in the Black Hills. On the other hand, the western-oriented Plumbeous Vireo and Pygmy Nuthatch, and the eastern-oriented American Redstart and Ovenbird, nest in the ponderosa pines and hardwood forests of both the Black Hills and Bighorns, but rarely or never breed in the Rockies of northwestern Wyoming.

Some eastern forest-nesting species reach the western edge of the breeding range in the Black Hills and Bighorns, such as the Red-eyed Vireo, Blue Jay, and Brown Thrasher. The Eastern Bluebird and Indigo Bunting breed in the Black Hills, but they only occasionally extend as breeders very far west into Wyoming, and the Baltimore Oriole is not yet known to breed in Wyoming.

Montane, or boreal-oriented species that reach the eastern edge of their central Great Plains ranges in the Bighorns and Black Hills include the Gray Jay, Clark's Nutcracker, Violet-green Swallow, Canyon Wren, Townsend's Solitaire, Swainson's Thrush, MacGillivray's Warbler and Western Tanager. The Common Raven once has a similar range pattern, but disappeared from the Black Hills after the extirpation of the bison (*Bison bison*) from the western plains. Curiously, the Steller's Jay is common throughout Wyoming's Rocky Mountains, but has so far failed to colonize either the Bighorns or Black Hills. However, it does occur in Wyoming's Laramie Range, not far to the south of the Bighorns (Faulkner, 2010).

Based on the present checklist's data, regional breeding has been confirmed for 190 species. Additionally, at least 323 species have been reported from the entire Bighorn region, as compared with a total of 427 species reported for all of Wyoming as of 2010 (Faulkner, 2010). Of the 323 species included in the present survey, 77 have breeding ranges that are considered by us to be either clearly eastern-oriented or western-oriented in North America. Of these, 55 (71 percent) were judged to be western-oriented and 22 eastern-oriented.

For a comparison with the topographically similar Black Hills of western South Dakota and eastern Wyoming, 226 species had been reported from the Black Hills as of 1965 (Pettingill and Whitney, 1965), or only about 70 percent the avian species diversity of the Bighorn region. Of the Black Hills breeders having either eastern or western geographic affiliations, 32 have breeding ranges that are mostly western-oriented (76 percent), and ten have mostly eastern-oriented ranges. On this basis, the incidence of western-oriented species in the Black Hills and Bighorns can be considered as essentially the same, with both having transitional avifaunas, with a substantial predominance of western species.

The Powder River basin has special ecological and ornithological interest, and is the center of development for coal and other energy sources that will greatly affect bird populations and diversity. In a long-term study of three counties in this basin (Johnson, Sheridan and Campbell) that extended from 2003–2001, a total of 1,142 raptor nests (counting multi-year repeats) were surveyed on BLM land. In descending abundance, the percentage species composition of these nests were Red-tailed Hawk, 38.1, Ferruginous Hawk, 21.5, Great Horned Owl, 12,9, Golden Eagle, 11.4, Long-eared Owl, 3.7, Burrowing Owl, 3.3, American Kestrel, 2.7, Prairie Falcon, 1.6, Swainson's Hawk, 1.6, Bald Eagle, 0.9, Cooper's Hawk, 0.8, Northern Harrier, 0.8, Short-eared Owl, 0.4, Peregrine Falcon, 0.3, Barn Owl, 0.2, and Turkey Vulture, 0.1 (Chalfaun *et al*., 2013).

Notes on Regional Birding

by Jacqueline L. Canterbury

People birding in the Bighorn Mountains should be aware of significant differences in the climate, vegetation, and bird life of the western and eastern slopes of these mountains. Because the western slope lies in a partial rain shadow of the Pryor and Owl Creek Mountains, it receives significantly less moisture than the eastern slope. Therefore, the western slope is available to birders later in fall and earlier in spring. Furthermore, the steep-walled canyons of the western Bighorns lie above lush riparian areas at their base. One can therefore observe cliff dwelling raptors and rock loving species such as Rock and Canyon Wrens. Common Ravens are also more prevalent on the western slope. In the lower altitudes of the canyons are mixed forests of hardwoods and conifers. Montane species such as Townsend's Solitaire and Mountain Chickadee can often be found in these mid-altitude woodlands.

In contrast, the eastern slope is not as accessible to birders in early spring and late fall. However, a surprisingly large number of species are more likely to be encountered on the eastern slope. These are birds associated with the denser and generally moister forests and the associated grassland species that find their way west as far as the eastern edge of the Big Horns.

Toward the northern end of the range and the Cloud Peak Wilderness Area, the many alpine areas are likely to host such tundra-adapted birds as

American Pipits and perhaps Black-Rosy-finches. In summer the alpine area may by used by additional species such as Golden Eagles, and passerines such as Mountain Bluebirds and Dark-eyed Juncos.

US Highway 16 traverses the southern end of the Bighorns and is open year-round. It provides access across the highest alpine pass, Powder Ridge, at 9,668 feet. US Highway 14 traverses north and provides access to excellent birding in the subalpine forest. Dayton Gulch is a good example of this habitat type. Useful sources of information can be found at the USDA Forest Service Visitor Centers in both Burgess Junction and at Shell Canyon, both on US Highway 14.

The Bighorn National Forest has campgrounds and picnic areas, and 1,500 miles of trails. Within the National Forest's borders is the Cloud Peak Wilderness, named for the Bighorn's highest peak. Most of the area is above 9,000 feet and offers a variety of trails. This area is limited to non-motorized travel, so birders can enjoy the solitude of the wilderness. There are 189,000 acres of designated wilderness, but much of it is subalpine and alpine, so species are alpine-specific. The alpine zone also does not become snow-free and accessible until July. On the east side of Cloud Peak itself, a deeply carved cirque currently holds the last remaining glacier in this range. Several hundred beautiful lakes are the sources of many montane streams. Specific information on local birding sites and regional maps can be obtained from Forest Service offices at Sheridan (307-672-0751), Buffalo (307-684-1100) and Lovell (307-548-6541).

Additional information on birding in Wyoming, such as bird lists, links to state birding organizations and birding hotspots, is available through Birding.com (http://www.birding.com/wheretobird/wyoming.asp). The Cheyenne High Plains chapter of the Audubon Society's website also has useful information on Wyoming birds and eastern Wyoming birding: http://home.lonetree.com/audubon/ .

Birding Areas by Vegetation Type

by Jacqueline L. Canterbury

Birding can be more rewarding when one learns to associate birds and their predominant habitat. To make this book more useful, I thought it would be appropriate to identify some local birding areas with their associated habitats. The following is a habitat-based list of those areas that can be found on maps and directions provided in the next section on birding locations:

Riparian: Ash Creek, Big Goose Creek, Buffalo Creek, Clear Creek, Tongue Canyon, Piney Creek, Little Piney Creek, North Piney Creek, South Piney Creek, Big Goose Creek, Tensleep Creek, Soldier Creek, Crazy Woman Creek, Paint Rock Canyon, Trapper Canyon, Medicine Lodge, Shell Creek Canyon

Reservoirs and Lakes: South Dam Pond, Lake DeSmet, Moore's Reservoir, Healy Reservoir, McClain's Pond, Piney Creek Diversion, Wagner Reservoir

Grassland: Powder River Basin, Wyarno, Arvada

Alpine: US Routes 16 and 14, Hunt Mountain Road

Subalpine: Dayton Gulch Road, Shell Creek Canyon

Mid-Elevation Conifer Forest: Paint Rock Canyon, Trapper Canyon, Medicine Lodge Canyon

Low-Elevation Conifer Forest: Clear Creek Trail

Juniper: Medicine Lodge, Shell Canyon Research Natural Area

Aspen: Paint Rock Canyon, US Routes 16 and 14

Sage: Beatty Gulch, Kumor Road, Decker Road, Wyarno Road, Fort Phil Kearney, SR Buffalo Creek Road

Urban: Bird Farm Road, Dayton-Beckton Road, Rock Creek Road, French Creek, Lower Prairie Dog Road, Lower Piney Creek Road, Red Grade Road, Sheridan Cemetery and Draw, Soldier Creek Road, Wagon Box Monument, Wolf Creek Road.

Suggested Birding Locations and Site Descriptions

by Jacqueline L. Canterbury

The purpose of this book is to share local knowledge about birding and birding sites, and to share the beauty of the Bighorn Mountain area of Wyoming. Below I have incorporated many of the birding locations that Helen Downing (1990) noted in her book into 5 distinct birding loops: Sheridan and South Sheridan, North Sheridan, Dayton, Story, and Buffalo. Maps have been incorporated to help you navigate each loop. The text provides directions, information on habitat, and a short list of expected birds. For more information on individual species, go to the species accounts in the annotated list of regional birds. I have also added four special roadless areas to explore on foot, and two of my favorite drives through the Bighorn Mountains.

Birding Loops

SHERIDAN AND SOUTH SHERIDAN LOOP

Sheridan Cemetery
South Park Trail
McClain's Pond
East Lane
Big Horn
Bradford Brinton Road
Bradford Brinton Museum
Bird Farm Road
Red Grade Road

The **Sheridan Cemetery** is located in south Sheridan. To access the cemetery from Sheridan's 5th and Main travel south on Main Street 0.8 miles onto West Burkitt Street. Take the second left onto Thurmond and follow 0.7 miles, turn right onto Huntington Street, take the first right onto Ash.

From the cemetery, return to Huntington Street, take a right onto Linden Avenue and a left onto Sioux. Street. Turn right onto Big Horn Avenue and travel south, turn left onto Brundage Lane. The **South Park Trail** is on the left. It is a newly established walking trail and natural area on 40 acres along Little Goose Creek. A trail goes through a deciduous forest of cottonwood. There is a grassland meadow and wetland complex, and on a walk one can often hear the Red-winged Blackbirds calling near their nests. Ring-necked Pheasants and Yellow Warblers can also be found here.

From the South Park Trail head west on Brundage Lane, turn left onto Big Horn Avenue and travel 2.8 miles and turn right on Swaim Road, and follow about 0.6 miles to **McClain's Pond** on the left. Previously, this was a very good birding spot, but has been compromised due to the increased density of houses. Yellow-headed Blackbirds and Common Yellowthroat are occasionally seen along the pond. Across the road is a grassland with Bobolinks present later in the spring.

From McClain's pond, return to Big Horn Avenue and continue south 1 mile. At the intersection, turn left onto US Route 87N. At mile 0.5 turn right onto **East Lane,** cross the bridge and observe the Great Blue Heron colony north of the road. Expect to see over 20 nests built on the top of the tall cottonwoods. The heronry is on private property, so please view only from the public roadway.

After East Lane you have two options: stay on State Route 332, which becomes State Route 335 and go to Big Horn, Bradford Brinton, Bird Farm Road, and Red Grade Road, or take US Route 87 to Story. To proceed to **Big Horn**, follow State Route 335. From East Lane travel about 4 miles until you see the Big Horn sign on the right. The town was named for the surrounding mountains. In 1894, one of the first colleges, Wyoming College and Normal School, was built at this site. Travel left off State Route 335 into Big Horn and you are on the **Bradford Brinton Road**. This is one of my favorite local birding roads. The habitat is very diverse, with abundant water including Little Goose Creek. Birders can see a variety of species, including a nesting Cooper's Hawk observed the summer of 2013. Also present along the road are the Least Flycatcher, Ruby-crowned Kinglet, and Black-and-White Warbler, a rare migrant. At 2.4 miles there is a sign and small lane into the Bradford Briton Memorial Museum, which is open to visitors during regular business hours, and has a wonderful art collection. The grounds are beautiful, and the variety of trees is noteworthy. Bradford Brinton was an eastern industrialist who raised horses and collected a variety of western art that is on display at the museum. Helen Brinton, his sister, willed the museum to the county in 1960 for all to enjoy. Birds likely to be observed here are the Calliope Hummingbird, Red-naped Sapsucker, Northern Flicker, Black-capped Chickadee, White-breasted Nuthatch, Belted Kingfisher, Bohemian and Cedar waxwings, and Black-billed Magpie. There is usually an American Dipper nest under the bridge along Little Goose Creek. In winter I have seen the Brown Creeper, Great Blue Heron, Cassin's Finch, and a flock of 200 Bohemian Waxwings. Also, Bald Eagles perch in the large trees on the Gallatin Ranch to the east, as do Rough-legged Hawks. I have observed as many as ten adult and juvenile Bald Eagles and five Rough-legged Hawks sharing the same tree.

After your visit, turn left at the entrance. Follow this road until it intersects with State Route 335. Take a left onto State Route 335 and climb up **Red Grade Road,** a gravel road that provides public access to the eastern slope of the Bighorn Mountains. Look for a small herd of antelope. Mountain Bluebirds can be seen at the higher elevations. The locals living along Red Grade Road feed birds year-round. In winter, large flocks of Gray-crowned Rosy-finches, Common Redpolls, Red Crossbills, and Evening Gros-

BIRDING LOOPS — SHERIDAN AND SOUTH SHERIDAN   39

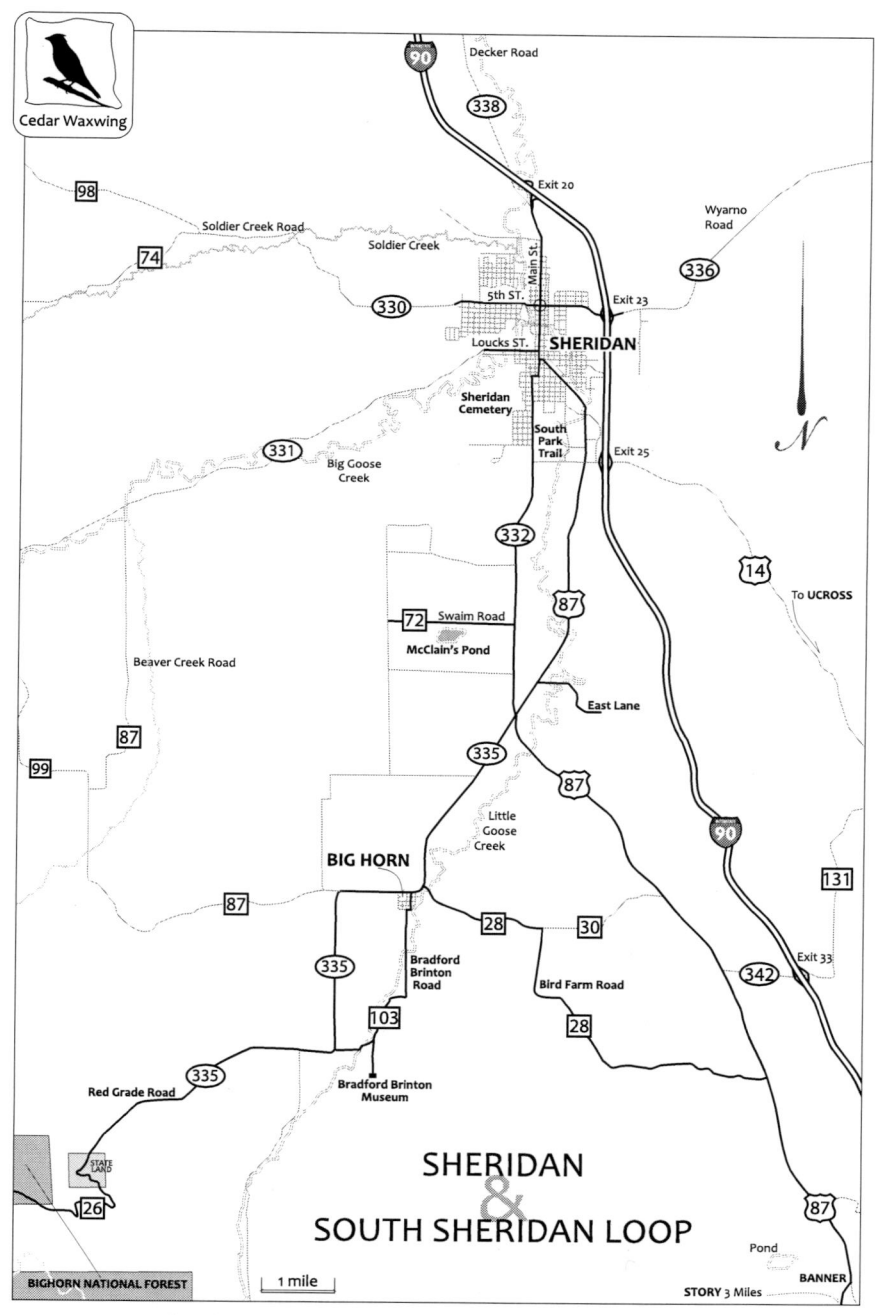

Map 2. Sheridan and South Sheridan Loop. Map by Wolfgang Schwartz

beaks can be seen (see species account of Gray-crowned Rosy-Finch for details on seasonal timing and numbers). I do not advise traveling far up Red Grade Road. It is a primitive road with low clearance, and the Forest Service allows the use of off-road vehicles, so noise can be a problem for birding.

After visiting Red Grade Road, continue back to Big Horn on State Route 335 or the Bradford Brinton Road. At the Big Horn Post Office turn right on State Route 335 for 0.2 miles, then take a right turn onto **Bird Farm Road (Co. 28)**. Go 1.7 miles and take a right, on County Route 28 and the Bird Farm Road. This road passes grasslands dotted with sage and purple lupine in spring. On the right is the private Flying H Polo Club, one of the oldest polo grounds in the country. Englishman Oliver Henry Wallop, younger son of an earl, realized the value of horses during the Boer Wars. He went into partnership with Malcolm Moncrieffe, son of a Scottish baronet. They brought in the first thoroughbred horses to the area. In 1898 Malcolm Moncreiffe moved to Bighorn, built the polo field and continued to breed horses. He subsequently established the area as a significant polo location. Currently, top international players compete at the Flying H and the Big Horn Equestrian Center. Follow the curve past the equestrian center. On the left is the sign for the "State Bird Farm" established in 1937 by the Wyoming Game and Fish Department as a pheasant-rearing farm. This farm is responsible for the pheasants commonly seen along the roadways and in local acreages. I have seen Mountain Bluebirds, Say's Phoebes, Black-headed Grosbeaks, and Sharp-tailed Grouse along this road. In winter, Rough-legged Hawks and Bald Eagles are common.

The road changes to gravel at 3.4 miles and the terrain becomes hilly, interspersed with small draws of cottonwood and chokecherry. A few houses along the road have stands of cottonwood that are good habitats for vireos and warblers in late spring and summer. At about 4.8 miles there is a small pond where I have seen Wood Ducks. Follow the road and notice the stands of aspen; good habitat for woodpeckers and Yellow Warblers. Bird Farm Road ends at 6.3 miles and offers two options, turn left and continue back to Sheridan or turn right toward Story on US Route 87. If you continue right to **Story**, there is a small pond on the left at 2.0 miles. This is a human-made pond where I have seen Tree Swallows, Canada Geese and Mallards in spring. At 0.8 miles State Route 344, Pinos Creek Road, is on the left. This was once a main road until a 50-year series of landslides occurred. The road was finally closed in 1997. Travel back to US Route 87 to Story and the junction of US Route 87 and State Route 194.

North Sheridan Loop

Soldier Creek Road
Wolf Creek Road
Acme
Kleenburn Recreation Area
Decker Road,
Welch Recreation Area
Beatty Gulch Road
Ash Creek
Young's Creek
Wyarno
S.R. Creek,
Buffalo Creek
Ucross

From Sheridan's 5th and Main, follow 5th Street west on State Route 330, which becomes County Route 74 or **Soldier Creek Road**. Travel along Soldier Creek until you come to **Wolf Creek Road**. This road follows Wolf Creek and offers a good example of a grassland riparian habitat. There is an Important Bird Area (IBA) along Wolf Creek. Walk along the road and observe the water-associated species such as the Northern Harrier, Sandhill Crane and Great Blue Heron. Sandhill Cranes are numerous in this area; I have seen as many as three pairs during the breeding season. The American Kestrel and Northern Harrier are also common. You can see the exposed rock entrance to Tongue Canyon in the distance. Wolf Creek Road then merges into I-90, which heads east and follows the Tongue River.

Another option is to travel north from Sheridan on Wyo. 338, a scenic road that follows Goose Creek and offers a chance to visit **Acme** and the **Kleenburn Recreation Area**. From 5th and Main Street in Sheridan travel about two miles until you see a sign for Wyo. 338, the Decker Road. There are a few scattered wetlands along the road worth viewing. At 6.3 miles turn left onto Wyo. 339 and merge onto I-90. Follow I-90 north 2.1 miles to the Acme exit and the Kleenburn Recreation Area. Turn right on **Acme Road** and proceed 0.6 miles. This is prime birding habitat along the Tongue River. There is a Walk-In-Area on the left, and on the right there is access to the river. At 1.2 miles there is a parking lot on the right and a short trail through a dense thicket of plains cottonwood, hawthorn and common chokecherry. Uncommon species such as the Yellow-breasted Chat and Lazuli Bunting might be observed, as well as the more common Spotted Towhee and Yellow Warbler, all found in the thickets along the river. Continue on to the Acme Public Ac-

42 PART I. THE BIGHORN MOUNTAINS OF WYOMING

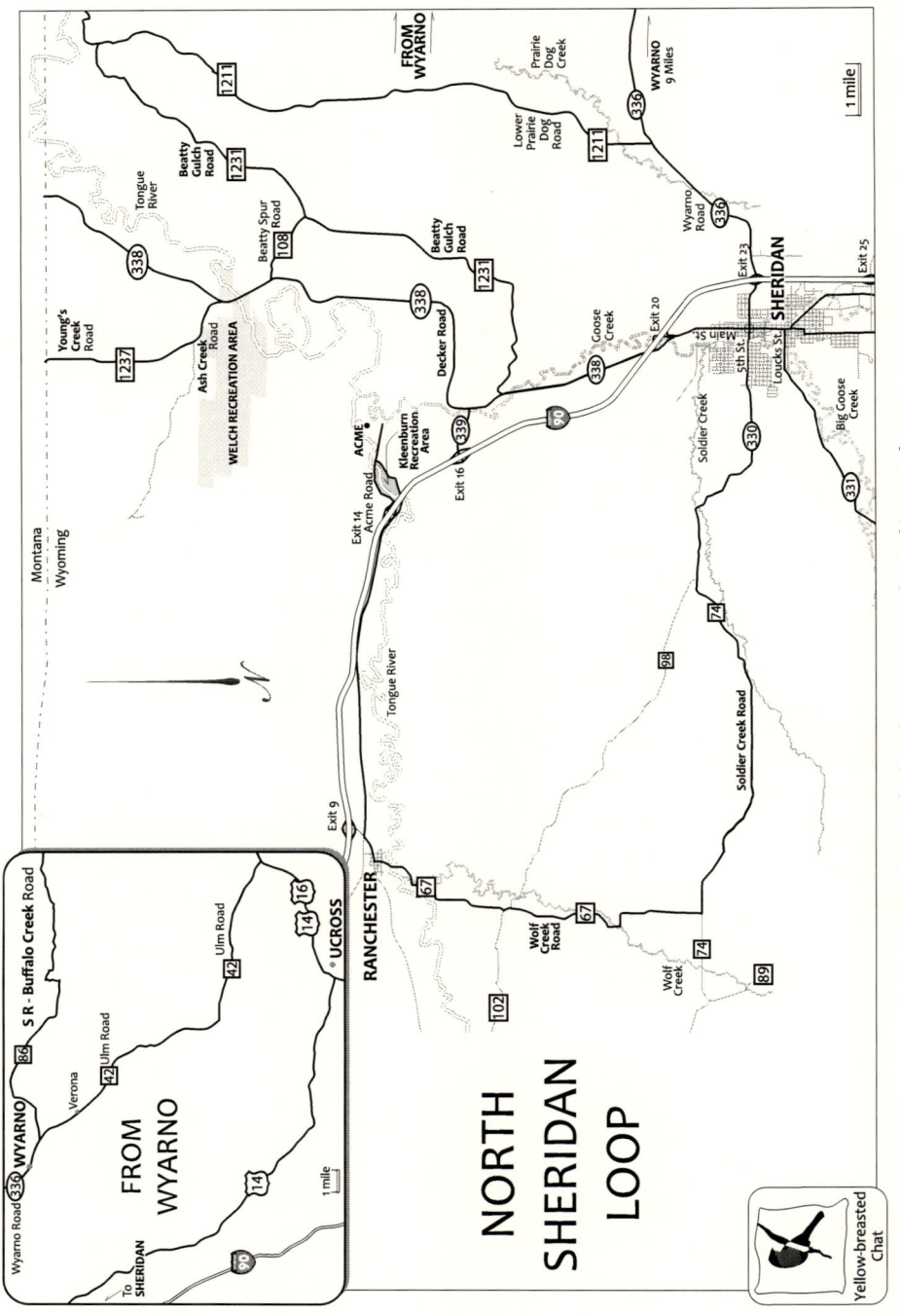

Map 3. North Sheridan Loop. Map by Wolfgang Schwartz

cess Area managed by Wyoming Game & Fish Department. Here you might observe a Say's Phoebe nesting in an old cattle shed, and Lark Sparrows on the old cattle fence. Across the road is Kleenburn Road, which leads to the **Kleenburn Recreation Area**, managed by Sheridan County Parks and Recreation Board (307-674-2980). It offers a walking trail, toilets, parking, and provides a landing for small boats. After seeing the recreation area, continue east on Acme Road 0.6 miles to a Walk-In-Area on the left. Park and walk along the river. This is a good place to watch for waterfowl, and is a likely site for seeing fledgling Canada Geese in late spring.

The **Decker Road** heads north into Montana and is classic sagebrush country. From the intersection of 5th Street and Main, follow Main Street north to I-90. Follow I-90 north 4 miles to the Decker exit (Wyo. 339). Turn right on 339 until the road forms a T. Turn left on Wyo. 338, the **Decker Road**. Follow the Decker Road north 6 miles to the **Welch Ranch Recreation Area**. Listen for Western Meadowlarks and an occasional Upland Sandpiper in the grasslands. This route follows the Tongue River. The Welch Ranch consists of 1,700 acres along the Tongue River, and is managed by the Bureau of Land Management. This riparian corridor offers good birding among the old cottonwoods. Bullock's Orioles can often be seen nesting, and Warbling Vireos can often be heard.

Either continue north to **Ash Creek and Young's Creek** or go back on Wyo. 338 to the **Beatty Spur Road (Co. Route 108)**. To bird **Ash Creek and Young's Creek,** travel north on Wyo. 338 crossing the Tongue River. In 0.4 miles there is a gravel road on the left called Young's Creek Road (Co. Route 1237). The surrounding land is private property and the future site of a coal mine. In the early days, Helen Downing was interested in the effects of coal mining on birds, so much of Helen's early work was done specifically in this area, to document the resulting local changes in bird numbers and distribution. If you continue on this road, follow Ash Creek for about 1.5 miles and head north to Young's Creek, and to the Montana line. On this road look for Golden Eagles, American Kestrels, and Prairie Falcons.

To bird **Beatty Gulch Road** continue from the Welch Ranch and head southeast 0.6 miles. Turn left on Beatty Spur Road that in 1.5 miles becomes the **Beatty Gulch Road (Co. Route 1231)**. Turn right here and head south to Wyo. 338. This makes a nice loop through a sagebrush–grassland community. In 0.2 miles there is a chain of three small ponds. From the road you might see Gadwalls and Mallards, along with several species of swallows. I have seen a pair of Sandhill Cranes here in summer, and saw six Northern Harriers in December of 2011. Continue on this road and look for Grasshopper, Vesper, Brewer's, Lark sparrows, Horned Larks, Lark Buntings, and Western Meadowlarks. This area was developed for coal-bed methane production in the late 1990s. You can see the well-houses along the road that contain the well-heads that extract the water from the coal seam beneath the earth. This process has caused new roads and power lines to fragment and thus compromise this landscape. At 6.3 miles turn left on Wyo. 338 and continue back to Sheridan, following Goose Creek.

A trip to **Wyarno** takes the birder to the eastern Powder River Basin. Follow 5th Street east from downtown Sheridan to Wyo. 336. Wyo. 336 follows Prairie Dog Creek, and at about 3.5 miles there is a series of small wetlands; a mile farther at 4.5 miles on the left is **Lower Prairie Dog Road (Co. Route 1211).** This road continues to the Montana border and the Tongue River Reservoir. Prairie Dog Creek flows northeast from the Bighorn Mountains to Dutch Creek and then into the Tongue River in Wyoming. The habitat is grassland–sage and the road parallels private land. Initially the road travels through grassland–sage, but at about 3.8 miles there are a few large cottonwoods on the right, and to the left is a small hill with juniper–sagebrush. I have seen Eastern and Western kingbirds along this road in early June, so I call it the "Kingbird Highway." Pronghorn antelope are also common here. At about five miles there is another grove of cottonwoods that is usually productive for warblers. At 5.6 miles there is cluster of cottonwoods that might have a Bullock's Oriole nest hanging at mid-canopy. In about eight miles you will see ponderosa pines and junipers atop a sandstone ridge. This road contains a diversity of habitats, thus also a diversity of birds. For example, in early June I have seen the Great Blue Heron, Turkey Vulture, Red-tailed Hawk, Killdeer, Black-billed Magpie, Barn Swallow, Yellow Warbler, Lark Sparrow, Western Meadowlark, and, of course, both Western and Eastern kingbirds. At 11 miles there is an intersection with Beatty Gulch Road. Here you can turn left to Beatty Gulch Road, or continue northwest. There the habitat opens to higher elevation grassland–sage tableland and the road becomes Badger Creek Road, which takes you into Montana. To return south, take a left on Quietus Road until you see a small slough at the southern end of the Tongue River Reservoir. This is a great wetland–riparian birding spot. Osprey should be first species to look for on your list.

From **Wyarno**, travel southeast on County Route 42 through Verona and Ulm. Where the road forks, take US Route 16 to **Ucross**. The town of Ucross was named for the cattle brand of the original owners of the land, which was a "U" with a cross beneath. There is a museum in Ucross operated by the Ucross Foundation. The foundation was established in 1981, and provides opportunities for artists of many disciplines to do their work. About 1,300 artists have spent time there since 1981. Ulm is a good area to view Sandhill Cranes in spring.

Another option is to continue east from Wyarno to **SR Creek and Buffalo Creek.** Buffalo Creek flows into the Powder River. The landscape is classic eastern Bighorn grassland and offers the opportunity to view a variety of grassland birds. The Powder River to the east is one of the major north-south routes for migratory birds in spring and fall. Large flocks of Sandhill Cranes have been observed in the Powder River area staging during spring migration. Cranes arrive in the Bighorns around March 17th, spend time in the Powder River area, then the birds start moving to their breeding grounds.

Dayton Loop

Dayton-Beckton Road
Amsden Creek Wildlife Habitat Management Area
Tongue River Canyon
Kerns Wildlife Habitat Unit
Little Bighorn Canyon

From Beckton travel north on Beckton Road 89 to Dayton, the **Dayton-Beckton Road**. This road travels through a sage–grassland complex and provides good viewing of grassland birds such as Vesper Sparrows. The road also provides panorama views of Walker Mountain and Wolf Creek. Beckton was named for George W. Beck, an early settler who built a flour-mill. A sign on the Beckton Road "No country for old rabbits" tells the ecological story of the surrounding countryside. Travel about 6 miles on Beckton Road 89 until you see the Eaton Ranch Road. Turn left and follow the signs. The Eaton Ranch was the first dude ranch in Wyoming, and was established in 1904 by the Eaton brothers. The ranch is still in family ownership. There is a hiking trail on the ranch that accesses a Forest Service trail into the Bighorn Mountains. After visiting Eaton's, go back to the main road and continue north on Beckton Road 89 to Dayton. Dayton is a small town named for a Sheridan banker, but is best known as the first town in the United States to elect a woman as mayor in 1911 (Urbanek, 1988).

To access **Amsden Creek Wildlife Habitat Management Area** and the **Tongue River Canyon** trailhead, turn right before the Dayton Bridge onto County Route 92 and follow the signs to Amsden Creek Wildlife Habitat Management Area. This road meanders along the Tongue River. The name "tongue" comes from a Cheyenne story of a large rock above the Tongue River that resembles a human tongue. On this road I have seen Black-billed Magpies, Chipping Sparrows, Northern Harriers, Sandhill Cranes, and once

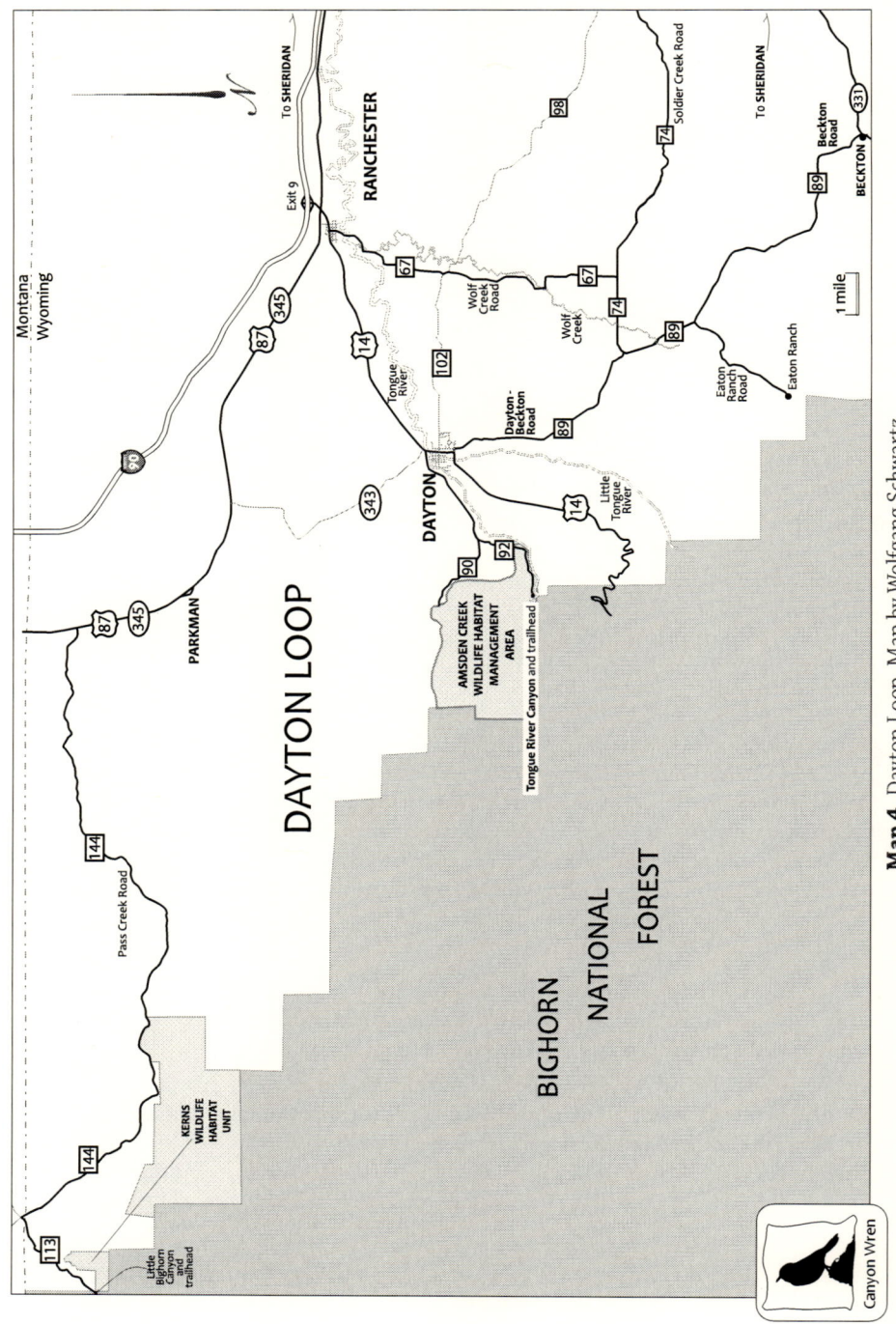

Map 4. Dayton Loop. Map by Wolfgang Schwartz

saw a Great Horned Owl perched on a roadside pole. Two Great Blue Heron colonies can be seen off the left side at mile 0.9, and also at mile 1.0. There was a recent fire that changed the landscape, but the old cottonwoods still stand and provide nesting habitat for a variety of arboreal species. County Route 92 follows the Tongue River, and at mile 2.2 intersects with County Route 90 that leads to Amsden Creek Wildlife Habitat Management Area, or continues as County Route 92 to the **Tongue River Canyon trailhead**. Once in the canyon, there is a Forest Service trail that traverses the Tongue River with views of sheer limestone walls. The Tongue River trail is open year-round and one can usually hear Townsend's Solitaires and Clark's Nutcrackers. On the south side of the canyon there are Rock Wrens, as well as the less common Canyon Wren. According to Scott (1988), this is a good place to see rare migrants such as the Chestnut-sided and Tennessee warblers. The Swainson's Thrush and MacGillivray's warbler can often be heard past the bridge on the first part of the trail. Also listen for the Veery. Look above the canyon rim for White-throated Swifts. If you follow County Route 90, you will enter the Amsden Creek Wildlife Habitat Unit, an elk reserve that is closed each year to vehicles from November 1–May 31, and to humans from November 16–April 30. When open to visitors, birding this area can be rewarding. It begins as grassland and transitions into mountain mahogany and ponderosa pine. There is a Mountain Bluebird box at the trailhead that usually supports a breeding pair.

After hiking in Tongue Canyon, travel back to Dayton and head northwest on Wyo. 343 to the **Kerns Wildlife Habitat Unit**. It is located 12 miles northwest of Parkman. Take Pass Creek Road (Co. Route 144) to the west and watch for the signs for the Kerns Wildlife Habitat Management Area. This area provides crucial winter range for about 800 elk. It consists of foothills and deep canyons, and provides habitat for Wild Turkeys, and grouse. After Kerns continue on Co. Rte. 144 to the **Little Bighorn Canyon,** a prime place for seeing raptors.

Story Loop

Story
Fish Hatchery Road
South Piney Creek Trailhead
North Piney Creek Road
Red Trailhead
Wagon Box Road
Wagon Box Monument
Little Piney Creek
Fort Phil Kearny
Fetterman Battlefield and Monument
Piney Creek Diversion
Lower Piney Creek Road

The northern entrance to **Story** is at a corner gas station at the intersection of US Route 87 and State Route 194. Story is a summer mountain resort named after Charles Story, a Sheridan newspaperman. This area offers some of the most accessible montane birding opportunities in the area. Here you can probably see the Calliope and Broad-tailed hummingbirds, American Redstart, Ovenbird, and all three Wyoming species of nuthatches. However, the roads are somewhat confusing. The locals describe the separation of North Piney Creek Road and South Piney Creek Road by what they call Piney Island.

Fish Hatchery Road (Wyo. 194) is the main road through Story. Watch for Wild Turkeys crossing the road, and notice the aspen trees (relatively rare in the Bighorns) along the way. Fish Hatchery Road dead-ends in about 3 miles at the Fish Hatchery, where you can picnic along the creek, or tour the hatchery. The hatchery was built in 1907-1908 and is the oldest operating fish hatchery in Wyoming. It was recently renovated. After viewing the hatchery and its grounds, turn around and follow Fish Hatchery Road for 0.2 miles to another good trail and birding area, the Thorne Rider Road (Sheridan County Road 6). Take a right onto Thorne Rider and follow the road 0.6 miles to the **South Piney Creek Trailhead**. This trail climbs through ponderosa pine forests and here you can seasonally see the Calliope Hummingbird, American Redstart, Western Wood-Pewee, Western Tanager, and Yellow-rumped Warbler. Also search for the less common Red Crossbill and the resident Mountain Chickadee.

To access **North Piney Creek Road (Wyo. 340)** from the Story gas station, travel one-half mile on Fish Hatchery Road and turn right on North

BIRDING LOOPS — STORY   49

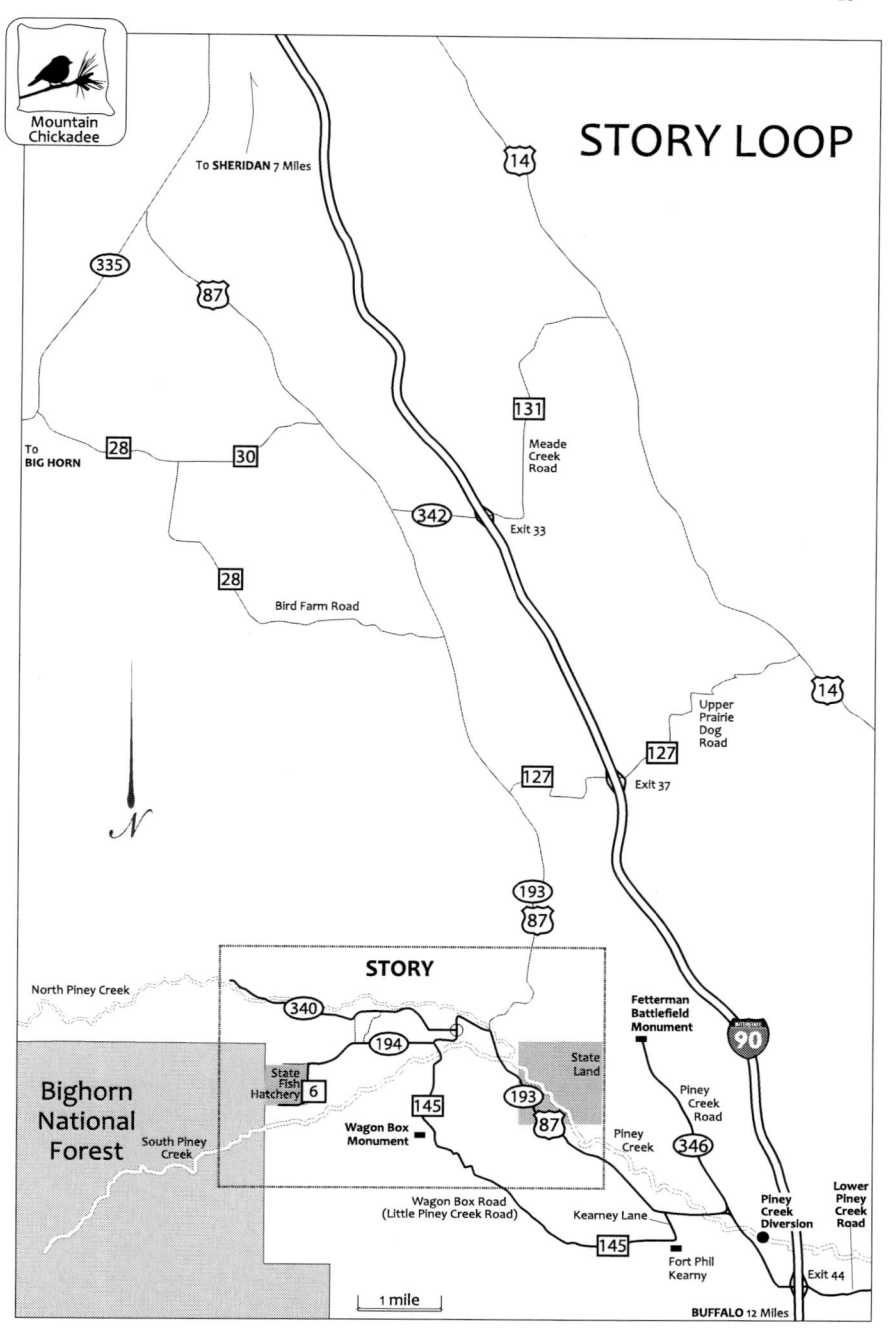

Map 5. Story Loop. Map by Wolfgang Schwartz

Piney Creek Road (Wyo. 340). Follow the road past the Wagon Box Inn. The pavement ends at mile 1.7, and the **Red Trailhead** is on the left side of the road at 2.5 miles. To the west you can see Moncreiffe Ridge, from which North Piney Creek flows south. To access the trail, park on the left side of the road. The 1-mile trail links with the Penrose Trail. The first 0.75 miles is a private property easement, so stay on the trail. At about 0.75 miles the trail enters public land (USFS). The trail passes through a forest of ponderosa pine, Douglas-fir, limber pine and aspen and then climbs to views of lupine and the bright yellow arrow-leaf balsamroot that share the forest understory. Common spring birds are the Ruby-crowned Kinglet, Western Tanager, Yellow-rumped Warbler, Mountain Chickadee, Red-breasted Nuthatch, and a variety of *Empidonax* flycatchers. This area of the Bighorn Mountains also has a small population of Ovenbirds.

Travel back to Fish Hatchery Road and continue 2.5 miles to **Wagon Box Road** (Sheridan County Route 145), which is called Little Piney Creek Road by the locals. Turn right and follow the Wagon Box Road to the **Wagon Box Monument**. The road travels through several productive birding miles. Go about 0.6 miles to the Catholic Church on the right. Here there are hawthorns and lilac bushes that provide good hummingbird habitat. Look on the electrical wires above, or at the feeders at the house below, for both the Calliope and the Broad-tailed hummingbirds. Both species are common in Story from late May into summer. In mid-July, the Rufous Hummingbird arrives, and replaces those species. Leaving the church, follow the road until the sign on the right for Wagon Box Road and Monument. Turn right and park. On August 2, 1867, Red Cloud's Lakota (Sioux) warriors attacked a group of soldiers. The soldiers removed the storage boxes from wagons, arranging them in a circle in an open area, and piled sacks of grain on top. Of the 32 men inside the resulting wagonbox fort, only three died, while all the others outside the fortress circle perished. This monument commemorates the memory of those men. The wildflowers in this area are magnificent in early June, and the open grasslands surrounding the historic site support Bobolinks, Savannah Sparrows and other grassland sparrows. From the monument, travel back to the main Wagon Box Road and turn right. At 0.3 is **Little Piney Creek** and the beginning of excellent riparian habitat of cottonwoods and aspen. Lazuli Buntings may be found in the brushy ravines, American Redstarts and MacGillivray's Warblers are known to nest in the area, and Ovenbirds can be heard from the trees. Sharp-tailed Grouse were once common to the hillsides, but housing developments have reduced their habitat. After about two miles of good birding habitat, houses begin to appear, and after three miles one reaches the rear entrance to **Fort Phil Kearny**.

Birding Loops — Story

The meadow here supports Bobolinks. At 3.9 miles turn to the Fort, or continue on to State Route 193. From there one may return north to Story, or go south to Buffalo.

From Story, travel on US Route 87 (State Route 193) to Buffalo. This road is called the **Piney Creek Road** by the locals. It follows Piney Creek and offers several birding stops en route. At 0.8 miles, stop at the Wyoming State Land Trust sign. The land provides public access to a portion of Piney Creek. Park on the left, enter through the gate, and follow the game trails to the creek. After that stop, continue 3.4 miles to the **Fort Phil Kearny** site, or turn left and go 2.0 miles to the site of the **Fetterman Battlefield and Monument**. Fort Phil Kearny and the Fetterman Battlefield were the focal point of a violent war between the U.S. Army and the Dakota (Sioux), Cheyenne, and Arapaho Indians. Both sites preserve the history of these conflicts. Today, visitors can walk in the footsteps of history on the Fetterman Battlefield, which includes interpretive signs explaining detailed battle tactics. The short hike offers incredible vistas of the mountains, foothills, and surrounding area, as well as excellent grassland birding and hawk-viewing. Watch for pronghorns along the mountain foothills. Benches along the trail provide a potential rest or lunch stop.

Continue back to US Route 87, turn left, and at 0.3 miles you will see the **Piney Creek Diversion** on the left. In 1907 Piney Creek and Clear Creek irrigators constructed a dam and built a canal to divert water from Piney Creek. At 0.8 miles there is an Osprey nesting platform. The Ospreys have access to good fishing at the Lake DeSmet, and are very successful at fledging young. At 1.4 miles you will enter Interstate 90 en route to Buffalo. There is another prominent Osprey nest platform along the interstate, about 2 miles past the freeway entrance.

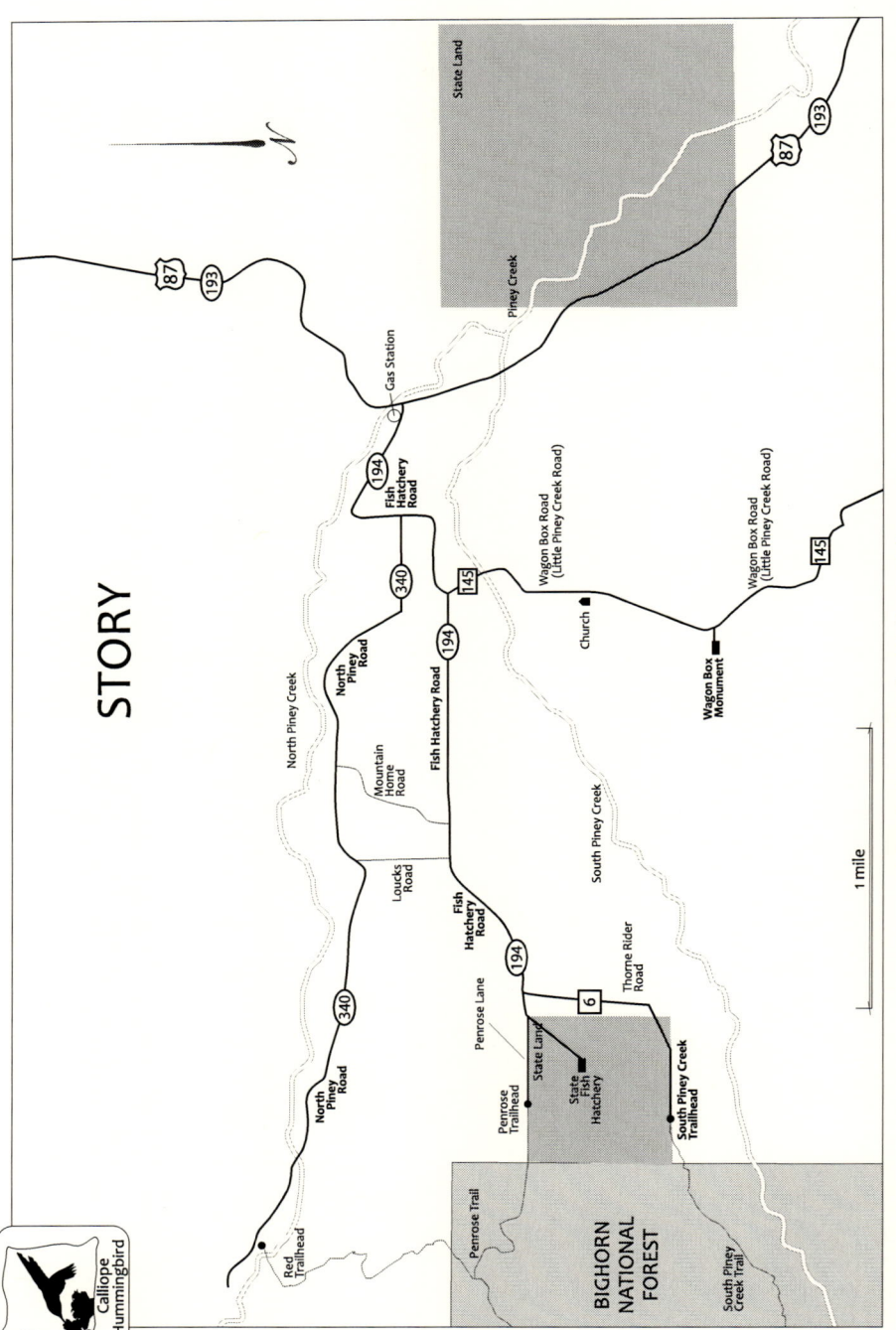

Map 6. Story. Map by Wolfgang Schwartz

Buffalo Loop

Lake DeSmet
Rock Creek Road
Buffalo
Clear Creek Trail
Mosier Gulch Picnic Area
Kumor Road
Moore's Reservoir
South Dam Pond
Healy Reservoir
Clear Creek Diversion
Ucross

From Story, continue on I-90 to the Shell Creek Road Exit and follow Shell Creek Road to Monument Road leading to **Lake DeSmet**. The road ends at a small boat dock with picnic tables. As you look at the lake, imagine the rich and colorful human and geological history. The Dakota and Crow Indians used this area, and referred to it as "Medicine Lake" (meaning a lake of great spiritual importance). Later, it was named for an early Catholic missionary, Father DeSmet (1801–1873). The lake-bed is underlain by coal deposits, which have been sought-after for decades. In 1957, Reynolds Mining purchased the lake's water and coal rights. In 1976, Texaco purchased the rights from Reynolds Mining, and began raising the water level of the lake. This inundated all of the mud flats, sandy beaches, and the large area of beach grass along the shore that had been used by shorebirds. The shoreline habitat was gone by 1980. The coal deposits and water rights were purchased in 2013 by Statoil, an international energy company and the world's leading expert on coal-to-fuels production.

Lake DeSmet has historically been one of the best local birding areas for waterfowl, loons, cormorants, grebes, and gulls, since there are few lakes in the Sheridan area. DeSmet is deep, so it freezes late, allowing birds to use it from April through December. There is a nesting colony of Double-crested Cormorants that was established in 1980 on a small island on the north end of the lake. Since the late 1920s this species has expanded its range as a Wyoming breeding species (Faulkner, 2012). These birds can be seen regularly flying over the lake from March through November. California, Ring-billed and Herring gulls can be seen from April through November. I saw a Tundra Swan in December of 2012 and I have watched Western Grebes and Common Loons congregate on the lake during spring migration in April. Rarities such as the Black, Surf, and White-winged scoters have

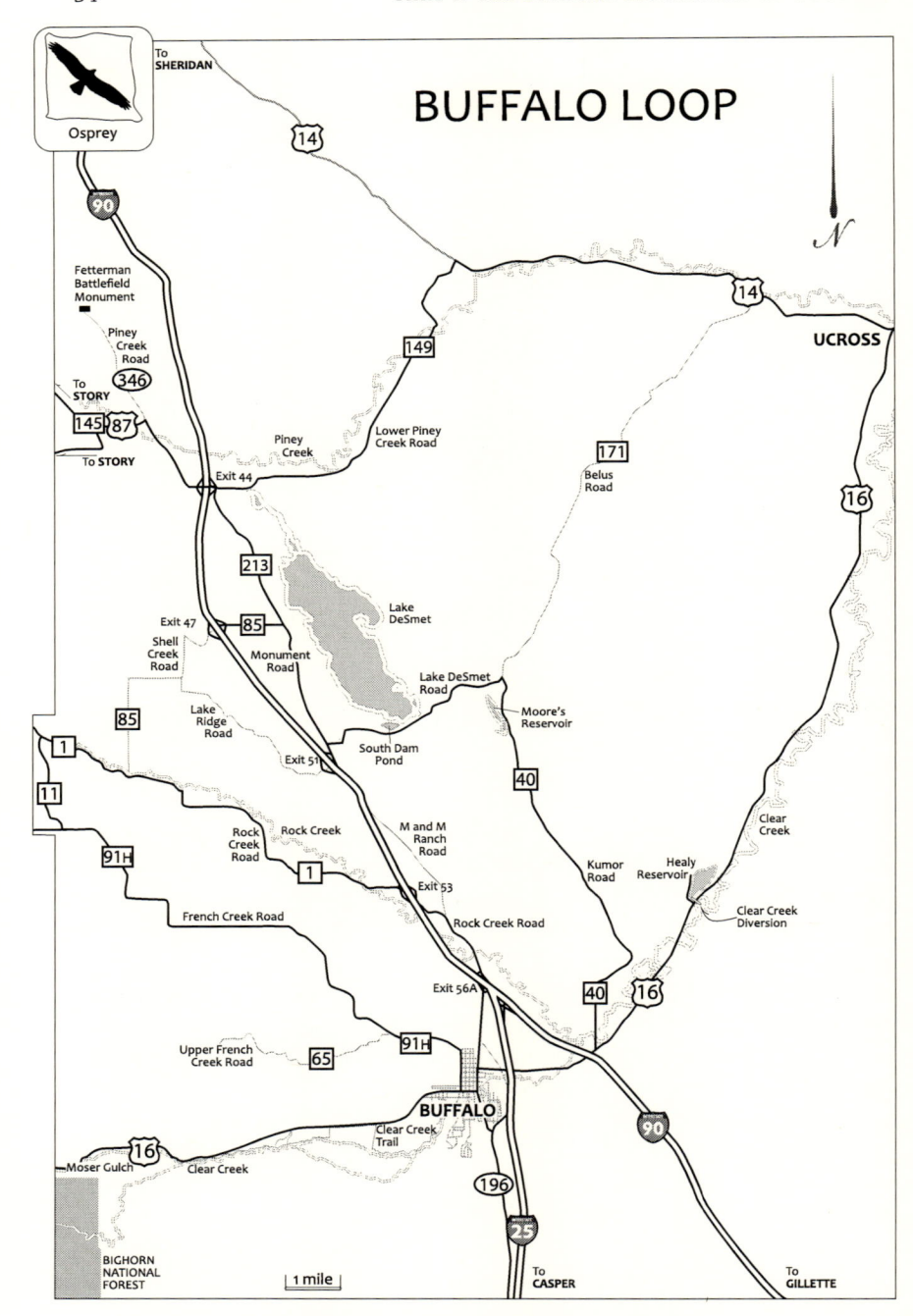

Map 7. Buffalo Loop. Map by Wolfgang Schwartz

been observed as well. In fact, of the 25 waterfowl on our *Checklist of Bighorn Mountain Birds* (Canterbury and Johnsgard, 2013), 22 have been observed on Lake DeSmet.

After viewing Lake DeSmet return to I-90 and take a right onto **Rock Creek Road.** The Rock Creek Road turns into Johnson Creek and the French Creek Road, eventually reaching Buffalo, or one may continue south on I-90 directly to Buffalo. **Buffalo** was home to the Johnson County Wars, pitting newly settled ranchers against wealthy long-time land-owners, and was named after Buffalo, New York. It is a quaint town with many options for birding and hiking along the **Clear Creek Trail**. The entire Clear Creek Trail System includes about 17 miles of trail along Clear Creek. The three forks of Clear Creek originate on the east face of the Bighorn Mountains and eventually flow into the Powder River. More than 60 species of birds can be found along the creek, including Warbling Vireos, Yellow-billed Cuckoos, and Ovenbirds. Begin hiking on Main Street and head west on Fetterman Street. At Klondike Drive, there is an access point and kiosk for the Clear Creek Trail. The walking path continues through the Veterans' Home of Wyoming pasture and then to US Route 16 bike path. The bike path merges into the 3.5-mile William Mentock Trail that traverses the ponderosa-pine foothills of the Bighorn Mountains. It ends at the **Mosier Gulch Picnic Area t**hat was created in 1986 from public lands remaining from the Fort McKinney Military Reserve. In 2011, 5.2 additional miles of new trail was built to access Grouse Mountain.

From Buffalo, travel east on US Route 16 and take a left onto **Kumor Road,** or travel north on Highway 16 to Ucross. The first option, Kumor Road, parallels agricultural lands for the first few miles then opens to native sagebrush. This is excellent hawk country and a wonderful place to walk. Red-tailed Hawks and Golden Eagles can be seen soaring in spring and summer, and Rough-legged Hawks and Bald Eagles frequent the area in winter. I have observed Upland Sandpipers, Kestrels, Upland Sandpipers, as well as Vesper and Lark Sparrows along Kumor Road. Continue 7.5 miles to **Moore's Reservoir**. Moore's Reservoir provides a shallow shoreline zone that supports many aquatic plants and insects important for ducks, geese, and grebes. Most lakes and ponds in this area have no vegetation to provide cover for wildlife; the vegetation that occurs most often are cattails, and very few have rushes. Moore's Reservoir is one of the very few with an extensive stand of rushes. This cover provides nesting sites for Pied-billed Grebes, Virginia Rails, Soras, American Coots, Canada Geese, a variety of ducks, and also attracts a number of migratory birds (Downing, 1990). The cattails along the shoreline provide habitat for Common Yellowthroats and Red-winged Blackbirds. I have also observed Northern Harriers flying low over the wetlands. Migrant Hooded Mergansers have been seen here, as well as Tundra Swans (Scott, 1993). Take a left off Kumor Road onto Lake DeSmet Road at the southern end of the lake. Continue to **South Dam Pond,** an area to look for American Coots. I watched a female with three juveniles feeding in this pond.

Another option is to head north on US Route 16 to Ucross. Travel US Route 16 about 7.1 miles to **Healy Reservoir**. This beautiful road follows Clear Creek. Healy Reservoir was built in 1957 for industrial and domestic water use, and also for electrical power. Continue about one mile to the parking lot. This is one of the best places for seeing ducks in the area. It often has Northern Shovelers, Northern Pintails, Mallards, Gadwalls, and American Wigeons. According to Scott (1993), rarities such as the Eurasian Wigeon and Red-throated Loon were seen here in October, 1985. Ospreys are common in spring and summer, because of the nesting platform that was created to keep the birds from nesting on power poles. There are several such nest platforms located near the fish resources of Lake DeSmet. Across the road from Healy Reservoir is the **Clear Creek Diversion**. The diversion dam was built to divert water from Clear Creek into the Healy Reservoir, which feeds water into Lake DeSmet. Waterfowl use this area during migration, and shorebirds are found here during times of peak irrigation demands, when water levels are low and the shoreline is exposed. After viewing the reservoir, continue north to **Ucross**.

Birding in the Bighorn Mountain Roadless Areas

by Jacqueline L. Canterbury

There are currently approximately 1,818 miles of roads in the Bighorn National Forest, or approximately 1.04 miles of road per square mile of National Forest, including both wilderness and private lands (Winters et al., 2004). The high road density in the Bighorn Mountains has compromised the integrity of the forest for wildlife, and for people who want solitude. Therefore, those areas that are currently roadless are very important to protect. According to the 2001 Roadless Area Conservation Rule, there are 640,000 acres of roadless lands remaining within the Bighorn National Forest (Bighorn National Forest, 2013). The birding areas described below remain without roads, and hopefully will remain so into the far distant future. Enjoy them, and work to keep them wild.

The western and eastern canyons of the Bighorn Mountains are very different from one another. The western side of the Bighorns is more arid and the western canyons are deep. The sandstone rock formations on the western slopes of the Bighorn Mountains appear to be painted red, and are carved into deep canyons with remarkably rich riparian systems at their base. These canyons also offer one the opportunity to experience marked clinal altitudinal transitions in habitats. For example, many of these canyon trails begin in subalpine habitats at about 9,000 feet, and end in much lower elevation riparian areas. In contrast, the canyons along the eastern edge of the Bighorns are shorter and less rugged. The highways to these areas are also great for birders and offer excellent drives. But hiking and birding in the canyons is an experience unto itself. Below I detail the roadless birding areas, including (from north to south) the Little Bighorn Canyon, Trapper Canyon, Medicine Lodge Canyon and Paint Rock Canyon. Only Crazy Woman Canyon is on the eastern side of the mountains, and an exception in that it is not roadless. For travel to the roadless sites I suggest getting information from the responsible land management agency offices. The land agencies are listed below:

USDA Forest Service, Bighorn National Forest
2013 Eastside 2nd Street, Sheridan, WY 82801. 307-674-2600

BLM Field Office: Wind River/Bighorn Basin District
District Manager: Steve Dondero
101 South 23rd Street, Worland, WY 82401, 307-347-5100

BLM Field Office: Medicine Wheel/Paintrock Ranger District
604 East Main, Lovell, WY 82431, 307-548-6541

BLM Field Office: Powder River Ranger District
1415 Fort Street, Buffalo, WY 82834, 307-684-7806

BLM Field Office: Tongue Ranger District
2013 Eastside 2nd Street, Sheridan, WY 82801, 307-674-2600

Suggested Roadless-Area Birding Trails

by Jacqueline L. Canterbury

Little Bighorn Canyon and the Little Horn Trail: The name Bighorn Canyon comes from its association with the Bighorn River, which was named by William Clark for the great numbers of bighorn sheep observed at its mouth (Urbanek, 1988). This canyon area of 134,760 acres of national forest land is the largest of the remaining roadless areas within the Bighorn National Forest. The habitat of the Little Bighorn Canyon ranges from high-elevation bunchgrass Palouse prairie (typical of the Pacific Northwest) at Bull Elk Park to low-elevation forests of Douglas-fir and ponderosa pine. The Little Horn Trailhead starts at the Kerns Wildlife Management Unit and follows the Little Bighorn River. After about 2.1 miles, the trail merges into the granite-faced inner gorge of the canyon. The trail continues about 16 miles from the mouth of the canyon to Forest Road 135. During fall the rare Harlequin Duck might be seen in the fast-moving waters. The Dusky Grouse and Ruffed Grouse are both present in the forest and might be readily seen or heard in spring. Passerine birds found here are include a variety of regional grassland, coniferous forest and riparian species.

Trapper Canyon: Trapper Canyon was named for the trappers who lived in canyon dugouts in the 1880s (Urbanek, 1988). Trapper Canyon contains 7,200 acres of remote BLM land that has been recommended as a Wilderness Study Area (WSA). This means that the BLM regards this land as suitable for a wilderness designation, and therefore it must be managed to reserve its wilderness characteristics. Trapper Canyon is located about five miles southeast of Shell. Although surrounded by private land, the BLM has an easement across private property on Trapper Creek Road (BLM Road 1114), located along the south boundary of the WSA. Access is from Shell southeast on Trapper Creek Road, drive straight to the southeast boundary. The habitat is varied, and changes from sagebrush steppe to Douglas-fir forest. This is a steep hike with no trail, and requires stamina and persistence. However, the birding rewards are great, and sightings may include Golden and Bald eagles, and Prairie and Peregrine falcons. The shrubby riparian area contains stands of mountain mahogany, sagebrush and other arid-adapted plants. This diversity provides birders the opportunity to see American Dippers, Violet-Green Swallows and various warblers. Common Ravens can be seen flying along the canyon walls, and are more common in the western canyons of the Bighorn Mountains than on the eastern slope.

Medicine Lodge Canyon: Medicine Lodge was named after the medicines Native Americans made at their winter camp on the banks of Medicine Lodge Creek (Urbanek, 1988). The Medicine Lodge Wilderness Study Area encompasses 7,740 acres of BLM-administered land and 20,760 acres of National Forest roadless land. Only 3,600 acres of this total were actually recommended for formal Wilderness designation. This, however, is too small a parcel to be recommended for Wilderness, so the designation may not be achieved until the agencies come together with a new proposal. Medicine Lodge Canyon is accessed from Cold Springs Road. The 6.4-mile hike starts at Captain Jack Creek, and ends at the Dry Medicine Lodge Road. Elevations in this canyon range between 5,100 and 8,500 feet. The habitat varies from sagebrush to juniper woodlands in the foothills to tall stands of Douglas-fir, which extend down to the canyon floor. There is mountain mahogany brushland on the side-slopes that provides forage for wintering elk. This plant diversity offers a chance to see some ecologically diverse species, such as Mountain Bluebirds, Canyon Wrens, Song Sparrows, Mountain Chickadees and Townsend's Solitaires.

Paint Rock Canyon: Paint Rock Canyon was named by Native American peoples who used the clay from the banks of the creek for ceremonial paint (Urbanek, 1988). This canyon area consists of 11,588 acres of unprotected BLM land, and 4,480 acres of National Forest land. The canyon can be accessed from Hyattville. Head north 0.5 mile to the Cold Springs Road and continue about four miles east to the trailhead. A very steep trail drops into the canyon and enters the rich bottomlands of Paint Rock Creek. The Paint Rock Canyon Trail extends 5 miles along Paint Rock Creek and follows an old road that enters BLM land and enters cottonwoods and riparian woodlands. This is the only canyon along the west slope of the Bighorn Mountains that does not involve bushwacking. The habitat ranges from sagebrush to Douglas-fir and lodgepole pine forest. Some ponderosa pine can be found along the stream and the canyon's upper walls. The steep limestone cliffs provide nesting sites for Golden Eagles and Prairie Falcons; I have seen both in the canyon. Spring arrives in late May and early June. I have heard the largest concentration of Yellow-breasted Chats in late May of 2013, when I heard the birds arrive, uttering a nocturnal symphony, from their wintering grounds in South America. The Spotted Towhee share the dense understory with the chats. Also present are the Yellow Warbler, Warbling Vireo, Lazuli Bunting, Violet-Green Swallow and Western Tanager. The White-throated Swift can usually be seen flying above the canyon rim.

Birding by Car in the Bighorn Mountains

by Jacqueline L. Canterbury

Shell Creek Canyon and Tensleep Canyon are both perfect places to see birds while driving through incredibly beautiful canyon country. There are pull-offs along the roadway, and Shell Falls offers the Bighorn National Forest Visitor Center.

Shell Creek Canyon: Shell Creek Canyon was formed by Shell Creek slicing into 2.9-billion year old Precambrian rock (Lageson and Spearing, 1988). Shell Canyon was named for the fossilized shells that are found in sediments above the earlier Precambrian bedrock (Urbanek, 1988). From Sheridan, travel north on I-90 to Ranchester and take US Route 14 to Burgess Junction. US Route 14 from the Bighorn National Forest to Shell is known as the Bighorn Scenic Byway. About half way down the canyon is the Shell Falls Visitor Canter, open from May to September. The Center puts out hummingbird feeders seasonally, and provides seats to enjoy the summer avian spectacle, as well as offering a wonderful view of Shell Falls. I have watched Calliope, Broad-tailed, and Rufous hummingbirds at Shell Falls. About six miles down the road there is a pullout above the creek that is a good site to look for Western Tanagers and Lazuli Buntings. One of my favorite spots on this route is the Shell Canyon Research Natural Area (on the left side) a few miles down the canyon from Shell Falls. This area offers a relatively easy hike through a juniper community. The best part of the hike is finding the Townsend's Solitaires that I have often heard singing in the junipers during both spring and winter months. This area seems to be an important area for this species, probably because of the abundance of juniper berries, a major winter food.

Tensleep Canyon: Tensleep Canyon was named by Native Americans because the canyon site was located "10 sleeps" from Fort Laramie to Yellowstone (Urbanek, 1988; Lageson and Spearing, 1988). Tensleep Canyon provides an exposure of a yellow sandstone, known geologically as the Tensleep Formation (Lageson and Spearing, 1988). From Buffalo, continue through town and then follow US Route 16. The Bighorn National Forest Boundary is about 13 miles west of Buffalo, and the Forest extends 45 miles along US Route 16. This 45-mile stretch through the Bighorn Mountains into Tensleep Canyon has many pullouts for viewing birds in different habitats and corresponding elevations. The trip starts in Buffalo at 4,650 feet elevation and climbs to 9,666 feet at Powder River Pass. The Nature Conservancy also owns the 9,000-acre Tensleep Preserve along a twelve-mile stretch of Canyon Creek, which is open to the public from May through October (Phone: 307- 366-2671). The Nature Conservancy's website suggests the preserve is home to some 120 bird species. This route also allows access to the last site: Crazy Woman Canyon. Tensleep's common grassland birds include the

Western Meadowlark, Lark Bunting, Lark Sparrow, Vesper Sparrow, Brewer's Sparrow and Sage Sparrow. The Violet-Green, Cliff, Barn, and Northern Rough-Winged swallows can all easily be seen here during summer.

Crazy Woman Canyon: This canyon is said to have been named for the legend of a woman who lost her mind after witnessing the death of her family, and yet remained in the mountains. Crazy Woman Creek begins near Clear Creek on the east face of the Bighorn Mountains and flows into the Powder River to the east. The eastern side of the Bighorn Mountains offers a different visual perspective and more accessibility than the western slope. Access to Crazy Woman Canyon is via US Route 16 from Buffalo, then along Forest Service Road 33 to Crazy Woman Canyon Road. Crazy Woman Mountain to the north is 7,205 feet in elevation. The canyon's walls are narrow, and the creek runs fast. The habitat is diverse, and this canyon has a corresponding high diversity of coniferous forest birds. The Mountain Chickadee, Townsend's Solitaire, Pine Siskin, Ruby-crowned Kinglet, Dark-eyed Junco, Chipping Sparrow, Mountain Bluebird, Western Wood-Pewee and Yellow-rumped Warbler have all been seen commonly in the canyon. In fact, according to the North American Breeding Bird Survey results, Crazy Woman Canyon had the highest number of birds per route, as compared to other BBS routes in the region (Table 3). It is important to note that the survey route was south of Crazy Woman Canyon.

Part II
Annotated List of Regional Birds

by Paul A. Johnsgard

The following list of regional birds closely follows the earlier edition, but includes updated taxonomy, more recent records, and additional relevant information. Newly included species include the Boreal Owl and Eurasian Collared-Dove, the former a species that is difficult to detect, and the latter a rapidly expanding invasive species, as well as several newly recognized species that have emerged as a result of recent taxonomic "splitting." Some species, such as the Snow Goose, Canada Goose, Osprey and Bald Eagle, have seemingly become more abundant in the region as a reflection of national population trends. Others, such as some grassland-dependent species and the sagebrush-obligate Greater Sage-Grouse, have been in a prolonged state of gradual decline, the result of extensive losses of critical habitats.

Some of the regional population changes might even be the result of climate change (global warming), such as the apparent national declines of rosy-finches, which depend upon their relatively rare and now rapidly shrinking alpine habitats needed for breeding. The most recently available national survey of North American bird populations, the annual Breeding Bird Surveys from 1966 through 2011, indicated that at least 140 species were then in statistically significant population declines, while 85 were increasing significantly.

With the advent of climate change, there has been a great increase in forest fires, intense droughts, and infestations of bark beetles in the coniferous forests of the region. The resulting losses of coniferous trees is likely to seriously impact the many finches that depend on conifer seeds, such as Cassin's finch, Red and White-winged crossbills, and Evening Grosbeaks, as well as other species such as Clark's Nutcrackers and seed-dependent mammals. On the other hand, several beetle-eating woodpeckers, including the relatively rare Black-backed, American Three-toed and Lewis's, will benefit from the increased supply of available insect foods.

Family Anatidae: Waterfowl

Hooded Merganser

Greater White-fronted Goose, *Anser albifrons*: extremely rare spring (April–May) and fall (Oct.–Dec.) transient L5. Most reports are from Lake DeSmet. Not reported regionally on eBird from 1-1-1990 through 4-25-2013. While on migration these birds sometimes fly in company with Canada Geese. Like Canada Geese, they forage in grain fields and other croplands, and usually roost in large, open marshes. Breeding is done on open arctic tundra, and in general the birds avoid forested areas.

Snow Goose, *Chen caerulescens:* uncommon spring and fall (Mar.–May, Oct.–Dec.) transient L4 & 5. A few flocks seen per season is usual; the highest substantiated number in one day was 1,000. Many are seen at Lake DeSmet and other reservoirs. Average spring arrival, 4-22. The dark-plumaged genetic morph ("blue goose") of the Snow Goose is extremely rare in this region, but is relatively common in the Great Plains. However, Snow Geese are increasing rapidly in the Great Plains and throughout North America, and both plumage morphs are likely to be seen more frequently in the Bighorn region.

Ross's Goose, *Chen rossii*: extremely rare fall (Oct.–Nov.) vagrant L4 & 5. One was at Healy Reservoir October 28, 1984, and one with a flock of Canada Geese at Rapid Creek, November 1, 1985. Not reported regionally on eBird from 1-1-1990 through 4-25-2013. Migrating birds have similar habitat needs to those of Snow Geese, and often mingle with them. Like the Snow Goose, this species' population is increasing rapidly, and is likely to be increasingly seen regionally.

Canada Goose, *Branta canadensis*: abundant spring and fall transient, fairly common summer resident, uncommon winter resident; breeding confirmed L4 & 5. Average spring arrival, 3-10. A pair began nesting activities in an Osprey nest in a dead cottonwood about 30 feet above the water at Healy Reservoir early in the spring of 1988; the late arriving Osprey had to move elsewhere. Migrating flocks of Canada Geese have been estimated to number 15,000 birds. The Canada Goose was observed during all 21 years of Spring Bird Counts in Johnson County, 1984–2004, during 16 of 26 years of Christmas Bird Counts at Buffalo, 1986–2011 and during all four Spring Bird Counts in Sheridan County, 2009–2012. This extremely adaptable goose increasingly nests within the city limits of large cities, but also occurs on prairie marshes, beaver ponds, and forest-edged mountain lakes. Beaver lodges or muskrat houses provide safe and favored nest sites in many areas. Breeding Bird Surveys indicate that national Canada Goose populations are increasing significantly at a remarkably high rate (8.8% annually, 1966-2011). In 2004, the tundra-nesting populations of very small "white-cheeked" geese were taxonomically split off from the larger forms of Canada Geese, and recognized as the Cackling Goose by the A.O.U. (see hypothetical species list).

Trumpeter Swan, *Cygnus buccinator*: extremely rare spring and fall vagrant L5. Six at the south end of Lake DeSmet November 18, 1968; an April

1984 observation was also at Lake DeSmet. Not reported regionally on eBird from 1-1-1990 through 4-25-2013. In the Rocky Mountain region this species is mostly limited to fairly large ponds having considerable aquatic vegetation and relative seclusion from disturbance by humans. Beaver ponds are most often used for nesting, and nests are sometimes built on their lodges. The Rocky Mountain flock has been in decline in recent years, although the introduced Great Plains population is rapidly expanding.

Tundra Swan, *Cygnus columbianus*: rare spring, uncommon late fall (Apr,–May, Oct.–Jan.) transient, rare winter visitant L4 & 5; usually seen in family groups with independent young. Average spring arrival, 4-20. Most often found at Lake DeSmet, but also at Shell Reservoir nearby, Tongue River at Dayton, Wagner Reservoir, and McClain's Pond. Reported once regionally on eBird from 1-1-1990 through 4-25-2013, at Lake DeSmet, 12-16-2012. The Tundra Swan was observed during one of 21 years of Spring Bird Counts in Johnson County, 1984–2004, and during one of 26 years of Christmas Bird Counts at Buffalo, 1986–2011. On migration, Tundra Swans frequent favored stopover points that are used every year. These are usually shallow marshes rich in submerged vegetation, which is the major food source for these birds. Field-feeding on dry land has also been observed rarely in migrating birds. Until the 1980s, this swan was considered a species distinct from the Eurasian Bewick's Swan, and until then had been called the Whistling Swan.

Wood Duck, *Aix sponsa*: uncommon spring and fall transient and summer resident (Mar.–Oct.); breeding confirmed L4 & 5. Average spring arrival, 4-21. Wood Ducks were reported only twice from 1966 through 1977 when there were few observers; since then Wood Ducks have been recorded almost every year. Successful rearing of young was reported on Tongue River near Dayton, the Ash Creek and Tongue River confluence, and on Clear Creek at Ucross. They are now found on all reservoirs and creeks during migration. The Wood Duck was observed during 11 of 21 years of Spring Bird Counts in Johnson County, 1984–2004, during two of 26 years of Christmas Bird Counts at Buffalo, 1986–2011, and during all four Spring Bird Counts in Sheridan County, 2009–2012. Breeding Bird Surveys indicate that national populations are increasing significantly (2.1% annually, 1966-2011). During the breeding season these birds are found among woodlands having fairly large trees offering nesting holes, and frequently also those having acorns or similar nutlike foods in abundance. Even outside the breeding season the birds are usually associated with flooded woodlands rather than open marshes.

Gadwall, *Anas strepera*: abundant spring and fall transient, common summer resident, extremely rare winter visitant (Feb.–Dec.); breeding confirmed L4 & 5. Average spring arrival, 3-23. Found at Lake DeSmet, Moore's Reservoir, McClain's Pond, ponds east of Arvada. The Gadwall was observed during all 21 years of Spring Bird Counts in Johnson County, 1984–2004, during one of 26 years of Christmas Bird Counts at Buffalo, 1986–2011, and during two of four Spring Bird Counts in Sheridan County, 2009–2012. This prairie-adapted dabbling duck prefers shallow marshes with grassy or weedy nesting cover, especially where low islands are present.

Eurasian Wigeon, *Anas penelope*: extremely rare fall vagrant L5. A male, with at least three females was found at the Lake DeSmet South Dam Pond 9-22-1983; and a male was at the same pond 10-18-1990. Three were seen at McClain's Pond, 4-10-1996 (Faulkner, 2010). Not reported regionally on eBird from 1-1-1990 through 4-25-2013.

American Wigeon, *Anas americana*: abundant spring and fall transient, common summer resident L4 & 5, extremely rare winter visitant L5; breeding confirmed L4 & L5. Average spring arrival, 3-24. Found at all reservoirs and ponds; largest numbers are seen at Lake DeSmet. The American Wigeon was observed during four of 21 years of Spring Bird Counts in Johnson County, 1984–2004, during five of 26 years of Christmas Bird Counts at Buffalo, 1986–2011, and during two of four Spring Bird Counts in Sheridan County, 2009–2012. Wigeons are associated with relatively open marshes and lakes having abundant aquatic vegetation at or near the surface, and in the breeding season favoring areas with sedge meadows or with shrubby or partially wooded habitats nearby. Wigeons are strongly vegetarian, and spend more time grazing grassy vegetation than do most ducks.

Mallard, *Anas platyrhynchos*: abundant early spring and fall, common to abundant summer and winter resident; breeding confirmed L4 & 5. The Mallard was observed during all 21 years of Spring Bird Counts in Johnson County, 1984–2004, during all 26 years of Christmas Bird Counts at Buffalo, 1986–2011, and during all four Spring Bird Counts in Sheridan County, 2009–2012. This highly adaptable species nests on nearly aquatic habitats, but prefers non-forested areas over forested ones, and shallow waters over deeper ones. Mallards quickly locate and utilize protected areas, even when close to human activities, and thus remain common in spite of intensive hunting pressures on them.

Blue-winged Teal, *Anas discors*: common spring transient and summer resident, abundant early fall transient, fairly common late fall (Apr.–Nov.); breeding confirmed L4 & 5. Average spring arrival, 4-17. Females with young found at Buffalo Creek northeast of Sheridan, McClain's Pond, and near Burgess Junction at about 8,000' elevation. The Blue-winged Teal was observed during all 21 years of Spring Bird Counts in Johnson County, 1984–2004. It was not observed during 26 years of Christmas Bird Counts at Buffalo, 1986–2011, but was reported during all four Spring Bird Counts in Sheridan County, 2009–2012. This species favors relatively small, shallow marshes over larger and deeper ones, especially those that are surrounded by grass or sedge meadows. Some birds winter south to South America. Migration in spring occurs fairly late, as does pair formation, but nonetheless renesting efforts are fairly common following nest failure.

Cinnamon Teal, *Anas cyanoptera*: uncommon spring and fall transient and summer (Apr.–Oct.) resident; breeding confirmed L4, assumed L5. Average spring arrival, 4-17. Found at Fletcher's, Forbes' and McClain's Beckton ponds, Lake DeSmet, Moore's Reservoir, a pond on Red Grade at about 7,000', and a pothole on Hazelton Road southwest of Buffalo off U. S. Hwy. 16, at about 8,000' elevation. The Cinnamon Teal was observed during 17 of 21 years of Spring Bird Counts in Johnson County, 1984–2004. It was not observed during 26 years of Christmas Bird Counts at Buffalo, 1986–2011, but was seen during two of four Spring Bird Counts in Sheridan County, 2009–2012. This species is associated with small, shallow and often somewhat alkaline marshes of western North America, overlapping with and variably replacing the Blue-winged Teal westwardly.

Northern Shoveler, *Anas clypeata*: abundant spring and fall transient, fairly common summer resident (Mar.–Dec.); breeding confirmed L4 & 5. Average spring arrival, 4-3. Found at all reservoirs and ponds. The Northern Shoveler was observed during 20 of 21 years of Spring Bird Counts in Johnson County, 1984–2004, during two of 26 years of Christmas Bird Counts at Buffalo, 1986–2011, and during two of four Spring Bird Counts in Sheridan County, 2009–2012. The specialized bill of this species allows for filter-feeding of surface organisms, and submerged plants sometimes also provide a supply of organisms that can be reached from the surface.

Northern Pintail, *Anas acuta*: abundant spring transient, fairly common summer resident, common fall transient (Mar.–Dec.); breeding confirmed L4 & 5. Average spring arrival, 3-15. First arrivals are usually found at Clear Creek Diversion. Females with young have been seen at Early Creek, Lake DeSmet, and McClain's Pond. The Northern Pintail was observed during 14 of 21 years of Spring Bird Counts in Johnson County, 1984–2004. It was not observed during 26 years of Christmas Bird Counts at Buffalo, 1986–2011. Not regularly observed during Spring Bird Counts in Sheridan County. This is a tundra- and prairie-adapted breeding species, and it is rarely found in heavily wooded wetlands. It can breed on small and temporary ponds as well as permanent marshes, and frequently nests on dry land in extremely exposed situations well away from water.

Green-winged Teal, *Anas crecca*: common spring and fall transient, fairly common summer resident, rare winter visitant; breeding confirmed L4 & 5. Average spring arrival, 3-7- Found on all reservoirs and creeks; recorded at Arrowhead Lodge, 7,656' elevation; and a marsh on Muddy Creek, 8,000' elevation. The Green-winged Teal was observed during 19 of 21 years of Spring Bird Counts in Johnson County, 1984–2004, during six of 26 years of Christmas Bird Counts at Buffalo, 1986–2011, and during two of four Spring Bird Counts in Sheridan County, 2009–2012. Nesting by this widely distributed teal frequently occurs in grasses, sedge meadows, or dry hillsides having brushy or aspen cover, near a pond or slough. On migration it is found on a variety of shallow wetlands.

Canvasback, *Aythya valisineria*: fairly common spring and fall transient, uncommon summer resident L4 & 5; extremely rare winter visitant (Mar.–Dec.); L5. Average spring arrival, 4-6. One known breeding occurrence, at Moore's Reservoir L5. Numbers in spring and fall migration are highly variable; up to 83 have been seen. The Canvasback was observed during five of 21 years of Spring Bird Counts in Johnson County, 1984–2004. It was not observed during 26 years of Christmas Bird Counts at Buffalo, 1986–2011, or in Sheridan County Spring Bird Counts, 2009–2012. In the breeding season, Canvasbacks are found on shallow prairie marshes with abundant growths of emergent vegetation and open water areas that frequently are rich in aquatic plants such as pondweeds.

Redhead, *Aythya americana*: common to abundant early spring transient, fairly common summer resident, common to abundant late fall transient (Mar.–Dec.); breeding confirmed L4 & 5. Average spring arrival,

3-26. Up to 2,000 have been seen found at Lake DeSmet and Moore's Reservoir. Highest known elevation sighting is at Sherd Lake, about 8,500'. The Redhead was observed during 20 of 21 years of Spring Bird Counts in Johnson County, 1984–2004, during five of 26 years of Christmas Bird Counts at Buffalo, 1986–2011, and during two of four Spring Bird Counts in Sheridan County, 2009–2012. Breeding habitats consist of non-forested country with water areas sufficiently deep to provide permanent, fairly dense emergent vegetation as nesting cover. Wetlands of an acre or more in area are preferred for nesting, especially those with substantial areas of open water for taking off and landing.

Ring-necked Duck, *Aythya collaris*: fairly common spring and fall transient, uncommon summer vagrant (Mar.–Dec.), L4 & 5; breeding not confirmed. Average spring arrival, 4-7. Pairs were seen several years at a pond on Hazelton Road between Hazelton and Dull Knife Reservoir in June at about 8,000' elevation. Moore's Reservoir is a good place to see this species in spring and fall; larger numbers occur at Lake DeSmet. The Ring-necked Duck was observed during 20 of 21 years of Spring Bird Counts in Johnson County, 1984–2004, during two of 26 years of Christmas Bird Counts at Buffalo, 1986–2011, and during one of four Spring Bird Counts in Sheridan County, 2009–2012. The Ring-necked Duck is strongly associated with beaver ponds and other forest wetlands, where it is often among the commonest of breeding ducks. Sedge-meadow marshes and boggy areas are preferred for nesting, and the presence of water lilies and associated heather cover seem to be an important part of breeding habitats.

Greater Scaup, *Aythya marila*: the status of this migrant is uncertain but it is probably an extremely rare spring (May) and fall (Nov.) vagrant. More than forty dates have been recorded in L4 & 5, but only three were well documented. They were: a male on 5-6-1979, another at Lake DeSmet on 11-9-1979, and six of both sexes at Holly Ponds 11-8-1981. A group of 10 was seen near Sheridan 10-19-1975 (Faulkner, 2010). Not reported regionally on eBird from 1-1-1990 through 4-25-2013. The Greater Scaup was observed during two of four Spring Bird Counts in Sheridan County, 2009–2012. It prefers rather larger water areas than do Lesser Scaups, such as lakes and deeper marshes.

Lesser Scaup, *Aythya affinis*: common to abundant spring and fall transient, rare summer visitor (Mar.–Dec.). L4 & 5; breeding not confirmed. Average spring arrival, 3-31. In 1975 a pair stayed at McClain's Pond all summer, but young were not seen. Migrant numbers vary from year to year; highest numbers have been 1,900 on 11-5-1978, and 2,700 on 11-15-1982, at Lake DeSmet. The Lesser Scaup was observed during all 21 years of Spring Bird Counts in Johnson County, 1984–2004, during three of 26 years of Christmas Bird Counts at Buffalo, 1986–2011, and during two of four Spring Bird Counts in Sheridan County, 2009–2012. This is largely a prairie-adapted breeder, and is associated also with ponds in the foothill woodlands, especially those supporting good populations of amphipods and other aquatic invertebrates.

Harlequin Duck, *Histrionicus histrionicus*: extremely rare in summer, but not enough records to determine if summer birds are vagrants, transients, or summer residents L4; breeding not confirmed. Four observations of males in Shell Creek Canyon ranged from May, 1978 to July 4, 1979. Two observations in the Little Bighorn River Canyon were: 5-22-1979 (male), and 5-21-1990 (male and female). Unconfirmed sightings in Story as well. Reported once regionally on eBird from 1-1-1990 through 4-25-2013, one at Twin Buttes 7-8-2007. Associated with clear, rapidly flowing streams, where aquatic insects such as caddis larvae abound; often found where American Dippers also occur.

Black Scoter, *Melanitta americana*: extremely rare fall (Oct.–Nov.) vagrant L5. Three observations: 10-9-1971, 11-1-1972, and 11-1-1975, two of the records were of females at Lake DeSmet. Not reported regionally on eBird from 1-1-1990 through 4-25-2013. Like the other scoters, this species is most likely to be encountered on large lakes or reservoirs while on migration. Female-like birds are most often seen; full-plumaged males are almost never seen regionally.

Surf Scoter, *Melanitta perspicillata*: rare spring (April–May) and fall (Oct.–Nov.) vagrant L5. Eleven observations of single birds, except two on 11-12-1983, and November 25, 1987; the first Surf Scoter reported in this area was found at Sheridan, 10-12-1970; also seen at Healy Reservoir, Lake DeSmet, the South Dam Pond. Not reported regionally on eBird from 1-1-1990 through 4-25-2013. The Surf Scoter was observed during one of 21 years of Spring Bird Counts in Johnson County, 1984–2004. It was not observed during 26 years of Christmas Bird Counts at Buffalo, 1986–2011. Like other scoters, this species is most likely to be encountered on large lakes or reservoirs while on migration; females or female-like immatures are typically seen.

White-winged Scoter, *Melanitta fusca:* rare spring (April) and fall (Oct.–Dec.) transient L4 & 5. Sixteen observations; the high count in one day (14) was on 10-26 and 28-1987, also seen at Healy Reservoir (four) and Lake DeSmet (ten); also seen at Fletcher's Pond. Not reported regionally on eBird from 1-1-1990 through 4-25-2013. Also seen 4-4-1982 at Sheridan (Faulkner, 2010). It is most likely to be seen on lakes and reservoirs, mainly during fall and winter.

Long-tailed Duck, *Clangula hyemalis*: rare fall (Oct.–Dec.) transient L5; eleven observations of one to three birds, both males and females in basic plumage, have occurrence at Lake DeSmet and Moore's Reservoir. Not reported regionally on eBird from 1-1-1990 through 4-25-2013. The Long-tailed Duck was not observed during 21 years of Spring Bird Counts in Johnson County, 1984–2004, but was reported during one of 26 years of Christmas Bird Counts at Buffalo, 1986–2011. Likely to be observed on reservoirs, lakes, or large rivers, while on migration. Known in North America as the Oldsquaw prior to 2000, when the racially inoffensive British name was adopted.

Bufflehead, *Bucephala albeola*: fairly common spring transient, extremely rare summer visitor, common to abundant fall transient (Mar.–Dec.), L4 & 5; breeding not confirmed. Average spring arrival, 4-24. Six summer records to 1990. Sometimes found on many small ponds, but larger numbers are at Lake DeSmet. The Bufflehead was observed during 13 of 21 years of Spring Bird Counts in Johnson County, 1984–2004, and during six of 26 years of Christmas Bird Counts at Buffalo, 1986–2011. Buffleheads nest in tree cavities as small as those of flickers, and might eventually be found breeding in the Bighorns.

Common Goldeneye, *Bucephala clangula*: uncommon spring transient, common fall transient and winter visitor (Sept.–May) L4 & 5. Most often found at Healy and Moore's reservoirs, Lake DeSmet, and on Tongue River; three were seen on Chill Lakes, between 10,000' and 10,400' elevation, 9-24-1987. The Common Goldeneye was observed during four of 21 years of Spring Bird Counts in Johnson County, 1984–2004, during 24 of 26 years of Christmas Bird Counts at Buffalo, 1986–2011, and during two of four Spring Bird Counts in Sheridan County, 2009–2012. This species occurs commonly on deeper marshes and lakes throughout the region during migration and during winter. It is Wyoming's most common wintering duck.

Barrow's Goldeneye, *Bucephala islandica*: rare vagrant (Nov.–May; July), L4 & 5; breeding presumed, L4. Found at Fetterman Hill Pond, Healy and Moore's reservoirs, Lake DeSmet, and on Lower Piney Creek. EBird reports from 1-1-1990 include: 7-9-2006, Yellowtail Wildlife Management Area, 6-11-2003, Bighorn National Forest, and 10-25-2008, eastern Bighorns. Seen in early July at Seven Brothers Lake, 9,000' elevation. The species was observed during seven of 21 years of Spring Bird Counts in Johnson County, 1984–2004. It was not observed during 26 years of Christmas Bird Counts at Buffalo, 1986–2011, but was reported during two of four Spring Bird Counts in Sheridan County, 2009–2012. This species occurs commonly on deeper marshes and lakes throughout the region on migration and during winter; summering birds suggest possible breeding. Breeding birds are associated with forested montane lakes, beaver ponds, and slowly flowing rivers; in some regions nesting in cliff or rock crevices also occurs. Nesting might eventually be found in the Bighorns.

Hooded Merganser, *Lophodytes cucullatus*: uncommon spring and fall transient, extremely rare summer and winter vagrant (Mar.–July; Oct., Jan.) L4 & 5; breeding not confirmed. Average spring arrival, 4-12. Three summer dates have been recorded: 6-6-1971; 6-19-1972; and 7-12-1988. One winter date recorded: 4 birds on Lake DeSmet 12-26-2012. Found on many small ponds, Healy and Moore's reservoirs, Lake DeSmet, Rapid Creek, Shell Reservoir and Tongue River. The Hooded Merganser was observed during two of 21 years of Spring Bird Counts in Johnson County, 1984–2004, and during two of 26 years of Christmas Bird Counts at Buffalo, 1986–2011. This species occurs commonly on deeper marshes and lakes throughout the region during migration and more rarely during winter. Breeding occurs along river areas bounded by woods and supporting good fish populations associated with clear water. Breeding Bird Surveys indicate that national populations are increasing significantly (3.2% annually, 1966-2011).

Common Merganser, *Mergus merganser*: common spring transient and summer resident, abundant fall transient, uncommon winter visitant in open winters; breeding confirmed L4 & 5. Found on all ponds and reservoirs, largest numbers occur at Lake DeSmet, but breeding birds found on the Goose Creek, Piney Creek, Rapid Creek, and Tongue River (including Tongue Canyon) drainages. In June of 2013, one adult female and 9 ducklings were seen on Little Goose Creek near the Bradford Brinton. The Common Merganser was observed during all 21 years of

Spring Bird Counts in Johnson County, 1984–2004, during four of 26 years of Christmas Bird Counts at Buffalo, 1986–2011, and during all four Spring Bird Counts in Sheridan County, 2009–2012. This fish-eating species occurs clear-water rivers or lakes supporting large fish populations, and is much the commonest merganser of the region. Nesting occurs in tree cavities, rock crevices, and sometimes under boulders or dense shrubbery.

Red-breasted Merganser, *Mergus serrator*: uncommon spring and fall transient (Mar.–May; Sept.–Dec.), L4 & 5. Average spring arrival, 4-11. Most records are of less than ten birds, but 50 or more have been recorded. Reported from a pond east of Arvada, at Healy and Moore's reservoirs, Lake DeSmet, Piney Creek and Clear Creek diversions, and Wagner Reservoir. The Red-breasted Merganser was observed during one of 21 years of Spring Bird Counts in Johnson County, 1984–2004, but not observed during 26 years of Christmas Bird Counts at Buffalo, 1986–2011. Generally found in similar habitats as the Common Merganser, but with a more northerly breeding distribution and a more coastal wintering distribution.

Ruddy Duck, *Oxyura jamaicensis*: fairly common spring, uncommon summer resident, common fall transient (Mar.–Dec.); breeding confirmed L4 & 5. Average spring arrival, 4-22. Found at the big reservoirs, also a pond near Arvada, Fetterman Hill Pond, McClain's Pond, Wagner Reservoir, and at a pond on Buffalo Creek Road northeast of Sheridan. The Ruddy Duck was observed during 14 of 21 years of Spring Bird Counts in Johnson County, 1984–2004. It was not observed during 26 years of Christmas Bird Counts at Buffalo, 1986–2011, but was reported during one of four Spring Bird Counts in Sheridan County, 2009–2012. This species occurs commonly on deeper marshes and lakes throughout the region during migration. Non-breeding birds are found on larger and generally deeper waters that have silty or muddy bottoms; breeding occurs on overgrown shallow marshes with abundant emergent vegetation and some open water.

Family Phasianidae: Partridges, Grouse & Pheasants

Dusky Grouse

Gray Partridge, *Perdix perdix*: introduced resident; abundance variable, from rare out to fairly common, depending upon weather severity; breeding confirmed L4 & 5. Often seen at Bud Love Game Management Unit, U.S. Hwy. 87 south of Banner, Healy Reservoir, and along Big Goose, Dow-Dutch, Prairie Dog, Rapid, Soldier and SR-Buffalo creeks. Observed during seven of 21 years of Spring Bird Counts in Johnson County, 1984–2004, and during 17 of 26 years of Christmas Bird Counts at Buffalo, 1986–2011, and reported during one of four Spring Bird Counts in Sheridan County, 2009–2012. Generally associated with grain fields and nearby edge habitats, such as shelterbelts, but also sometimes extending into sagebrush areas, especially where local water supplies are present. Nesting usually occurs in grain fields or hayfields, under grassy or herbaceous cover. Breeding Bird Surveys indicate that national populations are decreasing significantly (1.4% annually, 1966-2011). Often referred to as the Hungarian partridge.

Ring-necked Pheasant, *Phasianus colchicus*: common introduced resident; breeding confirmed L4 & 5. Abundance variable from uncommon to common, depending upon severity of weather. Pheasants can often be seen along rural roads around Sheridan, Big Horn, and Buffalo. They were introduced early in the 20th century and are mostly limited to low-altitude grasslands, croplands, and similar non-wooded environments. Breeding occurs mainly in native grasslands and grain croplands or their edges, but sometimes also in marsh edges, hayfields, or shelterbelts, as well as roadside ditches. Pheasants will come to ranch operations and suburban bird-feeding stations, so they survive better in winter than does the similarly introduced Gray Partridge.

Chukar, *Alectoris chukar:* common introduced (in 1934) resident in north-central Wyoming (Orabona *et al.,* 2009; Faulkner, 2010). Breeding confirmed, L4 & L5. The state introduced them and harsh winters have reduced their numbers is some areas. Primarily associated with sagebrush habitats during the breeding season, but extending into grassland and sometimes also riparian habitats at other times. Nearly always found in hilly, rocky topography. Unlike native quails, Chukars tend to flee by running rapidly upslope, rather than flying when frightened.

Ruffed Grouse, *Bonasa umbellus*: uncommon resident; breeding confirmed L4 & L5. They are found at Amsden Creek, Dry Fork, Kerns and Bud Love Game Management Units, Little Goose Canyon, Story, and at many locations on the face of the Bighorn Mountains as high as Black Mountain Fire Lookout at 9,489' elevation. The Ruffed Grouse was observed during three of 21 years of Spring Bird Counts in Johnson County, 1984–2004. It was not observed during 26 years of Christmas Bird Counts at Buffalo, 1986–2011. This species can often be found in aspen groves, and is especially associated with aspens during spring, the buds and catkins of which provide a major food source. Territorial display and nesting often occur in or near aspen clumps. However, it also occurs up to the spruce-fir zone of coniferous forest.

Greater Sage-Grouse, *Centrocercus urophasianus*: common resident; breeding confirmed L4 & 5. WG&F personnel counted more than 200 sage-grouse while tagging pronghorns 12-15-1985. Leks have been reported on Ash Creek-Monarch and SR–Buffalo Creek roads, along roads around Arvada in Sheridan County, and along Kumor and Red Hills roads in Johnson County. The species was not observed during 21 years of Spring Bird Counts in Johnson County, 1984–2004, but was reported during nine of 26 years of Christmas Bird Counts at Buffalo, 1986–2011. Occurs locally in sage to 9,000 feet elevation. Sage-grouse display socially in spring, with as many as 50 or more males seen at local display grounds, or leks. The densest regional breeding concentrations are probably in the sagebrush scrublands of south-central and southwestern Wyoming. Closely associated with sagebrush, which is the primary year-around food and also is used for nesting cover. The Greater Sage-Grouse has been badly impacted by the energy development in the Powder River Basin. Because of habitat losses, this species' numbers are declining rapidly, and a threatened national status is warranted. Breeding Bird Surveys indicate that national populations are declining significantly (2.7% annually, 1966-2011). A recent estimate of the species' total population is 150,000 (Rich *et al.*, 2004). Wyoming is believed to support the largest population of any state, a proportion estimated at about 37% of the total, or about 55,000 birds. To provide an indication of the rate of the species' decline, as recently as the late 1970s the annual Wyoming kill by hunters was as high as 83,000 birds. Previously named the Sage Grouse, but this English name had to be changed after the discovery in 2000 of a related but considerably smaller species, the Gunnison Sage-Grouse, in southern Colorado (Johnsgard, 2002).

Dusky Grouse, *Dendragapus obscurus*: common resident in the Bighorn Mountains; breeding confirmed L4 & L5. The highest number recorded was forty on Duncum Mountain September 25, 1982. The Dusky Grouse was observed during two of 21 years of Spring Bird Counts in Johnson County, 1984–2004. It was not observed during 26 years of Christmas Bird Counts at Buffalo, 1986–2011. This grouse usually is found at higher elevations in the Bighorn Mountains, but descends to lower elevations to breed. Observations are often low because they are difficult to see, but the birds can easily be heard hooting on the mountain in spring. Closely associated with coniferous forests, but also reaches alpine timberline, and as low as the ponderosa pine zone. Non-breeders move in late spring and summer into the sagebrush zone. Named the Blue Grouse prior to being split into a Rocky Mountain population

(Dusky Grouse) and a more westerly form in the Cascade and Sierra Nevada ranges, now recognized as a separate species, the Sooty Grouse (*Dendragapus fuliginosus*).

Sharp-tailed Grouse, *Tympanuchus phasianellus*: common resident; breeding confirmed L4 & 5. This species is regionally more abundant and more visible than the Greater Sage-Grouse. Grouse can be seen along Highway 335 in the windbreaks near Big Horn, especially as the road heads up to Red Grade Road. When the ground is snow-covered, Sharp-tails are often seen in treetops feeding on buds. Associated with grasslands, shrub-dominated transitional areas between grasslands and forest, and grassy sagebrush areas, and sometimes also mountain meadows during the breeding season, and extending into cultivated fields during fall and winter. In spring, male Sharp-tails "dance" on traditional display areas (leks) in groups of from a few to 20 or more males, during which dominance is determined and the associated relative access of individual males to females for fertilization is established. A very rare Greater Sage-Grouse x Sharp-tailed Grouse hybrid was observed north of Ash Creek from late March of 1979 until 1981. Other hybrids between seemingly very distinctive grouse species are also known, mostly between lek-breeding species whose mating choices are relatively spur-of-the-moment ones (Johnsgard, 2002).

Wild Turkey, *Meleagris gallopavo*: common resident, increasing in numbers since about 1985; breeding confirmed L4 & 5. A limited altitudinal migration takes place in April and May, as turkeys move upward from wintering to summering areas, often through the streets of Sheridan and Story. Usually found readily at Arvada, Ash Creek Road, Goose Canyon, Little Soldier Creek Road, U. S. Hwy. 14 east of Sheridan, and at various points along the Powder River. The Wild Turkey was observed during 20 of 21 years of Spring Bird Counts in Johnson County, 1984–2004, and during all 26 years of Christmas Bird Counts at Buffalo, 1986–2011, and during all four Spring Bird Counts in Sheridan County, 2009–2012. Present in the region as a result of 20th-century reintroduction efforts; mainly found in open forests of ponderosa pines or mixed woods, especially those with oaks or other mast-bearing trees. Breeding Bird Surveys indicate that national populations are increasing significantly (8.0% annually, 1966-2011).

Family Gaviidae: Loons

Common Loon

Red-throated Loon, *Gavia stellata*: extremely rare spring (May) and fall (Oct.–Nov.) vagrant L5. Found at Lake DeSmet (11-10-1981) and Healy Reservoir (10-24-1986). Has reportedly occurred seven times, all lone birds. Not reported regionally on eBird from 1-1-1990 through 4-25-2013. The Red-throated Loon was observed during one of 21 years of Spring Bird Counts in Johnson County, 1984–2004, and during one of 26 years of Christmas Bird Counts at Buffalo, 1986–2011. Like the other loons, this species is found on larger rivers and lakes.

Pacific Loon, *Gavia pacifica*: rare summer (July) and fall (Oct.–Nov.) vagrant L5. Found at Lake DeSmet and Healy Reservoir; 14 reports of one or two birds. One in alternate plumage was at Lake DeSmet 7-19-1979. Not reported regionally on eBird from 1-1-1990 through 4-25-2013. To be expected on large rivers and lakes. Previously included as part of Old World species Arctic Loon (*G. arctica*).

Common Loon, *Gavia immer*: common spring and fall transient, and rare summer (Mar.–Dec.) vagrant L4 & 5; breeding not confirmed. Average spring arrival, 4-16. Some loons are found throughout the summer months at Lake DeSmet, Healy Reservoir, and at Sibley Lake and other mountain lakes. These summer individuals are most often in basic or an intermediate plumage, suggesting the possibility of local breeding, but dependent young have not been observed. Also seen in winter on Lake DeSmet; 4 birds, 1-4-2013. The Common Loon was observed during 16 of 21 years of Spring Bird Counts in Johnson County, 1984–2004, during five of 26 years of Christmas Bird Counts at Buffalo, 1986–2011, and during three of four Spring Bird Counts in Sheridan County, 2009–2012. Mostly found on large rivers and lakes supporting good fish populations.

Yellow-billed Loon, *Gavia adamsii*: extremely rare vagrant (Nov.) L5; seen at Lake DeSmet 11-1, 4 & 5-1978. Not reported regionally on eBird from 1-1-1990 through 4-25-2013. To be expected on large rivers and lakes. There is one spring and several fall accepted Wyoming records (Faulkner 2010).

Family Podicipedidae: Grebes

Western Grebe

Pied-billed Grebe, *Podilymbus podiceps*: common spring and fall transient and summer (Mar.–Dec.); resident; breeding confirmed L4 & 5. Average spring arrival, 4-18. Downy young and adults have been observed at Beatty Gulch pond, Healy Reservoir, McClain's Pond, and Moore's Reservoir. The Pied-billed Grebe was observed during 13 of 21 years of Spring Bird Counts in Johnson County, 1984–2004, during one of 26 years of Christmas Bird Counts at Buffalo, 1986–2011, and during one of four Spring Bird Counts in Sheridan County, 2009–2012. Primarily found on heavily overgrown ponds or marshes, especially during the breeding season.

Horned Grebe, *Podiceps auritus*: uncommon spring transient, fairly common fall transient, extremely rare summer visitor (Apr.–Dec.); L4 & 5; breeding not confirmed. Average spring arrival, 4-18. Commonly found at Healy Reservoir, Lake DeSmet and Moore's Reservoir, and rarely in the Bighorn Mountains at Park Reservoir. The Horned Grebe was observed during two of 21 years of Spring Bird Counts in Johnson County, 1984–2004, and during four of 26 years of Christmas Bird Counts at Buffalo, 1986–2011. Observed January 11, 1981 on Lake DeSmet. During migration, marshes and lakes throughout the region attract this species. Breeding typically occurs on fairly small ponds (under 2.5 acres), with the pairs scattered and nesting in clumps of rather sparse emergent vegetation.

Red-necked Grebe, *Podiceps grisegena*: extremely rare fall (Sept.–Oct.) vagrant L5. Four were seen at Holly Pond 921-1975, one was at Lake DeSmet 10-18 &19-1981, and 10-8-1982, and two on 10-24-1982. Not reported regionally on eBird from 1-1-1990 through 4-25-2013. During migration, marshes and lakes throughout the region attract this species.

Eared Grebe, *Podiceps nigricollis*: common spring transient; fairly common summer resident; common to abundant fall transient; rare December vagrant (Apr.–Dec.); breeding confirmed L4 & L5. Average spring arrival, 4-19. Found at Lake DeSmet and all reservoirs and ponds. The Eared Grebe was observed during 20 of 21 years of Spring Bird Counts in Johnson County, 1984–2004, during six of 26 years of Christmas Bird Counts at Buffalo, 1986–2011, and was also reported during two of four Spring Bird Counts in Sheridan County, 2009–2012. Thirty-three birds were observed at Lake DeSmet May 5, 2013. During migration, marshes and lakes throughout the region attract this species. Associated in the breeding season with rather shallow marshes and lakes having extensive reedbeds and submerged aquatic plants. Generally found in larger and more open ponds than either pied-billed grebes or horned grebes and, unlike these species, typically nesting in large colonies. Resting migrants often form a tight "raft" on the water; as many as 600 individuals have been estimated in these groups.

Western Grebe, *Aechmophorus occidentalis*: fairly common early spring transient becoming common late spring, uncommon summer resident, common to abundant fall transient (Apr.–Dec.), L4 & 5; breeding suspected, L4. Average spring arrival, 5-3. Fall numbers are quite large, as many as 400 birds were estimated 11-5-1987, at Lake DeSmet. A group of 10 birds were reported in 5-2013 on Lake DeSmet and 2 birds were reported on 7-21-2011. The Western Grebe was observed during 20 of 21 years of Spring Bird Counts in Johnson County, 1984–2004, and during two of four Spring Bird Counts in Sheridan County, 2009–2012. Seen during one of 26 years of Christmas Bird Counts at Buffalo, 1986–2011. On December 1, 1987, at Lake DeSmet the temperature was 12 degrees Fahrenheit; yet one was seen diving and surfacing with ice crystals on its head. As many as 20 birds During migration, marshes and lakes throughout the region attract this and the following species. Breeding of both typically occurs on permanent ponds and shallow lakes that are often slightly brackish and have large areas of open water, as well as semi-open growths of emergent vegetation.

Clark's Grebe, *Aechmophorus clarkii*: This fairly recently (since 1985) recognized species was not recorded in this area prior to 6-22-1986. Because of the scarcity of information, the Clark's Grebe is presumed to be an uncommon spring and fall transient and summer resident (May–Aug.), L5; breeding not confirmed for region, but documented for Lovell Lakes, just beyond Latilong 4's western boundary (Faulkner, 2010). It has been found at Lake DeSmet and Rock Creek pond east of I-90. Some eBird reports from 1-1-1990 through 4-25-2013 are: Horseshoe Lake, Bighorn Canyon NRA, 7-8-2006, and Bighorn Canyon, Yellowtail Wildlife Management Area, 5-31-2010. The Clark's Grebe was observed during three of 21 years of Spring Bird Counts in Johnson County, 1984–2004, and during one of 26 years of Christmas Bird Counts at Buffalo, 1986–2011.

Family Phalacrocoracidae: Cormorants

Double-crested Cormorant

Double-crested Cormorant, *Phalacrocorax auritus*: common spring, summer and fall resident (Mar.–Nov); breeding confirmed L4 & 5. Average spring arrival, 4-15. A breeding colony was established in 1980 at Lake DeSmet, expanding each year with a maximum number of 59 nests. As of 2013, the number of nests has decreased but cormorants are commonly seen on the lake. This cormorant was observed during all 21 years of Spring Bird Counts in Johnson County, 1984–2004, during one of 26 years of Christmas Bird Counts at Buffalo, 1986–2011, and during all four Spring Counts in Sheridan County, 2009–2012. During migration, marshes, reservoirs and lakes throughout the region attract this species, especially those with good fish populations.

Family Pelecanidae: Pelicans

American White Pelican

American White Pelican, *Pelecanus erythrorhynchos*: this species has become more abundant since 1985, and is a fairly common spring transient and summer vagrant, uncommon fall transient (Apr.–July, Sept.–Dec.) L4 & 5; breeding not confirmed. Average spring arrival, 4-23. Found primarily at Lake DeSmet, but occurs also at the Clear Creek Diversion, Healy Reservoir and Moore's Reservoir. The American White Pelican was observed during nine of 21 years of Spring Bird Counts in Johnson County, 1984–2004. It was not observed during 26 years of Christmas Bird Counts at Buffalo, 1986–2011, or in Sheridan County, 2009–2012. Associated with lakes and rivers having large fish populations that can be reached by surface-feeding. Gregarious, typically foraging and nesting in groups, and sometimes foraging 30 or more miles away from the nesting grounds, which are typically low islands on large marshes or lakes. Breeding Bird Surveys indicate that national populations are increasing significantly (3.9% annually, 1966-2011).

Family Ardeidae: Bitterns & Herons

Black-crowned Night-Heron

American Bittern, *Botaurus lentiginosus*: rare spring (March–June) and fall (Aug.–Oct.) transient based upon the observations recorded to date, L4 & 5, but circumstantial evidence for breeding, L5 (Orabona *et al.*, 2010). However, the secretive nature of this species impedes observation. It is highly likely that this bittern nests in the region, although breeding has not been confirmed. Found on Buffalo Creek northeast of Sheridan, at Moore's Reservoir, and McClain's' Pond. It was observed during one of four years of Spring Bird Counts in Sheridan County, 2009–2012. Associated with reedbeds and other emergent marsh vegetation, and rarely observed feeding in open water like other herons. Foods include frogs, snakes, and other animals in addition to fish, and thus the species is not limited to areas where fish occur.

Ardeidae: Bitters & Herons

Great Blue Heron, *Ardea herodias*: common spring, summer, and fall resident, periodic winter visitant; breeding confirmed L4 & 5. Average spring arrival, 3-26. Heron colonies have been found on Piney Creek northwest of Ucross, Goose Creek on East Lane north of Sheridan, on the Tongue River near Ranchester and a few other sites. As of 2013, the Goose Creek heronry had 49 nests with 10 visibly occupied; the East Lane heronry had 26 nests with 6 visibly occupied. This heron was observed during all 21 years of Spring Bird Counts in Johnson County, 1984–2004, and during all four Spring Bird Counts in Sheridan County, 2009–2012. It was not observed during 26 years of Christmas Bird Counts at Buffalo, 1986–2011. This species occurs in a variety of habitats supporting fish, but usually breeds where there are tall trees. Large cottonwoods are a favored location for nesting colonies. However, it rarely nests on the ground, on rock ledges, or among bulrushes. In 1980, these herons built nests in a cottonwood grove occupied by Red-tailed Hawks near Shell Reservoir; both species raised young. In 1984 the hawks were successful in eliminating the herons as neighbors.

Great Egret, *Ardea alba*: extremely rare spring (April–May) vagrant L4 & 5. One was reported in May of 1979 on Clear Creek (exact date not known); one at Ranchester 4-27-1980; one south of Sheridan at a ranch pond 4-20 & 21-1984; one on Jackson Creek near Bighorn on 5-18, 19 & 25-1989. One eBird report from 1-1-1990 through 9-5-2011, was at Bighorn Canyon, 5-31-2010. Also seen 10-24–29-2000 at Healy Reservoir (Faulkner 2010). Found in similar habitats to those used by Great Blue Herons. Breeding Bird Surveys indicate that national populations are increasing significantly (2.4% annually, 1966-2011).

Snowy Egret, *Egretta thula*: extremely rare spring(April–June) vagrant L4 & 5. Nine observations have been made since 1968 on Tongue River, Big Goose Creek, Goose Creek, Lake DeSmet, and Moore's Reservoir. One early specimen record, Sheridan County 4-11-1904. Not reported regionally on eBird from 1-1-1990 through 4-25-2013. These birds occur in a wide range of aquatic habitats. When foraging the birds are fairly active, and sometimes rush about in shallow water in an apparent attempt to flush out their prey.

Cattle Egret, *Bubulcus ibis*: extremely rare spring (May) and fall (Oct.) vagrant L4 & 5. Two were found north of Bighorn 5-18-1982, one was in breeding plumage; an immature was observed near Lake DeSmet and Shell Creek 10-24-1982. On 1-6-1983, an immature was seen 1-6-1983 at the Saddlestring Ranch, west of Lake DeSmet, and was found dead two days later. Not reported regionally on eBird from 1-1-1990 through 4-25-2013. Besides using various aquatic habitats, this species also is regularly observed on agricultural lands, especially where there are cattle present. These birds forage on grasshoppers and other insects that are stirred up by the movements of the livestock. The species is highly social, and often nests among colonies of other herons. Breeding Bird Surveys indicate that national populations are decreasing significantly (1.0% annually, 1966-2011).

Green Heron, *Butorides striatus*: extremely rare spring (April–June) and fall (Oct.) transient L4 & 5; breeding not confirmed. Reported at Sheridan 4-28 & 30-1969; Lower Piney Creek near Lake DeSmet 5-18-1974; Barkey Draw 5-22-1979; Clear Creek east of Buffalo 10-24-1982; Tongue River near Acme 6-1-1987; and Jackson Creek 5-26 & 27-1989. Not reported regionally on eBird from 1-1-1990 through 4-25-2013. A wide variety of habitats are used by this adaptable species, which is usually found near trees but also sometimes breeds well away from tree cover. The birds are not very gregarious, and generally are seen as single individuals or territorial pairs. Foraging is done in shallow water; actual baiting of the water to attract prey has been observed in this species. Referred to by Downing as the Green-backed Heron, a name sometimes used for South American populations.

Black-crowned Night-Heron, *Nycticorax nycticorax*: uncommon spring and fall transient, and summer (Apr.–Oct.) vagrant L4 & 5. Average spring arrival, 5-6. They have occurred often enough in June and July to suggest breeding, but breeding has not been confirmed. Adults with independent young have been recorded. These herons have been found at Clear Creek Diversion, Fletcher's Pond, Hume Draw, Lake DeSmet, McClain's Pond, and Moore's Reservoir. The Black-crowned Night-heron was observed during four of 21 years of Spring Bird Counts in Johnson County, 1984–2004. It was not observed during 26 years of Christmas Bird Counts at Buffalo, 1986–2011. This is a highly adaptable species that can use a wide variety of habitats, but in this region it is likely to be associated with shallow bulrush or cattail marshes, often well away from woodlands. The species has very large eyes and, as its name implies, often forages in dim light when it is too dark for most herons to see their prey.

Yellow-crowned Night-Heron, *Nyctanassa violacea*: extremely rare summer vagrant (July–Aug.) L5. An immature bird was seen north of Sheridan near Goose Creek bridge on Wrench Ranch 7-27-1976; at a pond on the same ranch 7-28 & 7-29; and again from the bridge 8-22, presumably the same bird. Not reported regionally on eBird from 1-1-1990 through 4-25-2013. Found in much the same habitats as the previous species, but its ranger is more southward-oriented.

Family Threskiornithidae: Ibises

White-faced Ibis

White Ibis, *Eudomimus albus*: extremely rare fall vagrant L5. An adult was found by a ranch family on Lower Piney Road 9-12-1976, and was also seen the next day. The nearest breeding areas are along the Sea of Cortez and the Gulf Coast. Sheridan meteorologists said that a tropical depression near Baja, California, produced weather conditions favorable for bringing the White Ibis to this area. Not reported regionally on eBird from 1-1-1990 through 4-25-2013. There are two other state records (Faulkner, 2010).

White-faced Ibis, *Plegadis chihi*: uncommon spring transient, extremely rare summer and early fall vagrant L4 & 5. Average spring arrival, 4-30. Observed three times during summer months (June-July) causing speculations of breeding possibility, but breeding has not been confirmed in northern Wyoming; only one fall sighting. The White-faced Ibis has been found at many of the reservoirs, ponds and wet meadows in the area. It was observed during four of 21 years of Spring Bird Counts in Johnson County, 1984–2004. It was not observed during 26 years of Christmas Bird Counts at Buffalo, 1986–2011. Generally associated with freshwater or brackish marshes having an abundance of cattails, bulrushes or phragmites. Breeding Bird Surveys indicate that national populations are increasing significantly (3.2% annually, 1966-2011).

Family Cathartidae: American Vultures

Turkey Vulture

Turkey Vulture, *Cathartes aura*: fairly common spring and fall transient and summer (Apr.–Nov.) resident; breeding not confirmed, L4 & 5. Average spring arrival, 4-29. Seen often at Dayton, Lake DeSmet, Rapid Creek, Story, and Tongue River Canyon, and observed flying over many of the canyons. There is also a local population in Sheridan. This vulture was observed during 16 of 21 years of Spring Bird Counts in Johnson County, 1984–2004, and during all four years of Spring Bird Counts in Sheridan County, 2009–2012. It was not observed during 26 years of Christmas Bird Counts at Buffalo, 1986–2011. A scavenger species that consumes only dead remains of large animals, which it finds visually or by using its fine olfaction. Usually found below 8,000'; hilly areas near reservoirs are favored, and range country where road-kill carcasses are likely to be found. Nests are often located on cliff ledges or crevices, or in level country may occur in abandoned buildings. This species' range appears to be expanding northwardly, and vultures are roosting more frequently in tall trees within towns and cities. Breeding Bird Surveys indicate that national populations are increasing significantly (2.3% annually, 1966-2011). This and other New World vultures are not close relatives of the Old World vultures, and have at times been taxonomically associated with storks rather than with hawks and eagles.

Family Pandionidae: Ospreys

Osprey

Osprey, *Pandion haliaetus*: uncommon spring and fall transient, and uncommon summer resident (Mar.–Nov.) L4 & 5; breeding confirmed L4 & L5. Average spring arrival, 4-13. Ospreys were observed during all 21 years of Spring Bird Counts in Johnson County, 1984–2004. They was not observed during 26 years of Christmas Bird Counts at Buffalo, 1986–2011, but were reported during all four years of Spring Bird Counts in Sheridan County, 2009–2012. Commonly seen along clear rivers and lakes with good fish populations, these birds sometimes nest on rock outcrops but more often nest in tall trees near water. To avoid nest-building on power poles, nesting platforms were erected by the REA, WG&F, and the local Audubon chapter, starting in the 1970s. These were placed at Piney Diversion in 1973, Clear Creek Diversion in 1984, and Clearmont in 1988. As of 2013, the birds nesting on the platforms are very successful. These platforms are all close to Lake DeSmet, where they no doubt feed. Osprey have also built a new nest in a dead tree in the middle of a grassland in 2012 and returned in 2013 along Highway 335, close to Little Goose Creek. The osprey seems to be a common nester near Sheridan, possibly reflecting the national population increases. Breeding Bird Surveys indicate that national populations are increasing significantly (2.3% annually, 1966-2011).

Family Accipitridae: Hawks & Eagles

Golden Eagle

Mississippi Kite, *Ictinia mississippiensis*: extremely rare summer (June) vagrant, L4. One sub-adult was photographed on Rapid Creek 6-11-1987. The nearest breeding areas are in Kansas and Nebraska. Not reported regionally on eBird from 1-1-1990 through 4-25-2013. There were at least five Wyoming records by 2010 (Faulkner, 2010),

Bald Eagle, *Haliaeetus leucocephalus*: fairly common spring and fall transient, uncommon summer and early fall resident, fairly common winter visitant (common some winters) L4 & 5; breeding confirmed L4 & L5. A nesting pair on Tongue River fledged young each year, 1983 to 1989, except in 1987. Nesting occurred in 2012 near Wolf Creek Ranch (Robert Berry, pers. com.). Bald Eagles are commonly seen at Lake DeSmet, along Clear Creek and the Tongue River in spring, fall, and winter. They are quite common in winter at the Bradford Brinton and can be watched as they come in to roost on the large trees along the south end of the Bradford Brinton Road. In the winter of 2012, there were at least 15 adult and juvenile (or immature eagles) birds perched beside 3 Rough-legged Hawks. Eagle watching is also good along I-90 from Sheridan to Buffalo where the birds feed on road-kill. The Bald Eagle was observed during all 26 years of Christmas Bird Counts at Buffalo, 1986–2011, and during all four years of Spring Bird Counts in Sheridan County, 2009–2012. This species feeds almost exclusively on non-game fish, at least during the breeding season, but will also attack sick or wounded birds up to the size of geese and cranes. Breeding Bird Surveys indicate that national populations are increasing significantly (4.9% annually, 1966-2011).

Northern Harrier, *Circus cyaneus:* fairly common spring and late fall transient; common summer and early fall resident, rare winter visitant, breeding confirmed L4 & 5. Average spring arrival, 3-20. One was found in the Cloud Peak Wilderness Area between 9,000' and 10,000'; also a pair was observed at Circle Park off U. S. Hwy. 16 southwest of Buffalo at 8,000'. Records do not indicate a peak in abundance, except for the appearance of young in late August and early September. The Northern Harrier was observed during 20 of 21 years of Spring Bird Counts in Johnson County, 1984–2004, during 15 of 26 years of Christmas Bird Counts at Buffalo, 1986–2011, and during all four years of Spring Bird Counts in Sheridan County, 2009–2012. Grassy meadows, especially those near water, are favored by these birds, which nest in grasses on the ground rather than in trees, as is true of most hawks.

Sharp-shinned Hawk, *Accipiter striatus*: uncommon resident; breeding assumed L4 & 5. Reported at all elevations to the Bighorn Mountains at Arrowhead Lodge, 7,600', and on the east side of Edelman Pass, 13,000'; some altitudinal migration occurs spring and fall. They are often seen in the Sheridan Cemetery and at bird feeding stations during winter. This hawk was observed during five of 21 years of Spring Bird Counts in Johnson County, 1984–2004, and during three of 26 years of Christmas Bird Counts at Buffalo, 1986–2011. Mixed or coniferous forests are the preferred habitats of this species, which usually nests in dense woods such as Aspens, riparian woods, and coniferous forests.

Cooper's Hawk, *Accipiter cooperii*: uncommon spring and fall transient and resident, some migrate southward in severe winters; breeding confirmed L4 & 5. Reported at all elevations to 9,600' on Sheep Mountain Road. Like the Sharp-shinned, this accipiter is often seen in winter at Sheridan Cemetery and near feeding stations. It was observed during four of 21 years of Spring Bird Counts in Johnson County, 1984–2004, during seven of 26 years of Christmas Bird Counts at Buffalo, 1986–2011, and during two of four years of Spring Bird Counts in Sheridan County, 2009–2012. An active nest was reported on the Bradford Brinton Road in May, 2013. Associated with mature forests, especially deciduous or mixed, and less often in pure coniferous stands. Aspen groves are favored breeding locations; non-breeders use riparian woodlands, scrub oaks, and mountain meadows. Both this and the previous species often prey on birds near feeding stations in winter. Breeding Bird Surveys indicate that national populations are increasing significantly (2.3% annually, 1966-2011).

Northern Goshawk, *Accipiter gentilis*: probably a common resident but the goshawk appears to be uncommon as their habitat is not readily accessible to observers; a vertical migration takes place in winter and early spring; breeding confirmed L4 & 5. Found in timbered areas in the Bighorn Mountains; but sighted in Story, Piney Creek and Rapid Creek in winter. Also observed near the old game farm on Bird Farm Road where the pheasants made easy prey. In 2012, sightings have come from Little Goose Canyon Road. This elusive hawk was observed during two of 21 years of Spring Bird Counts in Johnson County, 1984–2004, during five of 26 years of Christmas Bird Counts at Buffalo, 1986–2011, and during one of four years of Spring Bird Counts in Sheridan County, 2009–2012. This species is found in many habitats from aspen groves to timberline, but favors dense conifers or aspens near water for breeding, and ranges into low woodlands, riparian woods, and sage areas at other seasons.

Broad-winged Hawk, *Buteo platypterus*: rare spring (March–June) and fall (Aug.–Nov.) transient L4 & 5. Average spring arrival, 4-27. In 1976 six Broad-winged Hawks were found in April and May, and in 1984 nine were recorded. Has been seen along Big Goose Creek, Piney Creek, Rapid Creek and in Sheridan Cemetery. The Broad-winged Hawk was observed during one of 21 years of Spring Bird Counts in Johnson County, 1984–2004. It was not observed during 26 years of Christmas Bird Counts at Buffalo, 1986–2011. Not reported regionally on eBird from 1-1-1990 through 4-25-2013. Associated with deciduous woodlands, including riparian woods and aspen groves. Usually found east of a line from Sheridan to Cheyenne on migration; breeding occurs in the Black Hills (Faulkner 2010).

Swainson's Hawk, *Buteo swainsoni*: fairly common spring and fall transient fairly common summer resident (Mar.–Nov.); breeding confirmed L4 & 5. Average spring arrival, 4-18. They are seen in migration almost anywhere; sometimes abundant in "kettles" during the last weeks of April and September. Pass Creek and Lake DeSmet are good in summer. Migrating flocks of up to 122 birds have been seen near Sheridan (Faulkner, 2010). The Swainson's Hawk was observed during eight of 21 years of Spring Bird Counts in Johnson County, 1984–2004, and during three of four years of Spring Bird Counts in Sheridan County, 2009–2012. It was not observed during 26 years of Christmas Bird Counts at Buffalo, 1986–2011. Associated with open grasslands, sagebrush, agricultural lands, and rarely with riparian areas, typically nesting in isolated trees, but sometimes in bushes, on man-made structures, or on cliffs. Breeding Bird Surveys indicate that national populations are increasing significantly (0.7% annually, 1966-2011).

Red-tailed Hawk, *Buteo jamaicensis*: of the several subspecies, the western subspecies, *B. j, calurus* is a common spring and fall transient; common spring, summer and fall resident. It is fairly common to uncommon in winter, depending upon the severity of weather; breeding confirmed L4 & 5. Red-tailed Hawk plumages are highly variable.

The "Harlan's Hawk", *B. j. harlani* is a melanistic plumage variant and probably an uncommon late fall and very early spring transient L4 & 5. Forty-two Harlan's have been reported from 1969 to 1988, but only ten had sufficient notes for adequate identification. All ten were seen from September to November, except one in mid-February, and presumably were migrants from western Canada or Alaska, where they breed. Wintering is common on the northern Great Plains.

The "Krider's Hawk," *B. j. krideri*, is a pale-plumaged and poorly differentiated subspecies of the Red-tailed Hawk that is an extremely rare spring and fall vagrant, L4 & 5. A Krider's was reported bathing in Little Goose Creek 12-17-2011. Its reputed breeding distribution is east of Wyoming, in the northern Great Plains, and has been regionally reported in March (3 times), April (3 times), and once each in September, November and December.

Red-tailed Hawks were observed during 20 of 21 years of Spring Bird Counts in Johnson County, 1984–2004, during 21 of 26 years of Christmas Bird Counts at Buffalo, 1986–2011, and during all four years of Spring Bird Counts in Sheridan County, 2009–2012. This typically tree-nesting buteo also extends to open woodlands and even treeless areas, where nesting may occur on cliffs. However, trees, especially large cottonwoods and pines, are favored nest sites. Breeding Bird Surveys indicate that national populations are increasing significantly (1.7% annually, 1966-2011).

Ferruginous Hawk, *Buteo regalis*: fairly common spring and fall transient; fairly common spring, summer and fall resident, uncommon winter resident; breeding confirmed L4 & 5. On 10-28-1979, 12 were counted in a wide area around Burgess Junction; 11 were recorded over the Sheridan area 3-25-1990, migrating northward, but one to five birds are typical. Often seen along the Powder River. The Ferruginous Hawk was observed during three of 21 years of Spring Bird Counts in Johnson County, 1984–2004, during two of 26 years of Christmas Bird Counts at Buffalo, 1986–2011, and during two of four years of Spring Bird Counts in Sheridan County, 2009–2012. Found during the breeding season in grasslands, sagebrush, and sometimes also mountain meadows, and nesting occurs in pygmy conifers, cliff ledges, rock outcrops, and sometimes on man-made structures such as windmills. Prairie dogs are this species' most frequent prey, and nests are often placed near their "towns." A recent estimate of the species' total population is 23,000 (Rich *et al.*, 2004); destruction of prairie dog towns has adversely affected this hawk's population.

Rough-legged Hawk, *Buteo lagopus*: uncommon early spring transient (Aug.–May), common fall transient and winter resident L4 & 5. Easily seen in open country, and the most common buteo in winter in the Sheridan area. The earliest arrival in the fall was 8-25-1984; five were seen from Owen Creek C. G., about 8,400' elevation. A dark-plumaged (melanistic) morph is occasionally seen. The Rough-legged Hawk was not observed during 21 years of Spring Bird Counts in Johnson County, 1984–2004, but was seen during all 26 years of Christmas Bird Counts at Buffalo, 1986–2011. Usually found hunting for small rodents in grasslands, sagebrush, or sometimes over marshes or mountain meadows.

Golden Eagle, *Aquila chrysaetos*: common resident, with a slight increase in numbers recorded in fall probably due to the presence of young and some transients; breeding confirmed L4 4 5. This species has been reported at all elevations as high as 10,000'. The Golden Eagle was observed during 16 of 21 years of Spring Bird Counts in Johnson County, 1984–2004, during all 26 years of Christmas Bird Counts at Buffalo, 1986–2011, and during all four years of Spring Bird Counts in Sheridan County, 2009–2012. A good place to view this eagle is in winter along I-90 between Sheridan and Buffalo and in the western canyons of the Bighorns. This species often occurs in grasslands, semi-desert areas, pinyon–juniper woodlands, the ponderosa pine zone of coniferous forests, and it sometimes forages above mountain meadows or alpine tundra. It nests over a broad altitudinal range, usually on cliffs or in trees, rarely on the ground. A recent estimate of the species' total population is 170,000 (Rich *et al.*, 2004). Wyoming is believed to support the largest Golden Eagle population of any state. Illegal killing, poisoning for predator control and electrocution at power lines are major causes of mortality. The expanding use of wind turbines in Wyoming has also caused recent significant mortality.

Family Rallidae: Rails & Coots

Virginia Rail

Yellow Rail, *Coturnicops noveboracensis*: extremely rare early fall (Aug.) transient, L5. One was observed 8-19-1968, a mile east of Sheridan off Wyarno Road. Not reported regionally on eBird from 1-1-1990 through 4-25-2013. Faulkner (2010) mentioned seven fall reports for Wyoming.

Virginia Rail, *Rallus limicola*: uncommon summer resident (May–Sept.); breeding confirmed L5, presumed L4. Average spring arrival, 4-17. Found at Ash Creek, Acme, McClain's Pond, Piney Diversion, Moore's Reservoir and, in seasons of plentiful precipitation, at Dietz Pond. The Virginia Rail was observed during one of 21 years of Spring Bird Counts in Johnson County, 1984–2004. It was not observed during 26 years of Christmas Bird Counts at Buffalo, 1986–2011. Inhabits marshes with dense stands of emergent vegetation, nesting on wet ground or over shallow water in such stands.

Sora, *Porzana carolina*: uncommon summer (Apr.–Oct.) resident; breeding confirmed L4 & 5. Average spring arrival, 5-15. Mating, nest building and young have been observed in past years at Dietz's pond, Holly Pond, Hume Pond, McClain's Pond, Parkman Pond, and Piney Diversion. Moore's Reservoir and the South Dam Pond at Lake DeSmet are also good Sora habitats. The Sora was observed during five of 21 years of Spring Bird Counts in Johnson County, 1984–2004. It was not observed during 26 years of Christmas Bird Counts at Buffalo, 1986–2011. Found in essentially the same marshy habitats as the Virginia Rail, and apparently with very similar niches.

American Coot, *Fulica americana*: abundant spring and fall transient and summer resident, rare winter vagrant; breeding confirmed L4 & 5. Average spring arrival, 4-3. A chick was observed at McClain's Pond 7-4-1981, begging for food from an adult; dependent young have also been seen on Beatty Gulch ponds, and in 2011 on South Dam Pond near Lake DeSmet. In the fall, numbers as high as 5,000 have been estimated at Lake DeSmet. Can be seen on all ponds and reservoirs. The American Coot was observed during all 21 years of Spring Bird Counts in Johnson County, 1984–2004, during six of 26 years of Christmas Bird Counts at Buffalo, 1986–2011, and during all four years of Spring Bird Counts in Sheridan County, 2009–2012. Associated with ponds and marshes having a combination of open water and emergent reed beds, in which nesting often occurs. Besides foraging on aquatic plants, coots sometimes also graze on nearby shorelines and meadows.

Family Gruidae: Cranes

Sandhill Crane

Sandhill Crane, *Grus canadensis*: uncommon spring and fall transient, uncommon summer resident (Mar.–Nov.); breeding confirmed L4 & 5. Average spring arrival, 4-17. As many as 400 have been seen migrating over the Sheridan–Buffalo area, but up to 4,800 have been estimated along the Powder River. Dependent young have been seen at Forbes' Pond near Beckton 5-31-1982; Upper Big Horn–Sheridan Road 5-20-1988 and 5-4-2013; and on Big Goose Road 5-27-1989, on State Route 332 in 2012, and on the North Tongue River on U. S. Hwy. 14A west of Burgess Junction at about 8,000'. An active nest was found in 2011 along Jackson Creek near Big Horn. Some eBird reports from 1-1-1990 through 9-5-2011 are: 7-9-06 and 5-31-2010, Yellowtail Wildlife Management Area, 6-30-2009 & 7-12-1999, Bighorn National Forest, Tongue River Road, 5-25-2011, Dayton Road, 8-21-10, Wolf Creek Ranch, 9-19-06, 8-6-2007 and 9-14-2009, Mountain Shadows, 9-5-

2011, Sheridan, 7-26-09, and Sheridan East 5, 9-18-2006. Breeding has been well documented on the western slope of the Bighorn Mountains (Faulkner, 2010), but Canterbury found evidence of birds breeding locally along the eastern slope of the Bighorns since 2009. The Sandhill Crane was observed during 11 of 21 years of Spring Bird Counts in Johnson County, 1984–2004, and during all four years of Spring Bird Counts in Sheridan County, 2009–2012. It was not observed during 26 years of Christmas Bird Counts at Buffalo, 1986–2011. Sandhill Cranes are especially associated with beaver impoundments, where the birds often nest along shorelines, or on muskrat houses, or beaver lodges, often in dense willow thickets. The birds are highly territorial and nests usually are well scattered. Their loud calls serve to advertise territories and to communicate over long distances. Breeding Bird Surveys indicate that national populations are increasing significantly (4.9% annually, 1966-2011), especially the Great Lakes population, whereas the hunted mid-continent and Rocky Mountain populations have remained relatively stable.

Whooping Crane, *Grus americana*: extremely rare vagrant (Mar., Oct.), L5. One was seen at Lake DeSmet. 10-4-1988 another was observed north of Buffalo, 3-25-1987 (Faulkner 2010). This is one of North America' rarest birds, with only four Wyoming records. Its normal migration route is through central Nebraska.

Part II. Annotated List of Regional Birds

Family Charadriidae: Plovers

Semipalmated Plover

Black-bellied Plover, *Pluvialis squatarola*: uncommon spring and fall transient, and summer vagrant L5. An alternate-plumaged bird was seen at Lake DeSmet 9-2-1973, and one in basic plumage was there on the 23rd. The only summer record was of two adults and six independent immature birds 7-14-1976. Lake DeSmet is the best place to observe this species. The Black-bellied Plover was observed during three of 21 years of Spring Bird Counts in Johnson County, 1984–2004. It was not observed during 26 years of Christmas Bird Counts at Buffalo, 1986–2011. Migrant birds are likely to be found along lakes or reservoirs, but sometimes also are seen on plowed fields, or forage in short meadows or pasturelands.

American Golden-Plover, *Pluvialis dominica*: extremely rare spring (May) vagrant L5. Plovers were flying about thirty feet directly overhead at Lake DeSmet along with hundreds of other migrating shorebirds on May 16, 1982. Observers were able to get diagnostic Golden-Plover field marks on three birds in each of two flocks. Not reported regionally on eBird from 1-1-1990 through 4-25-2013. Migrant birds are usually found along lakes or reservoirs, or on agricultural lands, during migration. They often occur on plowed or recently burned fields on migration, where surface-foraging opportunities are available. Previously known as the Lesser Golden Plover.

Semipalmated Plover, *Charadrius semipalmatus*: uncommon spring and fall (Apt.–Oct.) transient L4 & 5. Average spring arrival, 5-1. Very few weeks separate the northbound spring departure and the southbound fall arrival. May be found at Moore's and Healy reservoirs. The Semipalmated Plover was observed during four of 21 years of Spring Bird Counts in Johnson County, 1984–2004. It was not observed during 26 years of Christmas Bird Counts at Buffalo, 1986–2011. Migrating birds are usually observed on open sandy or gravelly habitats along rivers or beaches, where they feed by running about and picking up morsels from the surface, rather than probing for foods.

Piping Plover, *Charadrius melodus:* extremely rare spring (May) and fall (Aug.) vagrant L5. A photo was obtained of one seen at Healy Reservoir May 13, 1989. Previous sightings were at Lake DeSmet before its water level was raised. Not reported regionally on eBird from 1-1-1990 through 4-25-2013. The Piping Plover was observed during one of 21 years of Spring Bird Counts in Johnson County, 1984–2004. It was not observed during 26 years of Christmas Bird Counts at Buffalo, 1986–2011.

Killdeer, *Charadrius vociferus*: abundant spring and fall transient and summer resident; uncommon winter visitant; breeding confirmed L4 & 5. Average spring arrival, 34-16. May be found at all reservoirs, ponds, roadways and meadows up to about 8,000' elevation. The Killdeer was observed during all 21 years of Spring Bird Counts in Johnson County, 1984–2004. It was not observed during 26 years of Christmas Bird Counts at Buffalo, 1986–2011, but was reported during all four years of Spring Bird Counts in Sheridan County, 2009–2012. Widely distributed in open-land habitats, including pastures, roadsides, gravel pits, golf courses, airports, and sometimes even suburban lawns. Gravelly areas are favored, and graveled rooftops are sometimes used for nesting in urban areas. Migrating and wintering birds are more closely associated with water, but also use mud flats and open fields.

Family Recurvirostridae: Stilts and Avocets

American Avocet

Black-necked Stilt, *Himantopus mexicanus*: extremely rare spring (April) vagrant L5. Two records to 1990: three birds at Clear Creek Diversion 4-20-1989; and one was there 4-17 & 18-1990. Not reported regionally on eBird from 1-1-1990 through 4-25-2013. Often found in company with American Avocets, which use similar habitats. Breeding in this erratically occurring species usually occurs in the grassy shoreline areas of shallow freshwater or brackish pools of wetlands having extensive mudflats, or sometimes along the shorelines of salt lakes where vegetation is essentially lacking.

American Avocet, *Recurvirostra americana*: fairly common spring and fall transient and summer (Apr.–Nov.) visitant; breeding confirmed L4. Average spring arrival, 4-23. Has been found often at Clear Creek Diversion, Healy and Moore's reservoirs, Parkman Reservoir at higher elevation, and Lake DeSmet. This species was observed during 15 of 21 years of Spring Bird Counts in Johnson County, 1984–2004, but was not observed during 26 years of Christmas Bird Counts at Buffalo, 1986–2011. During breeding it favors ponds or shallow lakes with exposed and sparsely vegetated shorelines, and somewhat saline waters that have large populations of aquatic invertebrates, which are gathered by making scythe-like movements of the curved bill through the water.

Family Scolopacidae: Sandpipers & Snipes

Sanderling

Spotted Sandpiper, *Actitis macularia*: common spring and fall transient and summer resident (Apr.–Oct.); breeding confirmed L4 & 5. Fledglings have been recorded at 4,000' elevation at Healy Reservoir and Lake DeSmet, and at 8,000' on the North Tongue River and the West Fork South Tongue River. Spotted Sandpipers were seen up to 10,800' elevation at Horseshoe Lake and Dutch Oven Pass 6-19-1989 and at lower elevation Lake DeSmet in 2011. Observed North Tongue River, 6-30-2013, 8,500' elevation. The species was observed during all 21 years of Spring

Bird Counts in Johnson County, 1984–2004, and during all four years of Spring Bird Counts in Sheridan County, 2009–2012. It was not observed during 26 years of Christmas Bird Counts at Buffalo, 1986–2011. Lake DeSmet. Associated with forest streams, pools, and rivers, usually at lower elevations, but extending locally to alpine timberline and utilizing a wide array of open terrains with water present, and rarely even in the absence of nearby water. Shaded watercourses are favored, and sometimes the birds are found along rapidly flowing mountain torrents.

Solitary Sandpiper, *Tringa solitaria*: fairly common spring and fall transient and non-breeding summer (Apr.–Oct.) visitant L4 & 5. Average spring arrival, 5-4. Found at all the reservoirs and ponds, even very small ponds and standing water; one was seen at Park Reservoir, 8,285' elevation, on 7-28-1988. The Solitary Sandpiper was observed during six of 21 years of Spring Bird Counts in Johnson County, 1984–2004, and during one of four years of Spring Bird Counts in Sheridan County, 2009–2012. It was not observed during 26 years of Christmas Bird Counts at Buffalo, 1986–2011, Beaver ponds and farm or woodland ponds with fairly dense surrounding vegetation are attractive to migrants.

Greater Yellowlegs, *Tringa melanoleuca*: fairly common spring and fall transient (Mar.–Oct.) and non-breeding summer visitant L4 & 5. Average spring arrival, 4-12. May be found at McClain's Pond, Moore's and Healy reservoirs, Piney and Clear Creek diversions, the Powder River at Arvada, and along the Tongue River at Dayton. The Greater Yellowlegs was observed during four of 21 years of Spring Bird Counts in Johnson County, 1984–2004. It was not observed during 26 years of Christmas Bird Counts at Buffalo, 1986–2011, but was reported during one of four years of Spring Bird Counts in Sheridan County, 2009–2012. In migration these birds occupy the edges of marshes and slow-moving rivers, foraging along the shorelines and sometimes wading out belly-deep to probe in the mud, or skim the surface for invertebrates.

Willet, *Tringa semipalmata*: fairly common spring and fall (Apr.–Sept.) transient and summer visitant, breeding suspected L4 & 5. Average spring arrival, 4-28. Largest number seen in one day was 186 on June 26, 1985, at Lake DeSmet, Healy Reservoir and Clear Creek Diversion. USFS personnel saw Willets at Prune Creek C. G. at 7,652' elevation the first week in May 1981. The Willet was observed during eight of 21 years of Spring Bird Counts in Johnson County, 1984–2004, and during two of four years of Spring Bird Counts in Sheridan County, 2009–2012. It was not observed during 26 years of Christmas Bird Counts at Buffalo, 1986–2011. Breeding habitats of this species consist of prairie marshes, usually brackish to semi-alkaline, seasonal ponds, and sometimes also intermittent streams in grassland areas. The birds are effective probers, and spend much of their time feeding in this way, but also peck at items on the water surface.

Lesser Yellowlegs, *Tringa flavipes*: fairly common spring and fall (Apr.–Oct.) transient and non-breeding summer visitant L4 & 5. Average spring arrival,4-24. Found at Apache Village Pond on U. S. Hwy. 14, Healy and Moore's reservoirs, Hidden Hills ponds off U. S. Hwy. 14 east of Sheridan and near Ucross, Lake DeSmet and McClain's Pond. The Lesser Yellowlegs was observed during six of 21 years of Spring Bird Counts in Johnson County, 1984–2004, and during one of four years of Spring Bird Counts in Sheridan County, 2009–2012. It was not observed during 26 years of Christmas Bird Counts at Buffalo, 1986–2011. On migration these birds occur along mud flats and shallow ponds, often with vegetated shorelines, and sometimes visit flooded fields.

Upland Sandpiper, *Bartramia longicauda*: uncommon spring and early fall (May–Sept._ transient and summer resident; breeding confirmed L4 & 5. Average spring arrival, 5-12. An active nest was found on Young's Creek 727-1978, and dependent young were seen on Beatty Gulch 7-29-1980. Wyarno Road and Soldier Creek are other good areas. The Upland Sandpiper was observed during two of 21 years of Spring Bird Counts in Johnson County, 1984–2004, and during two of four years of Spring Bird Counts in Sheridan County, 2009–2012. It was not observed during 26 years of Christmas Bird Counts at Buffalo, 1986–2011. Generally associated with wet meadows, hayfields, mowed prairies, or mid-length prairies, avoiding both shortgrass sites and extremely tall grasses. Often found far from water, and rarely if ever wading for its foods. Winters in southern South America.

Whimbrel, *Numenius phaeopus*: uncommon spring (Apr.–May) transient L4 & 5. Average spring arrival, 5-11. They have been seen 13 out of 21 years, at times in large flocks of up to 86 birds; 43 were seen 5-16-1978, and 32 on 5-13-1989, at Lake DeSmet. The Whimbrel was observed during two of 21 years of Spring Bird Counts in Johnson County, 1984–2004. It was not observed during 26 years of Christmas Bird Counts at Buffalo, 1986–2011. Migrants are found on meadows, grassy shorelines and shallow wetlands.

Long-billed Curlew, *Numenius americanus*: uncommon (probably decreasing) spring and fall (Apr.–Sept.) transient and extremely rare summer resident (eight June-July records to 1990) L4 & 5; breeding confirmed L4, suspected L5. Average spring arrival, 4-20. An observer reported "breeding circumstantial 6-9-67, Soldier Creek, highly agitated adult circling us." This species often migrates north in large groups; 55 near McClain's Pond 4-18-1969; 17 on Spring Willow Road 4-16-1977; 28 at Lake DeSmet and 37 on Little Piney Road 5-16-1982. After 1982 the number of sightings dwindled severely, but 25 were at Bud Love Game Management Unit April 22, 1988. The Long-billed Curlew was observed during three of 21 years of Spring Bird Counts in Johnson County, 1984–2004. It was also not observed during 26 years of Christmas Bird Counts at Buffalo, 1986–2011. On the breeding grounds this species occurs in shortgrass areas, grazed taller grasslands, and overgrazed grasslands with scattered shrubs or cacti. Hilly or rolling areas seem favored over flatlands, and the birds often nest rather far from standing water. However, migrating birds usually are found on beaches or other shoreline habitats.

Hudsonian Godwit, *Limosa haemastica*: extremely rare fall (Aug–Sept.) vagrant L5. Only three records to 1990, of two to four birds, all at Lake DeSmet, on 8-5-1970, 9-22-1971, and 8-17-1976. Not reported regionally on eBird from 1-1-1990 through 4-25-2013. On migration this species is likely to be found along shorelines of prairie marshes, singly or in small numbers, and usually probing dowitcher-like for food. Winters in South America.

Marbled Godwit, *Limosa fedoa*: uncommon spring and fall (Apr.–Sept.) transient, nonbreeding summer visitant L4 & 5. Average spring arrival, 4-30. Over 100 Marbled Godwits were counted at Lake DeSmet 4-27-1977; 65 were there 7-6-1986. Found at Healy Reservoir, Clear Creek Diversion, and on May 16, 1985, four were seen at Bear Lodge, 8,038' elevation, in a rain-and-snow-mix storm. The Marbled Godwit was observed during five of 21 years of Spring Bird Counts in Johnson County, 1984–2004. It was not observed during 26 years of Christmas Bird Counts at Buffalo, 1986–2011. On migration and on its breeding grounds this species occupies wetlands associated with prairies, including intermittent streams, ponds, and shallow lakes ranging from fresh to strongly alkaline. Semi-permanent ponds and lakes are especially preferred, with nesting occurring in grassy flats nearby.

Ruddy Turnstone, *Arenaria interpres*: extremely rare spring (May) and fall (Sept.)vagrant L5. Three records to 1990: 9-20-1969, at Lake DeSmet; 9-26-1976, at Goose Creek bridge on the Wrench Ranch; and 5-11-1977, at Lake DeSmet before the lake was enlarged. Not reported regionally on eBird from 1-1-1990 through 4-25-2013. Rocky or gravelly shorelines are favored wherever this species occurs; most migration occurs coastally.

Red Knot, *Calidris canutus*: extremely rare spring (May) and fall (Sept.) vagrant L5. Two records to 1990: 9-13 &14-1970 (same bird), and 5-10-1972; the latter in alternate plumage; both were seen by two observers at Lake DeSmet. Not reported regionally on eBird from 1-1-1990 through 4-25-2013. Most migration of this species occurs coastally.

Sanderling, *Calidris alba*: uncommon spring and fall (Apr.–May, July–Oct.) transient, rare summer visitant L5. Average spring arrival, 5-15. Found at Lake DeSmet, Moore's and Healy reservoirs, and Clear Creek Diversion. Migrating birds are usually seen around the larger water bodies with wave-swept sandy beaches.

Semipalmated Sandpiper, *Calidris pusilla*: uncommon spring and fall (Apr.–May, July–Oct.) transient, rare summer visitant L5. Average spring arrival, 5-8. They have been found at Beatty Gulch, Clear Creek Diversion. Lake DeSmet, and Moore's and Healy reservoirs. The Semipalmated Sandpiper routinely migrates through this area. It was observed during seven of 21 years of Spring Bird Counts in Johnson County, 1984–2004. It was not observed during 26 years of Christmas Bird Counts at Buffalo, 1986–2011. A very close relative of the Western Sandpiper, this species is more prone to occur on wet and dry mud, where it often picks up surface organisms, while the Western Sandpiper is more often found standing in water or in wet mud, where it probes for food. The Semipalmated Sandpiper is also less prone to move out into grassy flats to forage than is the Baird's Sandpiper. Winters in Central and South America.

Western Sandpiper, *Calidris mauri*: uncommon spring (April-May) and rare fall transient, rare summer visitant L5. Average spring arrival, 5-9. Scarcely five weeks occur between this species' northbound departure in the spring (which mostly follows the Pacific Coast) and its southbound arrival in the fall, which begins in July and is largely centered in the Great Plains. Statewide, fall records are much more common than spring records (Faulkner, 2010). The Western Sandpiper was observed during two of 21 years of Spring Bird Counts in Johnson County, 1984–

2004. It was not observed during 26 years of Christmas Bird Counts at Buffalo, 1986–2011.

Least Sandpiper, *Calidris minutilla:* fairly common spring and fall (Apr.–Oct.) transient, rare summer visitant L4 & 5. Average spring arrival, 4-25. Only two June (1980) records to 1990 in twenty-one years to 1990. The Least Sandpiper was observed during eight of 21 years of Spring Bird Counts in Johnson County, 1984–2004. It was not observed during 26 years of Christmas Bird Counts at Buffalo, 1986–2011. While on migration these tiny sandpipers are found on a variety of moist habitats, often in company with Semipalmated, Baird's, or Western sandpipers, and probably feeding on much the same invertebrate foods as these species.

White-rumped Sandpiper, *Calidris fuscicollis:* extremely rare early fall (July–Aug.) transient L5. Found at Lake DeSmet 8-17 & 19-1971, and 8-25-1977; Healy Reservoir 8-4-1980 and 7-10-1982, and Clear Creek Diversion 8-9-1984. Not reported regionally on eBird from 1-1-1990 through 4-25-2013. Migrants utilize the same kinds of prairie ponds as do the other "peep" sandpipers. Most migration of this species occurs well to the east, through the Great Plains.

Baird's Sandpiper, *Calidris bairdii*: fairly common spring (April-May) transient, rare summer visitant, common fall (July–Oct.) transient L4 & 5. Average spring arrival, 5-2. Less than six weeks elapse between this species' northbound trip and the return southward. Found at all reservoirs and ponds. The Baird's Sandpiper was observed during four of 21 years of Spring Bird Counts in Johnson County, 1984–2004. It was not observed during 26 years of Christmas Bird Counts at Buffalo, 1986–2011. Migrants are associated with wet meadows and shallow ponds, often feeding in grassy areas somewhat away from water, but also along muddy shorelines, where they tend to peck at food sources, rather than to probe for them.

Pectoral Sandpiper, *Calidris melanotos*: extremely rare spring (May) transient, uncommon fall (July–Oct.) transient L4 & 5. Only two records to 1990 in spring: 5-11-1973, and 5-30-1985. Seen at Wagner Reservoir, Ash Creek, Lake DeSmet, Moore's Reservoir, and Clear Creek Diversion. Not reported regionally on eBird from 1-1-1990 through 4-25-2013. Migrants are commonly seen along prairie marshes or potholes, where they wade in shallow water and probe or peck for food. Often found near grassy cover or in meadows rather than on open mud flats. Winters in South America.

Dunlin, *Calidris alpina*: extremely rare fall transient (Aug.–Sept.) L5. Four records to 1990: 8-30-1969, and 9-11-1969 (unknown locations); 9-2 &3-1971, at Lake DeSmet; and 8-14-1980, at Clear Creek Diversion. Migrant birds are likely to be seen with other small sandpipers such as the "peeps," and usually occur on mud flats or sandy beaches, where they probe for food.

Stilt Sandpiper, *Calidris himantopus*: Uncommon spring and fall (May, July–Sept,) transient L5. Average spring arrival, 5-19. This species, as with other sandpipers that breed in the arctic tundra, doesn't spend much time on the breeding grounds. It uses Lake DeSmet, Moore's Reservoir and Clear Creek Diversion as a stopover. The Stilt Sandpiper was observed during one of 21 years of Spring Bird Counts in Johnson County, 1984–2004. It was not observed during 26 years of Christmas Bird Counts at Buffalo, 1986–2011. Migrants are usually found in company with the typical "peeps," but usually are wading in belly-deep water, and thrusting their bills at organisms or probing the bottom with their rather long bills. They are fairly gregarious on migration, and often occur in moderately large flocks.

Buff-breasted Sandpiper, *Tringites subruficollis*: rare fall (Aug.–Sept.) transient L5. Observed at Lake DeSmet in the short-grass area adjacent to the lake, 9-1-1968; 8-30-1970, and 9-4-1970; 9-1-1972; 9-4-1976; 8-25-1977, and at Beatty Gulch 8-5-1979. Not reported regionally on eBird from 1-1-1990 through 4-25-2013. Often forages on dry land, such as in agricultural fields. Winters in South America; most migration occurs through the central Great Plains.

Long-billed Dowitcher. *Limnodromus scolopaceus*: Common spring and fall (Apr.–May, July–Nov.) transient, L4 & 5. Average spring arrival, 5-1. Occurs on variety of ponds and shallow wetlands. The Short-billed Dowitcher (*L. griseus*) may also occur in this region but it has yet to be documented. The Long-billed Dowitcher was observed during nine of 21 years of Spring Bird Counts in Johnson County, 1984–2004. It was not observed during 26 years of Christmas Bird Counts at Buffalo, 1986–2011. On migration, dowitchers of both species are often found in grassy marshes and along pond edges, where they feed by probing their long bills in belly-deep water.

Wilson's Snipe. *Gallinago delicata*: Common spring and fall (Apr.–Oct.) transient and summer resident, rare in winter; breeding confirmed L4 & 5. Average spring arrival, 4-7. Can be seen at all reservoirs, ponds and streams. The Wilson's Snipe was observed during 18 of 21 years of Spring Bird Counts in Johnson County, 1984–2004. It was seen during 14 of 26 years of Christmas Bird Counts at Buffalo, 1986–2011, and was also reported during all four years of Spring Bird Counts in Sheridan County, 2009–2012. Snipes nest in marshy areas, often using beaver ponds in the Rocky Mountains, and muskeg ponds or other heavily vegetated marshes elsewhere in their extensive range. Peatland habitats are especially favored, but the birds may also occur along slow-moving rivers, marshy shorelines of lakes, or sometimes even wet hayfields. Previously (until 2002) known at the Common Snipe (*G. gallinago*), a name now limited to a very similar Eurasian species.

Wilson's Phalarope, *Phalaropus tricolor*: abundant spring transient, common summer resident and fall (Apr.–Oct.) transient; breeding confirmed L4 & L5. Average spring arrival, 5-2. Young have been seen as early as June 27, 1980, at Healy Reservoir. The Wilson's Phalarope was observed during all 21 years of Spring Bird Counts in Johnson County, 1984–2004, and during one of four years of Spring Bird Counts in Sheridan County, 2009–2012. It was not observed during 26 years of Christmas Bird Counts at Buffalo, 1986–2011. Breeding habitats are typically wet meadows adjoining shallow marshes. Ditches, river edges, and shallow lakes, especially alkaline lakes, also used for migrating and breeding. Winters in South America.

Red-necked Phalarope, *Phalaropus lobatus*: uncommon spring and fall (May–Sept.) transient, extremely rare summer vagrant L4 & 5; breeding not confirmed. Average spring arrival, 5-13. Usual numbers are of one to four birds at Healy Reservoir, Lake DeSmet and McClain's Pond. On 8-12-1969, 40–50 alighted on Lake Geneva, 9,283' elevation; and on 9-27-1978, an observer saw 80 at Lake DeSmet, 4,000' elevation. The Red-necked Phalarope was observed during one of 21 years of Spring Bird Counts in Johnson County, 1984–2004. It was not observed during 26 years of Christmas Bird Counts at Buffalo, 1986–2011. On migration the birds are usually found in the same areas as Wilson's Phalaropes, and often are seen in company with them. Winters pelagically off South America.

Red Phalarope, *Phalaropus fulicaria*: extremely rare fall (Nov.) vagrant L5. One record on 11-7-1973, at Lake DeSmet. Not reported regionally on eBird from 1-1-1990 through 4-25-2013. There are fewer than ten state records for this species (Faulkner 2010).

Family Laridae: Gulls & Terns

Forster's Tern

Sabine's Gull, *Xema sabini*: extremely rare summer (June) and fall (Sept.–Oct.) vagrant L4 & 5. Seven observations: an adult and an immature were seen repeatedly at Lake DeSmet 9-18-1977 to 10-6-1977; an individual with aberrant plumage was seen at Lake DeSmet 6-7-19-1981. An immature was at Healy Reservoir 9-23-1981; an adult at Wagner Reservoir 9-24-1981; one in alternate plumage and another in basic plumage at Lake DeSmet 9-27-1982. This arctic nester is most likely to be observed among flocks of migrating Franklin's or Bonaparte's gulls.

Bonaparte's Gull, *Chroicocephalus philadelphia*: uncommon spring and fall transient, extremely rare summer (Apr.–Nov.) vagrant L4 & 5. Average spring arrival, 5-6. Four were seen at Willow Park Reservoir 9-25-1987, elevation 8,625'. One individual at Healy Reservoir was in basic plumage 6-5-1981. Reported most often at Lake DeSmet and Healy Reservoir. Like many gulls, it is most common around lakes and reservoirs.

Franklin's Gull, *Leucophaeus pipixcan*: fairly common spring transient, rare summer visitor, uncommon fall (Mar.–Nov.) transient L4 & 5; breeding not confirmed. Average spring arrival, 4-18. An adult and four young following closely were seen at Healy Reservoir 6-19-1981; the young were able to fly. Often found in plowed fields and at reservoirs and ponds. The Franklin's Gull was observed during 12 of 21 years of Spring Bird Counts in Johnson County, 1984–2004, and during one of four years of Spring Bird Counts in Sheridan County, 2009–2012. It was not observed during 26 years of Christmas Bird Counts at Buffalo, 1986–2011. On migration these gulls typically feed on dry land, often in fields that are being cultivated prior to planting.

Ring-billed Gull, *Larus delawarensis*: common to abundant spring and fall transient (Mar.–Dec.), and non-breeding summer resident L4 & 5; uncommon December visitor L5; breeding suspected, L5. Average spring arrival, 4-3. Many young of the year are seen annually, but there is no evidence of nesting or of dependent young. Often seen at all the large reservoirs, and overhead at Big Horn, Buffalo and Sheridan. The Franklin's Gull was observed during 12 of 21 years of Spring Bird Counts in Johnson County, 1984–2004, and during one of four years of Spring Bird Counts in Sheridan County, 2009–2012. It was not observed during 26 years of Christmas Bird Counts at Buffalo, 1986–2011. This is a highly adaptable gull, often exploiting new habitats such as reservoirs. Breeding usually occurs on isolated and sparsely vegetated islands of lakes and reservoir impoundments, sometimes in colonies of a thousand pairs or more. Breeding Bird Surveys indicate that national populations are increasing significantly (1.9% annually, 1966-2011).

California Gull, *Larus californicus*: fairly common to common spring and fall transient (Mar.–Nov.), and non-breeding summer resident L5. Average spring arrival, 4-25. Young of the year are rarely seen. Found primarily at Lake DeSmet and Healy Reservoir. The California Gull was observed during 14 of 21 years of Spring Bird Counts in Johnson County, 1984–2004. It was not observed during 26 years of Christmas Bird Counts at

LARIDAE: GULLS & TERNS

Buffalo, 1986–2011. Like the Ring-billed Gull, this is an adaptable and easily seen species around diverse wetlands.

Herring Gull, *Larus argentatus*: uncommon spring and fall transient, and rare summer (Mar.–Nov.) visitant L5. Average spring arrival, 4-22. Found primarily at Lake DeSmet. The Herring Gull was observed during four of 21 years of Spring Bird Counts in Johnson County, 1984–2004. It was not observed during 26 years of Christmas Bird Counts at Buffalo, 1986–2011. These gulls usually winter coastally, but sometimes spend the winter on ice-free lakes or impoundments.

Least Tern, *Sternula antillarum*: Extremely rare fall (Sept.) transient, L5. Several reported at Lake DeSmet, 9-14-1978. Not reported regionally on eBird from 1-1-1990 through 4-25-2013. The nearest regular nesting area is in Nebraska's Platte Valley.

Caspian Tern, *Hydroprogne caspia*: rare spring, summer and early fall (May–Sept.) visitant L5; breeding not confirmed. Twelve observations of from one to six birds, 1969 through 1990, at Lake DeSmet and Healy Reservoir. Two eBird reports from 1-1-1990 through 9-5-2011 are: Buffalo Wetlands Park, Buffalo, 6-29-2011, and northeast of Buffalo, 7-8-2010. The Caspian Tern was observed during three of 21 years of Spring Bird Counts in Johnson County, 1984–2004. It was not observed during 26 years of Christmas Bird Counts at Buffalo, 1986–2011. Usually seen on or near larger bodies of water; local nesting occurs elsewhere in Wyoming.

Black Tern, *Chlidonias niger*: uncommon spring and fall transient and summer (Apr.–Sept.) visitant L5. Average spring arrival, 5-15. Loose flocks, of as many as 50 7-25-1981, at Healy Reservoir, and 80 on 7-14-1980, at Lake DeSmet. They are also found at many small ponds, but are declining nationally. The Black Tern was observed during four of 21 years of Spring Bird Counts in Johnson County, 1984–2004. It was not observed during 26 years of Christmas Bird Counts at Buffalo, 1986–2011. Typical habitat consists of small to large marshes with extensive stands of emergent vegetation and some areas of open water.

Common Tern, *Sterna hirundo*: rare spring (April) and fall (Aug.–Oct.)_ vagrant L5. Twelve reports 1967 through 1983. Two summer reports, 6-24 and 7-12, 1969, were unexplained. One regional eBird report from 1-1-1990 through 4-25-2013 is 7-26-2009, Sheridan.

Forster's Tern, *Sterna forsteri*: uncommon spring and fall (Apr.–Sept.) transient, and extremely rare summer visitor L4 & 5; breeding not confirmed. Average spring arrival, 5-6. Has been seen at Wagner Reservoir, McClain's Pond, Rock Creek pond east of I-90, Lake DeSmet, Healy Reservoir, and Clear Creek Diversion. The Forster's Tern was observed during 12 of 21 years of Spring Bird Counts in Johnson County, 1984–2004. It was not observed during 26 years of Christmas Bird Counts at Buffalo, 1986–2011. Large marshes having extensive reed beds or muskrat houses for nest sites are the typical migrant and summer habitats of this species, and migrant often occur along clear, shallow rivers where small fishes are common.

Family Stercorariidae: Jaegers

Parasitic Jaeger

Parasitic Jaeger, *Stercorarius parasiticus*: extremely rare summer (June) and fall Aug., Oct.) vagrant L5. Three records to 1990: 10-24-1977, and 8-28-1978, at Lake DeSmet; and 6-21-1985, at Healy Reservoir. The

1985 record was of an adult in alternate plumage. Not reported regionally on eBird from 1-1-1990 through 4-25-2013. The three species of jaegers are all arctic-breeders that normally migrate along coastlines to pelagic Southern Hemisphere wintering areas. All three species occasionally drift inland during migration, where they are most likely to be seen on larger bodies of water. Of the three, the Parasitic Jaeger is perhaps most often seen in the continental interior. The name "jaeger" means "hunter" in German, and refers to the predatory and piratic nature of these birds. On their tundra nesting grounds, lemmings, nestling birds, unfledged waterfowl and shorebirds are common prey, and untended nests are quickly raided. Parasitic Jaegers are not "parasitic" in the usual sense, but they effectively exploit other predators or scavengers such as gulls by harassing them and eventually forcing them to give up their catches. There are fewer than ten state records for this species (Faulkner 2010).

Family Columbidae: Pigeons & Doves

Mourning Dove

Rock Pigeon, *Columba livia*: abundant resident; breeding confirmed L4 & 5. Found in all urban areas. The Rock Pigeon was observed during 19 of 21 years of Spring Bird Counts in Johnson County, 1984–2004, during all 26 years of Christmas Bird Counts at Buffalo, 1986–2011, and was also reported during all four years of Spring Bird Counts in Sheridan County, 2009–2012. Found almost entirely near human habitations, such as farmyards and in cities. Buildings that provide narrow nesting ledges are preferred for nesting, but cliff ledges or crevices are sometimes also used. Previously (until 2003) known as the Rock Dove.

Band-tailed Pigeon, *Patagoenas fasciata*: extremely rare summer (July) and fall (Oct.) vagrant L4; breeding not confirmed. Three records to 1990: 7-18-1980, two birds, Tongue River Canyon Road; 10-1-1982, Tongue River Canyon campground; and 7-29-1983, on Wolf Creek. One regional eBird report from 1-1-1990 through 4-25-2013 is from northeast of

Buffalo, 7-8-2010. This species is generally associated with western oak woodlands or mixed oak and pine woodlands, and extending into the ponderosa pine zone locally, especially where oaks are also present.

Eurasian Collared-Dove, *Streptopelia decaocto*: a recent invasive (since 1998) self-introduced and still-expanding resident species. Breeding confirmed, L4. Now a common resident in north-central Wyoming, occurring statewide at lower elevations (Faulkner, 2010). The Eurasian Collared-dove was observed during two of 21 years of Spring Bird Counts in Johnson County, 1984–2004, during ten of 26 years of Christmas Bird Counts (initially in 2002) at Buffalo, 1986–2011, and was also reported during all four years of Spring Bird Counts in Sheridan County, 2009–2012. Usually found in smaller towns and villages, especially around feedlots or granaries where waste grain is abundant. Breeding Bird Surveys indicate that national populations are increasing significantly at an astonishing rate (18.2% annually, 1966-2011).

Mourning Dove, *Zenaida macroura*: common spring and fall transient and summer resident, becoming abundant in the fall (Mar.–Dec.); breeding confirmed L4 & 5. Average spring arrival, 4-7. Two were seen on a Christmas Bird Count 12-21-1980. Found in all areas, urban as well as rural. The Mourning Dove was observed during all 21 years of Spring Bird Counts in Johnson County, 1984–2004, and during all four years of Spring Bird Counts in Sheridan County, 2009–2012. Breeds from riparian woodlands and cultivated areas through grasslands and sagebrush to woodlands, aspen, and open coniferous forest habitats, as well as in cities and farmsteads. Nests either on the ground or, preferentially, in shrubs or trees.

Family Cuculidae: Cuckoos

Yellow-billed Cuckoo

Yellow-billed Cuckoo, *Coccyzus americanus*: uncommon summer (May–Aug.) resident L4 & 5; fewer records than of the Black-billed Cuckoo; breeding confirmed L5. Average spring arrival, 6-1. A fledgling, just able to fly, was seen in Sheridan 8-11-1980; singing had been heard in the same place the last half of July. A road-killed immature was found on U. S. Hwy. 14 northwest of Ucross, 7-13-1987. Associated with thickets near water, second-growth woodlands, deserted farmlands, and brushy orchards. Dense woodlands are avoided.

Black-billed Cuckoo, *Coccyzus erythropthalmus*: uncommon summer resident (May.–Sept.; breeding presumed L4 & 5. Average spring arrival, 6-8. The two cuckoo species are secretive, and their very late spring arrival is often noted only by their distinctive songs. Both species have been heard singing in the same general vicinity. Ash Creek, SR–Buffalo Creek Road, and Sheridan Cemetery Draw are good places to find either species. Associated during the breeding season with somewhat dense woodland cover, such as upland woods with a variety of trees, shrubs, and vines, offering shady hiding places and nest sites. Breeding Bird Surveys indicate that national populations of both cuckoos are decreasing significantly (1.5–1.6% annually, 1966-2011).

Family Tytonidae: Barn Owls

Barn Owl

Barn Owl, *Tyto alba*: Extremely rare vagrant, L5. Two were photographed at separate locations near Ucross, 1-7–8-2007 (Faulkner. 2010). There are only about 20 reports of this species from Wyoming (Faulkner, 2010), which is rather surprising owing to its widespread occurrence and extensive breeding in western Nebraska. The January Ucross reports are especially surprising, as Barn Owls are migratory, and should be gone from the region by January. Barn Owls prefer open to semi-open habitats, where small rodents are abundant and where hollow trees, old buildings, or caves are available to provide roosting and nesting sites are present. Rats, including kangaroo rats, are particularly favored as prey species, but many other rodents are also consumed. Barn owls are rodent-catchers without peer, and the presence of a pair at a farm may account for the disappearance of several thousand mice or rats per year. They are thus highly valuable birds, although farmers often seem unaware of their presence or, if so, may actually try to kill them.

Family Strigidae: Typical Owls

Northern Saw-whet Owl

Eastern Screech-Owl, *Megascops asio*: uncommon resident; breeding confirmed L4 & 5. Screech-Owls have been seen at Ash Creek, Big Goose and Bird Farm roads, Sheridan (including just-fledged young), Story, and Big Horn. Robert Berry (pers. comm.) has reported hearing the calls of both the eastern and western species within the Bighorn region and individuals in Big Horn have suggested both species are present there. An adult was observed in a cavity at Bradford Brinton in 2012. Across its wide range, this little owl is associated with a variety of wooded habitats, including farmyards, cities, and orchards, and from riparian edges through pinyon–juniper and oak-mahogany woodlands to aspens and ponderosa pine forests. In the Bighorn region the eastern species is found exclusively in large riparian cottonwood trees. There has been much confusion about the range of the Screech-Owls since they were recognized in 1998 as two species. The Eastern, *M. asio*, and Western, *M. kennicottii*, are geographically isolated from one another over nearly all of their ranges. Faulkner (2010) found no evidence of Western Screech-Owls in this region, or anywhere east of the Continental Divide in Wyoming

Great Horned Owl, *Bubo virginianus*: common resident; breeding confirmed L4 & 5. The Great Horned Owl was observed during 17 of 21 years of Spring Bird Counts in Johnson County, 1984–2004, during 17 of 26 years of Christmas Bird Counts at Buffalo, 1986–2011, and during three of four years of Spring Bird Counts in Sheridan County, 2009–2012. A powerful and adaptable owl, this species occurs everywhere from riparian woodlands through the coniferous forest zones, and extends into city parks, farm woodlots, and rocky canyons well away from trees. Nest sites are highly variable, but often are in abandoned hawk or squirrel nests, or on tree crotches, rock ledges, or even on the ground.

Snowy Owl, *Bubo scandiaca*: extremely rare winter (Nov.–Feb.) vagrant L5. Seven records from 1968 to 1980: Airport Road, East Fifth Street, on I-90 both north and south of Sheridan, and at Banner. An arctic-breeding species that periodically is forced south in winter when food supplies on the breeding grounds are limiting, such as the winter of 2011–2012, when a massive movement into the northern states occurred. In the Bighorns region there were records from Arvada (1-31-2012), Buffalo (2-23-2012) and (south of our study area) Kaycee (2-8-2012) .

Northern Pygmy-Owl, *Glaucidium gnoma*: extremely rare, status unknown. A "heard only" record at Story 4-7-12-1980, L5; and a well-documented sight record on Rapid Creek, 12-28-1988, L4. Not reported regionally on eBird from 1-1-1990 through 4-25-2013. A rare and elusive nester in the Rocky Mountain region.

Burrowing Owl, *Athene cunicularia*: fairly common spring, summer, and fall (Apr.–Oct.) resident; breeding confirmed L4 & 5. Average spring arrival, 4-20. Only three records 1966 to 1976, probably due to lack of observers; more than 50 records from 1977 to 1989. Reported from north of Arvada, Beatty Gulch-Prairie Dog Road, southeast of Buffalo, East Fifth Street, the Sheridan City Dump, and along Soldier Creek Road. This is the only North American owl closely associated with Great Plains rodents such as prairie dogs, and as the range and abundance of these mammals have decreased, so too has the status of the Burrowing Owl. It is migratory and largely insectivorous species, often eating large beetles in summer, but also eats many small rodents, especially during winter.

Barred Owl, *Strix varia*: extremely rare vagrant, L5; one reported southeast of Sheridan "near the Dutchman mine," NW' Section 27, T54N R82W, 7-23-1977. Downing relegated this species to her hypothetical list, on the basis of having only a single regional report, but the record was accepted by Faulkner (2010) as one of seven state records.

Great Gray Owl, *Strix nebulosa*: extremely rare summer (June) and fall (Oct.) vagrant, L$; reported from Kettle Gulch, hunting season, October 1973, 1974, 1975; also October 18 and 27, 1978. One regional eBird report from 1-1-1990 through 4-25-2013 was from east of Greybull, 6-29-2007. This is a rare and elusive nester in the Rocky Mountain region, and hard to locate in spite of its large size. It is often perched in tall coniferous trees at the edges of clearings, but is usually extremely difficult to detect.

Long-eared Owl, *Asio otus*: believed to be an uncommon resident; breeding confirmed L4 & L5. Only three records exist from 1966 to 1978, probably due to lack of observers, but 20 records from 1979 to 1989. Long-eared Owls have been found on Ash Creek and on Wyarno Road; one was seen in Sheridan 5-21-1982. Often associated with coniferous or deciduous forests, but also found in woodlots, orchards, large wooded parks, and even sagebrush or pinyon–juniper woodlands during the breeding season. Densely-foliaged trees surrounded by open country seem to be favored for nesting. The first known regional communal roost was in a hawthorn shrub draw on Rapid Creek 12-15 –12-27, 1987, when at least 20 Long-eared and ten or more Short-eared Owls were found together.

Short-eared Owl, *Asio flammeus*: probably an uncommon resident, more abundant in years of rodent outbreaks; breeding confirmed L4 & 5. Four flying young birds were seen on Beaver Creek Road December 28, 1974; two adults, engaged in courtship activity, were seen on the Sheridan City Dump Road 6-3-1982. This owl has been seen on SR–Buffalo Creek Road and elsewhere in open country. A single bird was seen in April of 2013 in a grassland field near Big Horn. It was not observed during 21 years of Spring Bird Counts in Johnson County, 1984–2004, but was reported during two of 26 years of Christmas Bird Counts at Buffalo, 1986–2011. It is a prairie-adapted species, usually breeding in areas of grassland, marshes, arctic tundra, and low brush land. Nests are usually on the ground, but sometimes are in burrows. More diurnal than most owls, these birds are often seen hunting while it is still daylight.

Boreal Owl, *Aegolius funereus*: probably an extremely rare resident L4, breeding confirmed, L4. There is no information on its Bighorn status, other than that regional breeding was reported in 2006 near Graves Creek (Woodrock area), in one of the owl nest boxes put out in 2005, when it was used by a Saw-whet Owl (unpublished report by Jon Warder, Biologist, Bighorn National Forest). Boreal owls are among the most nocturnal, and most secretive of North American owls, and are typically found in mature and old-growth high-altitude forests, where old woodpecker holes provide nesting cavities, and forest-dwelling voles such as the red-backed vole (*Clethrionomys gapperi*) are abundant.

Northern Saw-whet Owl, *Aegolius acadicus*: probably an uncommon resident L4 & 5, but records are insufficient to determine abundance; breeding confirmed, L4, L5. An immature was seen near a Sheridan feeding station in June of 1969, and breeding occurred in 2005 near Graves Creek (Woodrock area) (unpublished report by Jon Warder, Biologist, Bighorn National Forest). Saw-whets have been found at Little Piney Road, Ranchester Park, Red Grade Road above Big Horn, Story, and just below Seven Brothers Lake, 9,000' elevation. Occurs widely, from riparian woodlands through aspen groves to the coniferous forest zones, but not reaching timberline. The foothills and ponderosa pine zones are probably their favored habitats, where they nest in old woodpecker holes.

Family Caprimulgidae: Poorwills & Nighthawks

Common Nighthawk

Common Nighthawk, *Chordeiles minor*: common summer (May–Sept.) resident; breeding confirmed L4 & 5. Average spring arrival, 6-2. Nighthawks are often seen aerial feeding all summer at Sheridan and Buffalo. This species was observed during one of 21 years of Spring Bird Counts in Johnson County, 1984–2004. It was not observed during 26 years of Christmas Bird Counts at Buffalo, 1986–2011. This species forages entirely in the air, on flying insects, and is especially common over grassland and urban areas, sometimes extending to sagebrush and desert scrub. Nesting occurs on the ground, usually in grasslands, or at the edges of woods, and sometimes on the asphalt rooftops of buildings. Breeding Bird Surveys indicate that national populations are decreasing significantly (1.2% annually, 1966-2011).

Common Poorwill, *Phalaenoptilus nuttallii*: uncommon spring and fall (Apt.–Sept.) transient and summer resident; breeding confirmed L4, presumed L5. Average spring arrival, 5-20. Only two records from 1966 through 1977; 34 records from then to 1990. An active nest was found in Wall Rock Canyon, about 8,500' elevation, in July 1981, no other details available. USFS personnel found adults with two chicks in a dirt nest above Miller Creek in the Dry Fork area. 7-2-1988. Poorwills have been seen on Jim Creek Hill on U. S. Hwy. 14 east of Sheridan, on Kumor Road south of Moore's Reservoir, and one was found injured in a Sheridan garden. It was not observed during 26 years of Christmas Bird Counts at Buffalo, 1986–2011. Generally this species is associated with rocky habitats having a cover of arid-adapted shrubs or low trees, such as pinyon–juniper, saltbush, greasewood, sagebrush, and dry grasslands. Poorwills nest on the ground, often under scrub oaks, the dead leaves of which provide concealment for adults, eggs and young.

Family Apodidae: Swifts

White-throated Swift

Chimney Swift, *Chaetura pelagica*: extremely rare summer (May–Sept.) visitant L5; breeding not confirmed. Average spring arrival, 5-30. Two regional eBird reports from 1-1-1990 through 4-25-2013 are: Tongue River Road, 5-26-2011, and Welch Wildlife Area, 5-31-2010. An observer in a downtown Sheridan building reported watching swifts from 1982 through 1985. Swift records are scarce except in southeastern Wyoming, and there are no state nesting records (Faulkner, 2010). This is a familiar city bird over most of eastern North America, mainly in the vicinity of towns and cities where chimneys offer roosting and nesting sites. Caves and hollow trees were used before chimneys became available, and may occasionally still be used in some localities. Breeding Bird Surveys indicate that national populations are decreasing significantly (2.3% annually, 1966-2011).

White-throated Swift, *Aeronautes saxatalis*: common spring, summer and fall (Apr.–Oct.) resident; breeding confirmed L4 & L5. Average spring arrival, 5-17. They have been seen to enter nest crevices in Tongue River Canyon and at Twin Buttes. White-throated Swifts have also been found in Crazy Woman Canyon, North Piney Canyon, the West Fork of Little Bighorn River, and at Black Mountain Fire Lookout at 9,489' elevation. The White-throated Swift was observed during two of 21 years of Spring Bird Counts in Johnson County, 1984–2004, and during one of four years of Spring Bird Counts in Sheridan County, 2009–2012. It was not observed during 26 years of Christmas Bird Counts at Buffalo, 1986–2011. This swift is associated with steep cliffs, deep canyons, and generally mountainous terrain, sometimes as high as 13,000'. Nesting occurs in crevices of canyon walls.

Family Trochilidae: Hummingbirds

Calliope Hummingbird

Ruby-throated Hummingbird, *Archilochus colubris*: extremely rare spring (May) and early fall (Aug.–Sept.) vagrant, L5. Five reports from Sheridan: 7-25 & 28-1970; 9-3-1970; 9-8-1971; 9-8 & 9, 1972; 5-14-1976. Considered hypothetical regionally by Downing (1970), but the Bighorn records were accepted by Faulkner (2010).

Black-chinned Hummingbird, *Archilochus alexandri*: extremely rare spring and summer (May–Aug.) vagrant L5. Four reports, May 18 to August 5, 1978–1986. Three of these reports were at Story, from, 5,000–5,500', in open ponderosa pine woods. Also reported from Sheridan, 5-26-1991 (Faulkner, 2010). Not reported regionally on eBird from 1-1-1990 through 4-25-2013. Typically associated with riparian habitats in dry canyons, but also occurring in oak-juniper woodlands, edges of aspen groves, and other habitats that usually are near water and provide open areas with many flowering plants.

Anna's Hummingbird, *Calypte anna*: Extremely rare early fall (Aug.–Sept) vagrant L5. One record at Cory, 7-1-9-15, 1975. Not reported regionally on eBird from 1-1-1990 through 4-25-2013. Arizona is the nearest region of regular nesting.

Broad-tailed Hummingbird, *Selasphorus platycercus*: fairly common summer (May–Sept,) resident; breeding presumed L4 & 5. Average spring arrival, 5-19. The best viewing areas are Arrowhead Lodge, Little Piney at the Wagon Box Monument, Catholic Church in Story, and West Pass Creek, up to about 8,500'. This species is commonly seen at feeders in Story during May and June. The Broad-tailed Hummingbird was observed during two of 21 years of Spring Bird Counts in Johnson County, 1984–2004. It was not observed during 26 years of Christmas Bird Counts at Buffalo, 1986–2011. Typically associated with ponderosa pine forests and aspen groves, but also extending into mountain meadows, pinyon–juniper woodland and riparian cottonwoods. Willow-lined streams adjacent to flowering meadows and open parklands are favored foraging areas.

Rufous Hummingbird, *Selasphorus rufus*: fairly common late summer and early fall (June–Sept.) transient, breeding not confirmed, L4 & 5. Found at Buffalo, Sheridan, Story, and up to Burgess Ranger Station at about 8,100'. This hummingbird arrives around July in the Sheridan area when it replaces the Calliope and Broad-tailed. Typically associated with open ponderosa pine forests and aspen groves, but also extending into mountain meadows, pinyon–juniper woodland and riparian cottonwoods. Like the previous species, willow-lined streams adjacent to flower-rich meadows and parklands are favored foraging areas. Breeding Bird Surveys indicate that national populations are decreasing significantly (2.0% annually, 1966-2011).

Calliope Hummingbird, *Selasphorus calliope*: Common summer (May–Sept,) resident: breeding confirmed L4 & 5. Average spring arrival, 5-11. Can be found at Big Goose Creek, Story (where common), along Little Piney Creek Road at the Wagon Box Monument, West Pass Creek, and the foothills of Wolf Creek, from about 4,500–8,500'. The Calliope Hummingbird was observed during three of 21 years of Spring Bird Counts in Johnson County, 1984–2004, and during three of four years of Spring Bird Counts in Sheridan County, 2009–2012. It was not observed during 26 years of Christmas Bird Counts at Buffalo, 1986–2011. Open meadow areas near coniferous forests, especially low willow or sage areas rich in flowers such as Indian paintbrush and gilia, are favored habitats for this species in the Bighorn region.

Family Alcedinidae: Kingfishers

Belted Kingfisher

Belted Kingfisher, *Ceryle alcyon*: fairly common resident, but numbers diminish in winter; breeding confirmed L4 & 5. Found on all streams and ponds in the area, at Burgess Ranger Station and on Hazelton Road just over 8,000' elevation, and at the Wilderness Area boundary below Edelman Pass, 9,200'. It was observed during all 21 years of Spring Bird Counts in Johnson County, 1984–2004, during 15 of 26 years of Christmas Bird Counts at Buffalo, 1986–2011, and during all four years of Spring Bird Counts in Sheridan County, 2009–2012. Recorded at Bradford Brinton in December of 2012. Found near water rich in small fish populations, usually where road cuts, eroded banks, gravel pits, or other exposed earthen surfaces provide opportunities for nesting, and where nearby trees provide convenient perching and observation sites. It can be seen along most regional rivers or lakes that have good fish populations, steep clay banks for excavating nest sites, and nearby perching sites such as bare-branched trees adjacent to water.

Family Picidae: Woodpeckers

Lewis's Woodpecker

Lewis's Woodpecker, *Melanerpes lewis*: uncommon spring and fall transient and summer resident (May–Oct,); breeding confirmed L4 & 5. Average spring arrival, 5-19. Suitable nest trees for either species are becoming increasingly scarce, due to blow-downs. Ash Creek has been the most easily monitored Lewis's Woodpecker habitat; these woodpeckers have also been seen at Story, Tongue River Canyon Road, and on Wolf Creek. A probable sighting was on Red Grade Road near the burn area in May, 2013. The Lewis's Woodpecker was observed during four of 21 years of Spring Bird Counts in Johnson County, 1984–2004, and during one of 26 years of Christmas Bird Counts at Buffalo, 1986–2011. This blackish woodpecker is especially associated with rather open, burned-over pines or otherwise dead-tree areas having abundant snags or stumps. This preference means that its distribution tends to be flexible and adapted to local conditions. Streamside cottonwood groves in the ponderosa pine or pinyon–juniper zones are also used, and old cottonwoods are favorite nesting trees. This species was regarded as fairly common 1966–1982, but has declined since then. One reason may be the abundance of American Kestrels that also use cavities for nesting. It is thought that the kestrels capture the woodpecker fledglings as they emerge (see Kestrel account). Breeding Bird Surveys indicate that national populations of this woodpecker are decreasing significantly (2.0% annually, 1966-2011). A recent estimate of the species' total population is 130,000 (Rich *et al.*, 2004).

Red-headed Woodpecker, *Melanerpes erythrocephalus*: uncommon spring to fall (Apr.–Oct.) resident in the Sheridan and Buffalo areas, but fairly common to common along the Powder River at Arvada; breeding confirmed L4 & 5. Average spring arrival, 5-20. They have nested at Ash Creek, Buffalo, on Kumor Road east of Buffalo, Lower Prairie Dog Road, Sheridan, Upper Road (Swaim Pond area) and Young's Creek. Red-headed Woodpeckers were seen as high as 7,500' elevation at Doyle Creek, 10-15-1978, and at 8,038' at Burgess Junction 5-30-1989. The species was observed during one of 21 years of Spring Bird Counts in Johnson County, 1984–2004. It was not observed during 26 years of Christmas Bird Counts at Buffalo, 1986–2011. Associated with open deciduous forests, woodlots, and riparian areas, sometimes extending into the ponderosa pine zone. Aspens and riparian cottonwood forests are the species' major habitats in this region. Breeding Bird Surveys indicate that national populations are decreasing significantly (2.7% annually, 1966-2011).

Williamson's Sapsucker, *Sphyrapicus thyroideus*: uncommon spring, summer and fall (Apr.–Oct.) resident; breeding confirmed L4 & 5. Average spring arrival, 5-6. This sapsucker has been seen at Bear Lodge, Dayton Gulch, Nickle Creek, Story, and Twin Buttes, up to 8,500' elevation. One winter record, at Story-Big Horn, 12-28-1974 (Faulkner, 2010). Breeding in this region usually occurs in the aspen or coniferous zones, especially in ponderosa pine forests, with mixed aspens. High ridges in the Douglas-fir zone are also used for foraging, but nesting is usually done in aspens, the soft wood of which allows for easy excavation.

Red-naped Sapsucker, *Sphyrapicus nuchalis*: fairly common spring, summer and fall (Apr.–Oct.) resident; breeding confirmed L4 & 5. Average spring arrival, 5-5. Readily found from Little Piney Creek Road and Story, at 5,000', Twin Buttes and Burgess Junction at just over 8,000', to Black Mountain Lookout, at 9,489' elevation. This sapsucker was observed during 13 of 21 years of Spring Bird Counts in Johnson County, 1984–2004, and during three of four years of Spring Bird Counts in Sheridan County, 2009–2012. It was not observed during 26 years of Christmas Bird Counts at Buffalo, 1986–2011. Sapsuckers use coniferous forests, deciduous forests, and mixed woodlands, but aspens are a favorite habitat in this region. They excavate holes in these trees to drink the sap, and also nest in aspens, either in dead trees or living ones that have dead, rotting interiors. They breed as high in the mountains as the upper limit of aspens, the holes providing ideal nesting cavities for at least six other species of hole-nesting birds. Breeding Bird Surveys indicate that national populations are increasing significantly (1.3% annually, 1966-2011). Until the 1980s considered part of the more eastern-oriented Yellow-breasted Sapsucker (*S. varius*) by the A.O.U.; the two are now classified as separate, closely related species.

Downy Woodpecker, *Picoides pubescens*: common resident; breeding confirmed L4 & 5. Found in all wooded areas. The species was observed during all 21 years of Spring Bird Counts in Johnson County, 1984–2004, during all 26 years of Christmas Bird Counts at Buffalo, 1986–2011, and during all four years of Spring Bird Counts in Sheridan County, 2009–2012. A wide variety of wooded habitats are used by Downy Woodpeckers, including woodlots, orchards, city parks, and natural habitats ranging from riparian forests to pinyon–juniper woodlands, oak–mountain mahogany scrub, and aspen or coniferous forests.

Hairy Woodpecker, *Picoides villosus*: fairly common resident; breeding confirmed L4 & 5. Recorded nesting at 4,000' elevation at Sheridan, 5,000' at Story, and at 8,000' at Freezeout. They have been seen on Ash Creek, Big Horn and Sheridan, but are most easily found at Story. The species was observed during 15 of 21 years of Spring Bird Counts in Johnson County, 1984–2004, during 21 of 26 years of Christmas Bird Counts at Buffalo, 1986–2011, and also during all four years of Spring Bird Counts in Sheridan County, 2009–2012. Optimum breeding habitat consists of fairly extensive areas of woodlands of conifers (especially lodgepole pines) or hardwoods, but nesting occurs in riparian forests, in aspen groves, and in various coniferous forest types nearly to timberline.

Generally, aspens and other hardwoods are preferred over conifers for breeding. Breeding Bird Surveys indicate that national populations are increasing significantly (0.0% annually, 1966-2011).

American Three-toed Woodpecker, *Picoides dorsalis*: probably an uncommon resident L4 & 5; breeding confirmed L4, presumed L5. Finding this species is difficult because of its widespread distribution in mountain habitat. The only record at Story was December 16, 1980; other sightings are from Billy Creek, Bucking Mule Creek, Bull Creek, Dayton Gulch, Lake Geneva, Owen Creek, Pole Creek Campground, the Sourdough area, and Willow Creek, from 8,000' to over 9,500' elevation. The species was not observed during 21 years of Spring Bird Counts in Johnson County, 1984–2004. It was reported during one of 26 years of Christmas Bird Counts at Buffalo, 1986–2011. This is a fire-adapted woodpecker, typically moving into a burned forest area immediately after the fire, breeding, and dispersing four or five years later. Bluebirds, nuthatches, and many other cavity-nesters then use the nest cavities until the snags eventually topple. Partly open, high-elevation coniferous or aspen forests are typical habitats. Spruce–fir forests are favored habitats in the northern Rockies. Previously named the Three-toed Woodpecker, *P. tridactylus*, a name now reserved for a closely related Old World woodpecker. The related Black-backed Woodpecker, *P. arcticus*, has not yet been reported from the region, but it and the present species are both likely to occur regionally as forest fires become more prevalent, and bark beetle infestations increase. Breeding Bird Surveys indicate that national populations of both species are increasing nationally at still non-significant statistical levels.

Northern Flicker, *Colaptes auratus*: common resident; breeding confirmed L4 & 5. Many, if not most, of the flickers in this area are intergrades between the eastern yellow-shafted race, *C. auratus auratus*, and the western red-shafted race, *C. auratus cafer*. Pure yellow-shafted plumages are rare. Flickers nest at Sheridan and Buffalo elevations up to Big Goose Ranger Station at 7,858'; they have been reported at elevations as high as 9,800'. The red-shafted race was observed during all 21 years of Spring Bird Counts in Johnson County, 1984–2004, during all 26 years of Christmas Bird Counts at Buffalo, 1986–2011, and during all four years of Spring Bird Counts in Sheridan County, 2009–2012. The yellow-shafted race was also reported for four years in each of the first two locations. Flickers are unusual among woodpeckers in that much of their food consists of insects such as ants that are obtained by probing in the ground, rather than extracted from trees. However, they do excavate holes in trees for nesting, usually those that are already dead or have decaying interiors, especially in relatively softwood species such as cottonwoods and aspens. Open woodlands, such as orchards, parks, and similar areas offering foraging opportunities on grassy areas nearby are preferred over dense forests. Breeding Bird Surveys indicate that national populations are decreasing significantly (1.4% annually, 1966-2011).

Family Falconidae: Falcons

Peregrine Falcon

American Kestrel, *Falco sparverius*: common spring and fall transient and summer resident; a few occasionally overwinter; breeding confirmed L4 & 5. Ten pairs were recorded on a 3½-mile stretch of road on Rapid Creek, 6-29-1979, several pairs were recorded off Kumor Road and Wolf Creek Road in 2011; nesting occurs at elevations up to at least 9,000'. The American Kestrel was observed during all 21 years of Spring Bird Counts in Johnson County, 1984–2004, during seven of 26 years of

Christmas Bird Counts at Buffalo, 1986–2011, and during all four years of Spring Bird Counts in Sheridan County, 2009–2012. This is an open-country falcon, occurring in agricultural areas, grasslands, sagebrush, desert scrub, and nesting in tree cavities, rock or building crevices or cavities, and rarely in earthen holes. It avoids forests, but sometimes forages as high as mountain meadows. Kestrels have been observed nesting in the same tree with Lewis' Woodpeckers, always selecting a nest cavity above the woodpeckers. It was speculated that the kestrels contributed to the decline of Lewis' Woodpeckers, by catching the fledglings as they emerged from the nest. They also are known to have unusual dispersal patterns, making it difficult to track this bird. Breeding Bird Surveys indicate that national populations are decreasing significantly (1.5% annually, 1966-2011).

Merlin, *Falco columbarius*: fairly common spring and fall transient and uncommon year-round resident; breeding confirmed L4 & L5. At least three nests (one with five eggs) have been reported in riparian areas, and young fledged. Peak Merlin movements occur from 4-15 to 5-15, and from 9-1 to 10-10. Most observations are at about 4,000' elevation, but as high as 9,000' on Sheep Mountain Road. The Merlin was observed during six of 21 years of Spring Bird Counts in Johnson County, 1984–2004, during eight of 26 years of Christmas Bird Counts at Buffalo, 1986–2011, and during three of four years of Spring Bird Counts in Sheridan County, 2009–2012. This is a forest- and woodland-adapted falcon, usually breeding in tree clumps or open woodlands, often in bottomlands or valleys. Breeding Bird Surveys indicate that national populations are increasing significantly (2.8% annually, 1966-2011).

Gyrfalcon, *Falco rusticolus*: rare but fairly regular fall to spring (Sept.–April) visitant, L4 & 5. A total of 53 were reported 1969 to 1987, but only four were well documented to 1990. About half of Wyoming's sightings were from Sheridan County, between 1972 and 1993: many are from late March (Faulkner, 2010). The species was not observed during 21 years of Spring Bird Counts in Johnson County, 1984–2004, and during one of 26 years of Christmas Bird Counts at Buffalo, 1986–2011. Not reported regionally on eBird from 1-1-1990 through 4-25-2013. Gyrfalcons regularly winter in small number as far south as the western plains of the Dakotas, probably preying on larger resident birds such as Sharp-tailed Grouse. A recent estimate of the species' U.S. and Canadian population is 55,000 (Rich *et al.*, 2004). There are at least 50 Wyoming reports, many unverified.

Peregrine Falcon, *Falco peregrinus*: uncommon spring and fall transient (Mar.–June, Sept–Nov.), L4 & 5. Most commonly seen at Lake DeSmet, and at Healy's and Moore's reservoirs when ducks are plentiful, but also found at diverse locations, often at about 4,000'. The Peregrine Falcon was observed during three of 21 years of Spring Bird Counts in Johnson County, 1984–2004, and during two of 26 years of Christmas Bird Counts at Buffalo, 1986–2011. This is largely a cliff-nesting species, often breeding in wooded montane habitats. Non-breeders occur over a wide habitat range, from high mountain meadows to grasslands, marshes, and riparian habitats. Thanks to restoration efforts, by 2004, there were more than 60 nesting pairs in Wyoming (Faulkner 2010), and breeding is likely to occur eventually in the Bighorn Mountains.

Prairie Falcon, *Falco mexicanus*: fairly common resident with a decrease in numbers in severe winters; breeding confirmed L4 & 5. Most observations are of lone individuals except when nesting activities are reported. Often found around the large reservoirs at 4,000' elevation, but also at Woodchuck Pass and Paintrock Primitive Area at about 9,600' and at Medicine Lodge in 10-1-2010. The Prairie Falcon was observed during seven of 21 years of Spring Bird Counts in Johnson County, 1984–2004. It was not observed during 26 years of Christmas Bird Counts at Buffalo, 1986–2011, but was reported during two of four years of Spring Bird Counts in Sheridan County, 2009–2012. Breeding birds are largely associated with plains, sagebrush, or desert scrub habitats with steep cliffs nearby for nesting. Sometimes alpine areas also support breeders, and foraging may be done on mountain meadows or similar montane habitats. A recent estimate of the species' total population is 36,000 (Rich *et al.*, 2004).

Family Tyrannidae: American Flycatchers

Cordilleran Flycatcher

Olive-sided Flycatcher, *Contopus borealis*: an uncommon spring, summer, and early fall resident (Apr.–Sept.), breeding confirmed L4 & L5. Average spring arrival, 5-17. Recorded at Sheridan as early as April 16 (Faulkner, 2010). Fairly common in its mostly remote mountain habitat not often visited by birders. Some readily accessible sites are Arrowhead Lodge, Black Mountain Road, Canyon Creek Road, Cold Spring on Red Grade Road, Dayton Gulch, Hunter Creek Road, and Twin Buttes. The Olive-sided Flycatcher was observed during one of 21 years of Spring Bird Counts in Johnson County, 1984-2004, and during one of four years of Spring Bird Counts in Sheridan County, 2009–2012. It was not observed during 26 years of Christmas Bird Counts at Buffalo, 1986–2011. Associated with coniferous montane forests (especially Douglas-fir and lodgepole pine), burned-over or logged forests with standing snags, and muskegs. Typically tall conifers and open, often boggy or meadow-like areas are present in territories. Breeding Bird Surveys indicate that national populations are decreasing significantly (3.3% annually, 1966-2011).

Western Wood-Pewee, *Contopus sordidulus*: common spring and fall transient and summer resident (May–Sept.); breeding confirmed L4 & 5. Average spring arrival, 5-20. Found at all elevations from the Powder River near Arvada to Freezeout, Owen Creek and Dull Knife Reservoir, up to about 8,600' elevation. The Western Wood-Pewee was observed during seven of 21 years of Spring Bird Counts in Johnson County, 1984–2004, and during three of four years of Spring Bird Counts in Sheridan County, 2009–2012. It was not observed during 26 years of Christmas Bird Counts at Buffalo, 1986–2011. Breeds in most coniferous forest types, and also to a varying extent in aspens, riparian hardwood forests, and various open deciduous or mixed woodland habitats. Open forests are favored, especially those dominated by conifers. Breeding Bird Surveys indicate that national populations are decreasing significantly (1.6% annually, 1966-2011).

Note: The following *Empidonax* group of small flycatchers ("empidonaces") that are found in this area include the Cordilleran Flycatcher, Dusky Flycatcher, Least Flycatcher and Willow Flycatcher. All are very difficult to distinguish in the field except by song.

Willow Flycatcher, *Empidonax traillii*: fairly common spring, summer and early fall (May–Sept.) resident; breeding confirmed L4 & 5. Average spring arrival, 5-26. Fairly common is typical most years, but eleven were counted 6-23-1982, an exceptional summer. Found on Dayton-Beckton Road, Soldier Creek and Wolf Creek roads, Tongue River Canyon, U. S. Hwy. 16-Hazelton Road, West Pass Creek, and up to 8,300' at Hideout Creek on U. S. Hwy. 14A. The Willow Flycatcher was observed during seven of 21 years of Spring Bird Counts in Johnson County, 1984–2004. It was not observed during 26 years of Christmas Bird Counts at Buffalo, 1986–2011. Especially associated with riparian or wetland habitats in this region, including willow thickets, prairie coulees, and low gallery forests along streams. Breeding Bird Surveys indicate that national populations are decreasing significantly (1.2% annually, 1966-2011).

Least Flycatcher, *Empidonax minimus*: fairly common spring, summer and early fall (May–Sept.) resident; breeding confirmed L4 & L5. Average spring arrival, 5-17. Twelve were counted 5-26-1982, in Tongue River Canyon; ten or more were seen on Little Piney Road, 7-7-1980. Four were counted at the Bradford Brinton 6-17-2012. This bird seems to be one of the most common flycatchers along Little Goose Creek near Sheridan. The Least Flycatcher was observed during 12 of 21 years of Spring Bird Counts in Johnson County, 1984–2004, and during one of four years of Spring Bird Counts in Sheridan County, 2009–2012. It was not observed during 26 years of Christmas Bird Counts at Buffalo, 1986–2011. Associated with open and edge-dominated habitats such as mature deciduous floodplain forests with shrubby understories in prairie areas, scattered prairie groves, shelterbelts, woody lake margins, and urban parks or gardens. Breeding Bird Surveys indicate that national populations are decreasing significantly (1.8% annually, 1966-2011).

Dusky Flycatcher, *Empidonax oberholseri*: uncommon spring, summer and early fall (May–Sept.) resident; breeding confirmed L4 & 5. Average spring arrival, 5-23. Reliable-appearing records indicate this species migrates at Sheridan's elevation, 4,000'. It summers on Wolf Creek and Bud Love Game Management Unit, at Story and on U. S. Hwy. 16-Hazelton and Billy Creek roads. to 8,000' elevation. The Dusky Flycatcher was observed during four of 21 years of Spring Bird Counts in Johnson County, 1984–2004. It was not observed during 26 years of Christmas Bird Counts at Buffalo, 1986–2011. Associated with open woodland with dense shrubby understories, ranging from riparian edges through oak–mountain mahogany woodlands, to aspens and open ponderosa pine woods.

Cordilleran Flycatcher, *Empidonax occidentalis*: fairly common spring, summer and fall (May–Sept.) resident; breeding confirmed L4, presumed L5. Average spring arrival, 5-22. Found in Tongue River Canyon at 4,000' elevation; at Story on Piney Creek, 5,000'; Nickle Creek, 7,600'; found as high as Pole Creek at 8,000'. The species was observed during five of 21 years of Spring Bird Counts in Johnson County, 1984–2004. It was not observed during 26 years of Christmas Bird Counts at Buffalo, 1986–2011. This is a widespread and adaptable flycatcher, ranging from riparian woodlands through aspens through the coniferous forest zones, up to the upper spruce-fir zones. Shrubby riparian areas with cottonwoods are favored. The closely related Pacific-Slope Flycatcher (*E. diffici-*

lis) is not yet known to occur in Wyoming (Faulkner, 2010). Until 1989, these two species had been collectively considered a single species by the A.O.U., namely the Western Flycatcher, *E. difficilis*. Breeding Bird Surveys indicate that their collective national populations are decreasing significantly (0.6% annually, 1966-2011).

Eastern Phoebe, *Sayornis phoebe*: extremely rare summer (June) vagrant L4 4 5. Two observations lacked details: Kerns Game Management Unit, 6-26-1982, elevation unknown; and at Buffalo 6-10-1985, elevation 4,645'. Reported at Sheridan from May to August, 1966–1971, and during July, 1972, at McClain's Pond area and Home Ranch Road. There is one eBird report from 1-1-1990 through 11-5-2013; one bird at Tongue River Road, 5-26-2011. The Eastern Phoebe was observed during one of 21 years of Spring Bird Counts in Johnson County, 1984–2004. It was not observed during 26 years of Christmas Bird Counts at Buffalo, 1986–2011. Associated with woodland edges, wooded ravines near water, woodlots, and lakes or streams in partially wooded areas. Often breeds close to humans, nesting on building ledges, or on the understructure of bridges.

Say's Phoebe, *Sayornis saya*: common spring, summer and fall (Apr.–Oct.) resident; breeding confirmed L4 & 5. Average spring arrival, 4-17. Most observations are at 3,700' to 4,000' elevation in grasslands. The species was observed during 19 of 21 years of Spring Bird Counts in Johnson County, 1984–2004, and during all four years of Spring Bird Counts in Sheridan County, 2009–2012. It was not observed during 26 years of Christmas Bird Counts at Buffalo, 1986–2011. Generally associated with grasslands, sagebrush, and agricultural areas in the region, especially prairie coulees and steep, eroded riverbanks. The birds sometimes reach foothill areas, but do not breed in the wooded mountain zones. Breeding Bird Surveys indicate that national populations are increasing significantly (1.1% annually, 1966-2011).

Ash-throated Flycatcher, *Myiarchus cinerascens*: extremely rare nonbreeding summer (July) vagrant L4. One record for Wolf Creek, 7-16-1982. There is also a western Sheridan County record (Faulkner 2010). Not reported regionally on eBird from 1-1-1990 through 4-25-2013, but reported from Bighorn National Forest 7-17-1971. A desert species associated in this region with open pinyon–juniper woodlands, grasslands with scattered trees, and gulches or riparian edges.

Cassin's Kingbird, *Tyrannus vociferans*: rare spring, summer, and early fall (May–Aug.) visitant L5; breeding not confirmed. An adult was seen carrying an insect on Beatty Gulch, 6-30-1976. This species has been reported at least once since 1983, with an eBird report of on bird seen at Dayton, 5-26-2011. Associated with open country, usually with scattered trees, or with open woodlands, and extending out into grasslands and agricultural lands where there are locally available trees for nesting.

Western Kingbird, *Tyrannus verticalis*: Common spring, summer and fall (May–Oct.) resident; breeding confirmed L4 & 5. Average spring arrival, 5-14. The species was observed during 15 of 21 years of Spring Bird Counts in Johnson County, 1984–2004, and during all four years of Spring Bird Counts in Sheridan County, 2009–2012. It was not observed during 26 years of Christmas Bird Counts at Buffalo, 1986–2011. Recorded at Sheridan as late as 10-5-1971 (Faulkner, 2010). This species is always associated with edge habitats near open country, such as shelterbelts, hedgerows, margins of forests, tree-lined residential districts, riparian forests, and the like. It occupies more open country and occurs at somewhat lower elevations than the Cassin's Kingbird.

Eastern Kingbird, *Tyrannus tyrannus*: Common spring, summer and fall (Mar.–Oct.) resident; breeding confirmed L4 & 5. Average spring arrival, 5-12. The species was observed during 16 of 21 years of Spring Bird Counts in Johnson County, 1984–2004, and during two of four years of Spring Bird Counts in Sheridan County, 2009–2012. It was not observed during 26 years of Christmas Bird Counts at Buffalo, 1986–2011. Associated with open areas with scattered trees or tall shrubs, such as forest edges, fencerows, riparian areas, agricultural lands and farmsteads. In Wyoming these birds occur statewide at lower elevations, especially where scattered mature trees or utility poles occur in otherwise open landscapes (Faulkner, 2010). Breeding Bird Surveys indicate that national populations are decreasing significantly (1.2% annually, 1966-2011).

Family Laniidae: Shrikes

Loggerhead Shrike

Northern Shrike, *Lanius excubitor*: fairly common very late fall, winter and early spring, (Aug.–Apr.) resident L4 & 5. Found in all areas up to Willow Creek at 8,100' elevation. This shrike was observed during one of 21 years of Spring Bird Counts in Johnson County, 1984–2004, and during 24 of 26 years of Christmas Bird Counts at Buffalo, 1986–2011. Invariably associated with open landscapes such as agricultural lands or grasslands that have scattered observation points such as fence posts or small trees.

Loggerhead Shrike, *Lanius ludovicianus*: fairly common spring, summer and fall (Mar.–Sept.) resident; breeding confirmed L4 & 5. Average spring arrival, 4-15. Loggerheads may be more common along the Powder River. They are found along the Powder River to about 4,500'; only one mountain record, Burgess Junction area 8-18 & 21-1981, at 8,038'. The species was observed during 18 of 21 years of Spring Bird Counts in Johnson County, 1984–2004, and during two of four years of Spring Bird Counts in Sheridan County, 2009–2012. It was not observed during 26 years of Christmas Bird Counts at Buffalo, 1986–2011. Like the Northern Shrike, this species is associated with open habitats having scattered perching sites, and ranges altitudinally from agricultural lands on the prairies in winter to summer montane meadows. Thorny trees or barbed-wired fences are used for impaling and storing prey. Sagebrush areas, desert scrub, and pinyon–juniper woodlands offer ideal nesting and foraging areas, but some nesting also occurs in woodland edge situations, farmlands, and similar habitats. In Wyoming these birds occur statewide at elevations up to the foothills zone (Faulkner 2010). Breeding Bird Surveys indicate that national populations are declining significantly (2.5% annually, 1966-2011).

Family Vireonidae: Vireos

Red-eyed Vireo

Plumbeous Vireo. *Vireo plumbeus*: uncommon late spring, summer, early fall (May–Sept.) resident; breeding confirmed L4 & L5. Average spring arrival, 5-22. A family group was seen at Trail End grounds in Sheridan, August 30. Found also on Prairie Dog Creek and Ash Creek roads, Little Piney Creek, and Powder River near Arvada. Open, coniferous or mixed forest with considerable undergrowth seem to be the Plumbeous Vireo's favored habitat, especially those that offer open branches for foraging at low to medium tree levels. Fairly dry and warm forests are favored by the Plumbeous Vireo over moist and cool ones, and breeding extends from the open oak or aspen and ponderosa pine zones upward through the lower coniferous communities. Breeding Bird Surveys indicate that national populations are decreasing significantly (2.2% annually, 1966-

2011). Previously considered part of the "Solitary Vireo" complex, which was split in 1998 by the A.O.U. into three species: the Plumbeous Vireo, *V. plumbeus*, Cassin's Vireo, *V. cassinii*, and Blue-headed Vireo, *V. solitarius*. The Cassin's Vireo is a very rare migrant in Wyoming, and the Blue-headed Vireo is a vagrant (Faulkner, 2010). Neither has been reported in latilongs 4 or 5 (Orabona et al.,2010).

Warbling Vireo, *Vireo gilvus*: common to abundant spring and summer resident, fairly common fall (May–Oct.), breeding confirmed L4 & 5. Average spring arrival, 5-16. Begging young were seen at Tongue River Canyon 7-11-1976. Also found at Big Horn, Buffalo, Dayton Park, Hunter Creek Road, Hume Draw, Sheridan Cemetery, Story, Wolf Creek, and elevations up to Burgess Ranger Station, just over 8,000'. Recorded at Sheridan as late as 10-9-1981 (Faulkner, 2010). The Warbling Vireo was observed during 15 of 21 years of Spring Bird Counts in Johnson County, 1984–2004. It was not observed during 26 years of Christmas Bird Counts at Buffalo, 1986–2011. Fairly open woodlands, especially of deciduous trees, are favored by this species. It is probably most common along riparian forests supporting tall trees, but also occurs in aspen groves and well-wooded residential or park areas, especially where tall cottonwoods are present. In coniferous forest areas the birds favor areas where single or clumped broad-leaved trees such as aspens or birches occur.

Philadelphia Vireo, *Vireo philadelphicus*: extremely rare spring (May) vagrant L4 & L5. About 19 observations were recorded to 1990. Faulkner (2010) evidently discounted many of these records. One was seen 5-16-1978, by two observers at Shell Creek. Not reported regionally on eBird from 1-1-1990 through 4-25-2013.

Red-eyed Vireo, *Vireo olivaceus*: fairly common spring and summer, uncommon fall resident (May–Sept.); breeding presumed L4, confirmed L5. Average spring arrival, 5-23. Most often reported at Story, the highest elevation on record, at about 5,000'. Found at Barkey Draw near Lake DeSmet, Big Horn, Dayton City Park, Little Goose Canyon Road, Tongue River Canyon Road and Canyon, UM Ponds, and Young's Creek. The species was observed during one of 21 years of Spring Bird Counts in Johnson County, 1984–2004. It was not observed during 26 years of Christmas Bird Counts at Buffalo, 1986–2011. This species is primarily associated with deciduous forests, especially those with semi-open canopies. In the Rocky Mountains it is largely limited to broad-leaved riparian forests in prairie areas, especially where large, mature cottonwoods occur.

Family Corvidae: Crows, Jays & Magpies

Blue Jay

Pinyon Jay, *Gymnorhinus cyanocephalus*: erratically reported, variably common permanent resident; breeding presumed L4 & 5. Most often seen on Ash Creek but have also been reported on Piney Creek, Tongue River Canyon, Big Goose Canyon and west of Big Goose Canyon, on Red Grade; as high as 8,000' at Penrose Park and 8,500' at Willow Park. Generally associated with pine forests growing on dry substrates, especially the pinyon–juniper association, but extending during the non-breeding period into oak–mountain mahogany, sagebrush, and desert scrub habitats. Breeding Bird Surveys indicate that national populations are decreasing significantly (3.8% annually, 1966-2011).

Gray Jay *Perisoreus canadensis*: fairly common permanent resident; breeding confirmed L4, presumed L5. Gray Jays have been reported near Burgess Junction, Caribou Mesa, Circle Park, Dayton Gulch, Elgin Park, and at many mountain locations. Occasionally seen at Story. This species is associated with a wide variety of boreal and montane coniferous forest types, and occasionally extends into aspens and riparian woodlands outside the breeding season.

Steller's Jay, *Cyanocitta stelleri*: extremely rare and geographically limited vagrant L4 & 5; reported Oct.–June, breeding not confirmed. The first report was of two birds at Story in late fall 1977; they were recorded from 12-1977, through 4-1978, again in 11-1978, and four times in 11-1979 and 12-1979; also once in 10-1985. In 5-1978 and 6-1978, this jay was seen in Tensleep Canyon, and one was found at Dayton Gulch in 6-1985. It is puzzling why this species is not a regional breeding resident, as the habitat seems suitable. Both of Wyoming's subspecies occur within 75 miles of the Bighorns (Faulkner, 2010), being found at Billings, Montana, to the north, and Casper, Wyoming, to the south. Not reported regionally on eBird from 1-1-1990 through 4-25-2013. This species is centered in the ponderosa pine zone, but also extends down into the pinyon–juniper zone, and occurs as high as the Douglas-fir zone.

Blue Jay, *Cyanocitta cristata*: uncommon permanent resident L4 & 5; breeding confirmed L4 & L5. The westward range expansion of this species reached this area in 6-1968, but jays were not seen again until 11-1972. They re-appeared in 9-1975, and became resident; their abundance has vacillated between rare and uncommon. Found at the Sheridan Cemetery and the streets adjacent to Cemetery Draw, along Big Goose Creek and residential areas near the creek. They have been reported in Arvada, Big Horn and the Upper Road at Big Horn, Buffalo, Dayton, Ranchester and Story. The Blue Jay was observed during one of 21 years of Spring Bird Counts in Johnson County, 1984–2004, during ten of 26 years of Christmas Bird Counts at Buffalo, 1986–2011, and during two of four years of Spring Bird Counts in Sheridan County, 2009–2012. Widely distributed in deciduous woodlands, city parks, suburbs, and almost anywhere there is an intersection of woods and open grassy areas. Riparian woods, with large willows or cottonwoods, are favored habitats on the Great Plains. Breeding Bird Surveys indicate that national populations are decreasing significantly (0.7% annually, 1966-2011).

Western Scrub-Jay, *Aphelocoma californica*: extremely rare spring (March, June) vagrant L5. A single bird was seen on Prairie Dog Creek 6-8-1966, and another on Ash Creek 3-16-1970. Associated with low arid woodlands, including pinyon–juniper and oak–mountain mahogany, and less frequently extending into the ponderosa pine zone where oaks are also present. It is often found along brushy ravines or wooded creek-bottoms.

Clark's Nutcracker, *Nucifraga columbiana*: fairly common to common permanent resident; breeding confirmed L4 & 5. Nutcrackers can be found in most mountain locations; sometimes at Ash Creek, Story and Tongue River Canyon. Observed Lodge Grass Creek, 6-28-2013, 9,372' elevation. The species was observed during four of 21 years of Spring Bird Counts in Johnson County, 1984–2004, and during 15 of 26 years of Christmas Bird Counts at Buffalo, 1986–2011. Widespread in coniferous habitats, from the ponderosa pine zone to timberline. More common in the higher coniferous zones (limber and whitebark pine zone in summer, but descending during winter to the pinyon zone and sometimes out onto the plains areas. Largely dependent on large pine seeds, including limber pine, white pine, and, to a lesser degree, ponderosa pine. An "invasion" occurred in 1977; 65 were counted on the Tongue River Canyon Riparian survey, September 14, 1977, and were seen in all areas, even at McClain's Pond south of Sheridan.

Black-billed Magpie, *Pica hudsonia*: common permanent resident; breeding confirmed L4 & 5. Found in all areas and occasionally seen in the mountains. The species was observed during all 21 years of Spring Bird Counts in Johnson County, 1984–2004, during all 26 years of Christmas Bird Counts at Buffalo, 1986–2011, and during all four years of Spring Bird Counts in Sheridan County, 2009–2012. Of widespread occurrence, but especially common in riparian areas with thickety vegetation, agricultural areas with scattered trees, sagebrush, aspen groves, and the lower levels of the coniferous forest zones. Small, thorny trees are especially favored nest sites, but junipers and similar thornless trees are also used. Magpies were seen with Bald and Golden eagles, Gray Jays, and Common Ravens 12-1-1979–1-18-1980, feeding on a moose carcass on Bull Creek west of Burgess Junction, elevation 8,180'.

American Crow, *Corvus brachyrhynchos*: common permanent resident; breeding presumed L4, confirmed L5. Found in all areas. The American Crow was observed during all 21 years of Spring Bird Counts in Johnson County, 1984–2004, during all 26 years of Christmas Bird Counts at Buffalo, 1986–2011, and during all four years of Spring Bird Counts in Sheridan County, 2009–2012. Forested areas, wooded riverbottoms, orchards, woodlots, large parks, and suburban areas are all used by this species, but it is often replaced by Common Ravens in rocky canyons and higher montane areas.

Common Raven, *Corvus corax*: uncommon spring and winter, occasional summer and fall visitant on the east side of the Bighorn Mountains; fairly common permanent resident on top and west side of the Bighorns; breeding confirmed L4. Only five records exist from 1966 to 1976, all at high elevations. Since 1987 it has been seen often on the eastern slope at Big Horn, Dayton, Lake DeSmet and Sheridan, along I-90 to Ranchester, and along Dayton-Beckton, Decker, Piney Creek, and Red Grade roads. The species was observed during 14 of 21 years of Spring Bird Counts in Johnson County, 1984–2004, during all 26 years of Christmas Bird Counts at Buffalo, 1986–2011, and during all four years of Spring Bird Counts in Sheridan County, 2009–2012. Generally associated with wilderness areas of mountains and forests, especially where bluffs or cliffs are present for nesting. Breeding Bird Surveys indicate that national populations are increasing significantly (2.4% annually, 1966-2011).

Family Alaudidae: Larks

Horned Lark

Horned Lark, *Eremophila alpestris*: Common permanent resident, becoming nearly abundant with winter visitants; breeding confirmed L4 & 5. Nests as low as Kumor Road south of Moore's Reservoir at 4,000' and at all elevations to above timberline on Hunt Mountain Road, and occurs nationally from deserts to arctic tundra. Larks are seen in large flocks along roads and airports in winter, and anywhere in July and August, when the young are independent. The Horned Lark was observed during 15 of 21 years of Spring Bird Counts in Johnson County, 1984–2004, and during 18 of 26 years of Christmas Bird Counts at Buffalo, 1986–2011. Open-country habitats, ranging from shortgrass plains through agricultural lands such as pastures, desert scrub, mountain meadows, and alpine tundra, are the basic requirements for this species, which has an enormous ecological and geographic range in North America. The same species is widespread in Eurasia (and is called the Shorelark in Britain), where many other members of the lark family also exist. These include the similar Skylark (*Alauda arvensis*), famous for its spectacular territorial flights and accompanying musical song. Horned larks also perform song flights but they are less famous. Breeding Bird Surveys indicate that the Horned Lark's national populations are decreasing significantly (2.4% annually, 1966-2011).

Family Hirundinidae: Swallows

Tree Swallow

Hirundinidae: Swallows

Purple Martin, *Progne subis*, extremely rare spring (May) vagrant, L5. Reported from near Sheridan, 5-27-1972, and near Kearny, 5-10-1995 (Faulkner, 2010).

Tree Swallow, *Tachycineta bicolor*: common spring, summer and early fall (Apr.–Sept.) resident; breeding confirmed L4 & 5. Common at Story and at Bear Lodge, about 8,000'; also seen at Caribou Mesa, over 9,600' elevation. Commonly seen flying over water for insects in many areas. The Tree Swallow was observed during all 21 years of Spring Bird Counts in Johnson County, 1984–2004, and during all four years of Spring Bird Counts in Sheridan County, 2009–2012. It was not observed during 26 years of Christmas Bird Counts at Buffalo, 1986–2011. Breeding in the region extends from riparian woodlands through the aspen zone and into the lower levels of the coniferous forest zone. Outside the breeding season it is often seen over lakes or rivers, as well as over other open habitats. Nesting is especially prevalent in the aspen stands where old woodpecker holes are available, but also nests in bird houses erected for bluebirds. Breeding Bird Surveys indicate that national populations are decreasing significantly (1.1% annually, 1966-2011).

Violet-green Swallow, *Tachycineta thalassina*: fairly common spring, summer and early fall (Apr.–Sept.) resident; breeding confirmed L4 & 5. Average spring arrival, 5-8. Adults were feeding young in a cliff fifteen feet above the roadway at Sand Turn on U. S. Hwy. 14 above Dayton, 7-19-1975. Prefers areas such as Trapper Canyon, where it uses the cliff for nesting. The species was observed during 15 of 21 years of Spring Bird Counts in Johnson County, 1984–2004, and during all four years of Spring Bird Counts in Sheridan County, 2009–2012. It was not observed during 26 years of Christmas Bird Counts at Buffalo, 1986–2011. Generally associated with open coniferous forests, often open ponderosa pine stands, but also breeds in aspen groves, riparian woods, and sometimes also in urbanized areas. Nesting sites are rather variable, and include old woodpecker holes, natural tree or cliff cavities, and occasionally birdhouses. They have been seen to enter crevices in Tongue River Canyon and lower Crazy Woman Canyon.

Northern Rough-winged Swallow, *Stelgidopteryx serripennis*: common spring, summer and fall (Apr.–Sept.) resident L4 & 5; breeding presumed. Average spring arrival, 5-3. Rough-winged Swallows have been seen to enter holes in the banks of Goose Creek, Ash Creek, and Piney Creek on Tunnel Hill; they are also common along the Powder River. This swallow was observed during all 21 years of Spring Bird Counts in Johnson County, 1984–2004, and during three of four years of Spring Bird Counts in Sheridan County, 2009–2012. It was not observed during 26 years of Christmas Bird Counts at Buffalo, 1986–2011. Associated with open areas, including agricultural lands, rivers, lakes, and grasslands near water. Breeding almost exclusively done in cavities dug in earthen banks of clay, sand, or gravel. Pre-existing rock cavities are also used.

Bank Swallow, *Riparia riparia*: uncommon spring, summer and fall(Apr.–Sept.) resident L4 & 5; breeding not confirmed. Average spring arrival, 5-12. Sometimes found at McClain's Pond, Lake DeSmet, Healy Reservoir, and along the Powder River. The Bank Swallow was observed during eight of 21 years of Spring Bird Counts in Johnson County, 1984–2004, and during three of four years of Spring Bird Counts in Sheridan County, 2009–2012. It was not observed during 26 years of Christmas Bird Counts at Buffalo, 1986–2011. Breeding almost always occurs near water, such as in steep banks along rivers, road-cuts near lakes, gravel pits, and similar areas with steep slopes of clay, sand, or gravel. Outside the breeding season the birds are of broader distribution, sometimes foraging over agricultural lands. Breeding Bird Surveys indicate that national populations are decreasing significantly (4.6% annually, 1966-2011).

Cliff Swallow, *Hirundo pyrrhonota*: abundant spring, summer and early fall (Apr.–Sept.) resident; breeding confirmed, L4 & 5. Average spring arrival, 5-8. Nests under almost all the underpasses, and at low elevations (3,700') at Bradford Brinton up to Dry Fork, Burgess and Big Goose Ranger Stations above 8,000'. The Cliff Swallow was observed during 20 of 21 years of Spring Bird Counts in Johnson County, 1984–2004, and during all four years of Spring Bird Counts in Sheridan County, 2009–2012. It was not observed during 26 years of Christmas Bird Counts at Buffalo, 1986–2011. A wide variety of nesting areas are used by this colonial species, but vertical cliff-sides and the sides or undersides of bridges are perhaps most commonly used regionally.

Barn Swallow, *Hirundo rustica*: common spring, summer, and fall(Apr.–Oct.) resident; breeding confirmed L4 & 5. Average spring arrival, 4-18. Recorded at all elevations up to 8,400' at Crazy Woman Camp Ground. USFS personnel found feathered nestlings frozen in a nest at Burgess

Ranger Station 11-2-1982. The Barn Swallow was observed during 20 of 21 years of Spring Bird Counts in Johnson County, 1984–2004, and during all four years of Spring Bird Counts in Sheridan County, 2009–2012. It was not observed during 26 years of Christmas Bird Counts at Buffalo, 1986–2011. This is the swallow species that is most closely associated with humans in the Rocky Mountain region. Although it may occasionally nest on cliff or cave walls, its normal current nesting sites are the horizontal beams or upright walls of buildings and similar structures. Breeding Bird Surveys indicate that national populations are decreasing significantly (1.2% annually, 1966-2011).

Family Paridae: Titmice & Chickadees

Black-capped Chickadee

Black-capped Chickadee, *Poecile atricapillus*: common permanent resident; breeding confirmed, L4 & 5. Found in all areas from Powder River near Arvada to Bald Mountain Campground at 9,200'. An altitudinal migration probably occurs. The Black-capped Chickadee was observed during all 21 years of Spring Bird Counts in Johnson County, 1984–2004, during all 26 years of Christmas Bird Counts at Buffalo, 1986–2011, and during all four years of Spring Bird Counts in Sheridan County, 2009–2012. Associated with a wide variety of wooded habitats, both of coniferous and hardwood types, and breeding wherever suitable nesting cavities exist. These typically consist of old woodpecker holes, but sometimes the birds excavate their own nest cavities in the rotted wood of dead stumps. Bird houses are also occasionally used.

Mountain Chickadee, *Poecile gambeli*: permanent resident, common in the mountains in all areas (recorded to 10,000'). Fairly common at Story, elevation 5,000' to 6,000', common there in winter; uncommon in Sheridan and Buffalo except for an occasional invasion; breeding confirmed L4 & 5. Juvenile birds observed on Hunt Mountain Road, 6-29-2013, 9,601' elevation. There is evidence of some altitudinal migration. The species was observed during 13 of 21 years of Spring Bird Counts in Johnson County, 1984–2004, during all 26 years of Christmas Bird Counts at Buffalo, 1986–2011, and during two of four years of Spring Bird Counts in Sheridan County, 2009–2012. Largely limited to montane coniferous forests, and usually absent from deciduous stands, although aspens are frequently used for nesting. Prefers open coniferous forests, especially pines, including both ponderosa pines and pinyons. Breeding Bird Surveys indicate that national populations are decreasing significantly (1.3% annually, 1966-2011).

Family Sittidae: Nuthatches

White-breasted Nuthatch

Red-breasted Nuthatch, *Sitta canadensis*: fairly common permanent resident; breeding confirmed L4 & 5. Readily found at Story, less often at Sheridan Cemetery vicinity, and at Ash Creek, Dayton, Ranchester and Tongue River Canyon. They have been recorded up to 9,000' elevation at Tensleep Meadows. The species was observed during 14 of 21 years of Spring Bird Counts in Johnson County, 1984–2004, during all 26 years of Christmas Bird Counts at Buffalo, 1986–2011, and during one of four years of Spring Bird Counts in Sheridan County, 2009–2012. Limited largely but not entirely to coniferous forests, primarily with relatively tall trees, and much of the foraging occurs at rather high portions of the trees. To a limited degree aspens and riparian woodlands are sometimes also used. Breeding occurs trunk cavities of dead trees or the rotting portions of live trees, with the birds typically excavating their own nesting holes.

White-breasted Nuthatch, *Sitta carolinensis*: fairly common permanent resident; breeding confirmed L4 & L5. Easily seen at Story; also observed at Ash Creek, Dayton, Ranchester, Sheridan Cemetery vicinity, and Tongue River Canyon. Recorded up to 9,600' at Caribou Mesa and near Dome Lake; The species was observed during 14 of 21 years of Spring Bird Counts in Johnson County, 1984–2004, during all 26 years of Christmas Bird Counts at Buffalo, 1986–2011, and during all four years of Spring Bird Counts in Sheridan County, 2009–2012. Largely confined in eastern states to deciduous forests, but associated in the Rocky Mountains with lower elevation coniferous forests, especially the ponderosa pine and pinyon–juniper zones. Nesting occurs in old woodpecker holes, or in self-excavated holes in rotted wood of dead or partially dead trees, often aspens.

Pygmy Nuthatch, *Sitta pygmaea*: uncommon and erratic permanent resident; breeding presumed L4, confirmed L5. First recorded 3-27-1971, on U. S. Hwy. 16 near Clear Creek west of Buffalo. Most records are from Story but also Young's Creek, Wolf Creek at the foothills, Amsden Creek, and at Bud Love Game Management Unit. A specimen was found on Piney Creek northwest of Ucross 7-21-1988. The species was observed during one of 21 years of Spring Bird Counts in Johnson County, 1984–2004, and during nine of 26 years of Christmas Bird Counts at Buffalo, 1986–2011. Primarily associated with the ponderosa pine zone, but also occurring locally in the pinyon–juniper zone. It generally forages fairly high in tall pines, but nests closer to the ground in snags or stubs that have rotted trunks providing excavation opportunities.

Family Certhiidae: Creepers

Brown Creeper, *Certhia americana*: fairly common permanent resident; breeding confirmed L4, presumed L5. Altitudinal migration takes place. In winter they are found at Bradford Brinton, Kendrick Park, Sheridan Cemetery, Story, and Trail End grounds They have also been seen in the mountains at Arrowhead Lodge, south of Snowshoe Pass, on Black Mountain Road, Big Goose and Burgess Ranger Stations, as well as on Blue Creek, Hunter Mesa, and Lake Geneva at 9,283' elevation. The species was not observed during 21 years of Spring Bird Counts in Johnson County, 1984–2004, but was reported during 21 of 26 years of Christmas Bird Counts at Buffalo, 1986–2011, and during one of four years of Spring Bird Counts in Sheridan County, 2009–2012. Associated with forests throughout the year, including both deciduous and coniferous forests. Virtually all foraging is done on the trunks of fairly large trees, where the birds forage for insects in bark crevices and grooves. In Wyoming, this inconspicuous species occurs almost statewide, and can often be found during winter in most towns and cemeteries. During summer it might be seen in high-altitude coniferous forests statewide.

Family Troglodytidae: Wrens

Marsh Wren

Rock Wren, *Salpinctes obsoletus*: common spring, summer, and fall (Apr.–Oct.) resident; breeding confirmed L4 & 5. Average spring arrival, 5-2; they are readily found at Ash Creek, the North Dam of Lake DeSmet, SR–Buffalo Creek, Tongue River Canyon, and on rock outcroppings up to 9,600' elevation. An adult and an immature were seen between Buckley Creek and Elk Mountain, 10,000' and 11,000', 7-29-1989. Observed Hunt Mountain Road, 6-29-2013, 9,892' elevation. The species was observed during 12 of 21 years of Spring Bird Counts in Johnson County, 1984–2004. It was not observed during 26 years of Christmas Bird Counts at Buffalo, 1986–2011. Closely associated with eroded slopes, badlands, rocky outcrops, cliff walls, talus slopes, and similar rock-dominated habitats at generally rather low elevations, but also in alpine areas.

Canyon Wren, *Catherpes mexicanus*: uncommon L4 & 5, status uncertain due to few records. First recorded October 28, 1976, in Tongue River Canyon where the species has most often been reported; also in Big Goose Canyon, Little Bighorn Canyon, and a canyon near Wolf Creek. Also recorded 3 Canyon Wrens singing at the Red Wall along the Red Fork of the Powder River 11-24-2012. This population may be partially migratory, but it is uncertain. Only one observation in L5, Ash Creek 5-14-1968. Rocky canyons, river bluffs, cliffs, rockslides, and similar topographic sites are favored, especially those offering shady crevices.

House Wren, *Troglodytes aedon*: common spring, summer, and fall (Apr.–Nov.) resident; breeding confirmed L4 & 5. Average spring arrival, 5-6. House Wrens are found in nearly all areas, and are easily found at Ash Creek, Little Piney Creek, Powder River near Arvada, and Story. Recorded up to 8,500' in the Dry Fork area. They are a common bird in local artificial nest boxes. This wren was observed during 20 of 21 years of Spring Bird Counts in Johnson County, 1984–2004, and during all four years of Spring Bird Counts in Sheridan County, 2009–2012. It was not observed during 26 years of Christmas Bird Counts at Buffalo, 1986–2011. Generally most common in the lower elevation forests, but occasionally reaching timberline. In this region the birds favor riparian woodlands, aspen groves, and the lower and more open coniferous forest zones, as well as areas of human habitations. A wren house in Sheridan was said to have been occupied by House Wrens for 14 consecutive years. A total of 3,937 pieces of nest materials were found in the house one year.

Winter Wren, *Troglodytes hiemalis*: extremely rare winter (Dec.–Jan.) visitant L5. One record December 27, 1974, through January 8, 1975, at the WG&F Fish Hatchery Picnic Ground; seen by several observers. Not reported regionally on eBird from 1-1-1990 through 4-25-2013. Two were reported from the Bighorn Mountains, 6-14-2004, and there have been "clustered" fall sightings around Story (Faulkner, 2010); the central Wyoming status of the recently described Pacific Wren, *T. pacificus*, is not yet clear, but it has been found in the northwestern part of the state, and has also been reported from the Black Hills. The Winter Wren is typically found in heavy forests, usually coniferous, and often occurs in moist and shady canyons where brush piles and tangles of vegetation cover the ground.

Marsh Wren, *Cistothorus palustris*: rare spring (April) and fall (Oct.–Dec.) transient L4 & 5. Four observations have full documentation: a pond at a ranch near Big Horn 11-22-1981; Hume Draw in Sheridan 10-18-1987; Hume Draw 12-30-1988; and a pond near Jackson Creek 4-8-1990. Reported regionally on eBird from 1-1-1990 through 4-25-2013 at Buffalo Wildlife Habitat Project, 10-5-1996. The species was observed during three of 21 years of Spring Bird Counts in Johnson County, 1984–2004. It was not observed during 26 years of Christmas Bird Counts at Buffalo, 1986–2011. Typically found in marshes heavily overgrown with cattails and bulrushes.

Family Polioptilidae: Gnatcatchers

Blue-gray Gnatcatcher

Blue-gray Gnatcatcher, *Polioptila caerulea*: extremely rare spring (May) vagrant L5. One was seen in a Sheridan residential area 5-18-1966, and one was seen near Moore's Reservoir 5-17-1976. Gnatcatchers are expanding their range in Wyoming so they are likely to be seen regionally in the future, but were not reported regionally on eBird from 1-1-1990 through 5-25-2013. Breeding of the Rocky Mountain race occurs in pinyon–juniper and also adjacent oak woodland or sagebrush areas, up to at least 7,000 feet elevation. Arid park-like areas, with scattered thickets, are preferred for foraging, and nests are usually placed in low junipers.

In Wyoming generally, gnatcatchers are most common in the southwest, but have expanded their range since the middle of the 20th century. They now breed east into both Nebraska and South Dakota (Faulkner, 2012), and have also expanded their Nebraska range across the entire state. Breeding Bird Surveys indicate that national populations are increasing significantly (0.6% annually, 1966-2011). Their distinctive nests are deep cups made of plant down, bark, plant fibers, catkins, feathers, and hair. They are lined with plant down or feathers, and held together with spider webbing and covered with flakes of lichens. Once classified with kinglet and the Old World warblers gnatcatchers are now considered to represent a unique family.

Family Cinclidae: Dippers

American Dipper

American Dipper, *Cinclus mexicanus*: fairly common resident; breeding confirmed L4 & 5. Dippers have been recorded at Lake Geneva at 9,283' elevation 7-28-1967, and 8-13-1969, and between 10,000' and 11,000' between Buckley Creek and Elk Mountain 7-29-1989. They have been recorded at Story on Piney Creek, and on Little Goose Creek (2013) where they have occupied a nest for several years. Male singing along a tributary of the North Tongue River, 6-30-2013, 8,500' elevation. Most of the clear mountain streams have dippers that are a sure sign of the health of the stream. A seasonal altitudinal migration occurs, no doubt because of the scarcity of food resources during hard freezes. The species was observed during 14 of 21 years of Spring Bird Counts in Johnson County, 1984–2004, and during 23 of 26 years of Christmas Bird Counts at Buffalo, 1986–2011, and was reported during all four years of Spring Bird Counts in Sheridan County, 2009–2012. Rapidly-flowing mountain streams, often with waterfalls or cascades present, and ledges or crevices providing safe nesting sites, are this species' prime habitat. Nests have been seen in Tongue River Canyon on inaccessible vertical walls above the river; one nested in a drainpipe under the bridge over South Piney Creek at Story, 6-1988. Nesting is often done on rock walls or overhangs near or even sometimes behind waterfalls. Often the globular, waterproof nests are often constructed under bridges that cross creeks or rivers. The birds are highly territorial, and pairs tend to be well separated.

Family Regulidae: Kinglets

Golden-crowned Kinglet

Golden-crowned Kinglet, *Regulus satrapa*: uncommon permanent resident; breeding presumed L4 & 5. Recorded near Arrowhead Lodge and at Bald Mountain Campground July 29, 1987, at 7,656' and 9,000' respectively; at Hazelton Road about a quarter-mile beyond U. S. Hwy. 16, 6-14,-1990, at 8,000'; at East Tensleep Meadows 7-8-19-1981, about 9,000'; at Upper Powder River 7-6-1977, over 9,500'; and on east side of Edelman Pass 9-3-1989, at 10,000'. The species was observed during one of 21 years of Spring Bird Counts in Johnson County, 1984–2004, during two of 26 years of Christmas Bird Counts at Buffalo, 1986–2011. Seasonal vertical migration occurs; this species summers at very high elevations. During the breeding season primarily associated with spruce-fir forests, but otherwise generally present in all the coniferous zones and sometimes extending out into riparian woodlands. Nesting occurs in dense and fairly tall coniferous trees, usually spruces, and nests usually are placed rather high in the tree. Breeding Bird Surveys indicate that national populations are decreasing significantly (1.1% annually, 1966-2011).

Ruby-crowned Kinglet, *Regulus calendula*: fairly common to common spring, summer and fall resident, extremely rare winter vagrant; breeding confirmed L4 & 5. Average spring arrival, 4-5. These kinglets have been found along Black Mountain Road, Circle Park C. G. on U. S. Hwy. 16, Sheridan Cemetery, Story and Big Horn. Can be heard in spring and summer in most forested canyons. Reported as high as 11,000 feet during the breeding season. Three winter dates: 12-28-1975, east of Big Horn; 12-16-1979, at the VA Hospital grounds; and 1-3-1990, at Story. This kinglet was observed during 17 of 21 years of Spring Bird Counts in Johnson County, 1984–2004, and during three of four years of Spring Bird Counts in Sheridan County, 2009–2012. It was not observed during 26 years of Christmas Bird Counts at Buffalo, 1986–2011. Breeding occurs in coniferous forests from the lower zones almost to timberline in the subalpine zone, but usually in tall and dense forests of medium altitude.

Family Turdidae: Thrushes

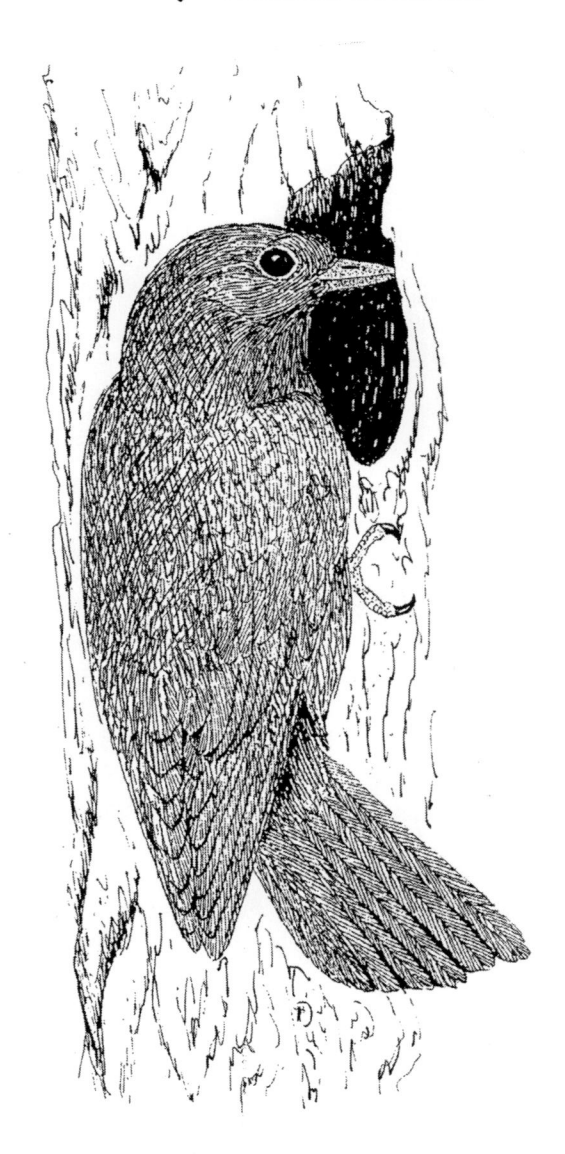

Mountain Bluebird

Eastern Bluebird, *Sialia sialis*: extremely rare spring, summer and fall (March–July, Nov.) vagrant L4 & 5; breeding not confirmed. Nine reports: Ash Creek, Ash Creek–Young's Creek Road, Bradford Brinton Memorial grounds, Sheridan City Dump, SR–Buffalo Creek Road, Tongue River Canyon, U. S. Hwy. 14 near Ucross and Wyarno; also seen with Mountain Bluebirds west of Little Piney Creek, through July, 1988. The species was observed during one of 21 years of Spring Bird Counts in Johnson County, 1984–2004, and during one of 26 years of Christmas Bird Counts at Buffalo, 1986–2011. Generally associated with open deciduous woods that are close to grasslands, such as riparian forests, shelterbelts, farmsteads, and city parks. Nesting occurs in old woodpecker holes, natural cavities of dead trees, dead limbs, or sometimes utility poles. Birdhouses are also frequently used, especially where natural cavities are relatively rare.

Mountain Bluebird, *Sialia currucoides*: common early spring and fall transient (Feb–Nov.), and summer resident; breeding confirmed L4 & 5. Average spring arrival, 3-11. The Mountain Bluebird was observed during 19 of 21 years of Spring Bird Counts in Johnson County, 1984–2004, and during one of 26 years of Christmas Bird Counts at Buffalo, 1986–2011, and during all four years of Spring Bird Counts in Sheridan County, 2009–2012. Habitats used are much like those described for the Eastern Bluebird, but include open coniferous forests. During breeding season, these bluebirds are mostly absent from Sheridan at lower elevations (3,700 feet), and more common on Red Grade Road at higher elevations (5,200 feet) where they are in closer proximity to forests. Birds were observed in krummholz on 6-29-2013, Hunt Mountain Road at 9,666' elevation. Nesting occurs in cavities from high elevation alpine rock crevices to mid-elevations. Breeding Bird Surveys indicate that national populations are decreasing significantly (0.7% annually, 1966-2011).

Western Bluebird, *Sialia mexicana*: probable rare spring (April–June) and fall (Sept.) migrant. Reports include: Clearmont-Ulm Road, 7-12-1982; south of Clearmont, 5-25-1983; near Ulm, 6-2-1983; and Ash Creek, 4-28-1986. There are four regional eBird reports through 11-5-2011: unstated numbers seen in Bighorn National Forest 5-15-2005 and 9-15-2009, six seen at Wolf Creek Ranch 9-19, 2006, and one seen northwest of Sheridan, 9-19-2006. Rather open timberlands, either of deciduous or coniferous trees, seem to be this species' favored habitats. It breeds in both aspens and ponderosa pine woodlands, nesting in preexisting cavities, but breeding in Wyoming is still unproven.

Turdidae: Thrushes

Townsend's Solitaire, *Myadestes townsendi*: fairly common resident; breeding confirmed L4 & 5. Sheridan Cemetery, Ash Creek, and Tongue River Canyon are favored winter spots where Solitaires defend feeding territories by singing and calling. Solitaires occur along the Powder River; it is unlikely they nest there. The highest elevation on record is 9,489' at Black Mountain Lookout. These birds are common in winter in the Shell Canyon Research Natural Area where juniper berries are abundant. I have heard over 20 birds singing there the winter of 2011 and 2012. The species was observed during 12 of 21 years of Spring Bird Counts in Johnson County, 1984–2004, during 24 of 26 years of Christmas Bird Counts at Buffalo, 1986–2011, and during one of four years of Spring Bird Counts in Sheridan County, 2009–2012. Forested mountain slopes that provide snow-free areas for nesting on or near the ground, and that also offer sources of berries for food, are favored for breeding. There is an upward migration the first week of April and a return to lower elevations the last week of August. The latter movement is more food-related than weather-related, as wild berries are ripening at the end of August.

Veery, *Catharus fuscescens*: fairly common spring, summer and early fall (May–Sept.) resident (common some years); breeding confirmed L4 & 5. Average spring arrival, 5-19. One individual was seen daily in Story 6-9 –7-29-1982. Recorded most often on Little Piney Creek Road and at Story, but also in Tongue River Canyon and along Clear Creek west of Buffalo City Park; highest elevation, 9,000' at Seven Brothers Lake 7-4-1980; lowest elevations at Kendrick Park in Sheridan 7-23-1981; and the USFS Work Center on Fort Road 7-1-1987, and Red Grade 6-15-2013. The Veery was observed during eight of 21 years of Spring Bird Counts in Johnson County, 1984–2004, and during all four years of Spring Bird Counts in Sheridan County, 2009–2012. It was not observed during 26 years of Christmas Bird Counts at Buffalo, 1986–2011. In this region its favored habitats consist of wooded river valleys and canyons that range from deciduous gallery forests through aspen forests of the foothills, and willow-lined mountain streams. Areas with heavy and thickety undergrowth that are difficult for humans to penetrate are its favorite habitats, and most of its foraging is done on the ground. Breeding Bird Surveys indicate that national populations are decreasing significantly (0.9% annually, 1966-2011).

Gray-cheeked Thrush, *Catharus minimus*: extremely rare vagrant, L5. Reported from Sheridan, 6-1-1971 and 6-4-1968 (Faulkner 2010). Not listed by Downing (1990).

Swainson's Thrush, *Catharus ustulatus*: common spring transient, fairly common summer and early fall (Apr.–Sept.) resident; breeding presumed L4, confirmed L5. Average spring arrival, 5–11. A female with two nestlings was photographed at Story Fish Hatchery grounds 7-2-1986. Found most often at Little Piney Creek Road, Story, and Tongue River Canyon. Also seen on Dayton Gulch Road in the northern Bighorns and Walker Prairie at 7,068' elevation 7-12-2010. The species was observed during 20 of 21 years of Spring Bird Counts in Johnson County, 1984–2004, and during one of four years of Spring Bird Counts in Sheridan County, 2009–2012. It was not observed during 26 years of Christmas Bird Counts at Buffalo, 1986–2011. On migration these birds are likely to be found in almost any fairly dense woodlands, but during the breeding season the birds are found at higher and cooler elevations. Then they use shaded canyons where there are also fairly large areas of tangled brushy undergrowth, permitting ground-level foraging. Riparian thickets, often of willows or alders, and moist mountain slopes supporting aspens, are usually used for nesting in this region. Overlap in the distribution of Swainson's and Hermit Thrushes occurs; the Hermits are more abundant at higher elevations. Breeding Bird Surveys indicate that national populations are decreasing significantly (1.0% annually, 1966-2011).

Hermit Thrush, *Catharus guttatus*: uncommon spring and early fall migrant (May–Oct.), common summer resident in mountains; breeding confirmed L4, presumed L5. Average spring arrival, 5-16. An immature was photographed above Robin Lakes 7-28-1967; also found at Horseshoe Lake and Dutch Oven Pass 7-20-1989, both at about 10,000' elevation. Dayton Gulch and Hunt Mountain roads are favored locations. Observed an adult feeding young at Walker Prairie 7-12-2010 at 7,505' elevation, and heard a male singing on Dayton Gulch Road at 9,165' elevation 7-14-2010. Observed Hunt Mountain Road, 6-29-2013, 9,980' elevation. The species was observed during one of 21 years of Spring Bird Counts in Johnson County, 1984–2004, and during one of four years of Spring Bird Counts in Sheridan County, 2009–2012. It was not observed during 26 years of Christmas Bird Counts at Buffalo, 1986–2011. Moist woodlands, especially of coniferous or mixed hardwoods and conifers, are preferred for breeding. Spruces, ponderosa pines, and higher zones of coniferous forests nearly to timberline are sometimes used. Shady and leaf-littered forest floors are favored for foraging, and the altitudinal range of breeding often spans several thousand feet.

Wood Thrush, *Hylocichla mustelina*: extremely rare spring and summer (May–Aug) vagrant L5. Four records to 1990; unspecified location, 5-14-1977; Sheridan, 7-?-1977 (unspecified day); Buffalo 5-7-1983; Story, 6-3-1983. Not reported regionally on eBird from 1-1-1990 through 4-25-2013. Breeding Bird Surveys indicate that national populations are decreasing significantly (2.2% annually, 1966-2011).

American Robin, *Turdus migratorius*: abundant spring and fall transient, abundant spring, summer and fall resident; common to rare in winter, subsisting on wild fruits, mostly juniper berries; breeding confirmed L4 & 5. Local birds might move south in the fall, to be replaced by more northerly ones. Robins are abundant during breeding season up to 10,000'; dependent young have been recorded at Black Mountain Lookout, 9,489'. The species was observed during all 21 years of Spring Bird Counts in Johnson County, 1984–2004, during 23 of 26 years of Christmas Bird Counts at Buffalo, 1986–2011, and during all four years of Spring Bird Counts in Sheridan County, 2009–2012. Open woodlands, whether natural or artificial, such as suburbs, city parks, and farmsteads, are typical habitats. The birds tend to occur almost anywhere there are at least scattered trees, soft ground suitable for probing, and where mud can be gathered for nests. Nesting on human-made structures seems to be preferred over natural nest sites such as trees, at least in protected areas. A recent estimate of the species' total population is 320,000,000 (Rich *et al.*, 2004), making this one of America's most abundant land birds.

Varied Thrush, *Ixoreus naevius*: extremely rare early spring (March–April) and fall (Oct.) vagrant L4 & 5. A report from the Saddlestring Ranch northwest of Buffalo on an unspecified day in October 1978 lacked details. Two records prior to 1990; 3-16-1982, at Story, and 4-13-1983, on Wolf Creek, were well documented. Another record, 12-27-1986, was incomplete. Individuals in Big Horn have pictures of this thrush near Jackson Creek. Not reported regionally on eBird from 1-1-1990 through 4-25-2013. In this region this thrush is associated with mature coniferous forests, especially rather wet forests that have completely shaded floors and a relatively open understory vegetation permitting ground foraging. Breeding Bird Surveys indicate that national populations are decreasing significantly (2.2% annually, 1966-2011).

Family Mimidae: Mockingbirds & Relatives

Brown Thrasher

Gray Catbird, *Dumetella carolinensis:* fairly common spring, summer and fall (May–Oct.) resident; breeding confirmed L4 & 5. Average spring arrival, 5-15. Found along Clear Creek west of Buffalo City Park, Kendrick Park and Trail End grounds in Sheridan, Dow-Dutch Creek and Rapid Creek roads, Little Piney, and Powder River near Arvada. Observed as high as Red Grade Road and the foothills area of Wolf Creek. As many as 331 seen in Sheridan 5-18-1986 (Faulkner, 2010). The species was observed during 19 of 21 years of Spring Bird Counts in Johnson County, 1984–2004, during one of 26 years of Christmas Bird Counts at Buffalo, 1986–2011, and during two of four years of Spring Bird Counts in Sheridan County, 2009–2012. Dense thickets, ranging from riverine forests or prairie coulees, city parks and suburbs, orchards, woodland edges, shrubby marsh borders, and similar overgrown areas that provide a combination of dense vegetation and transitional "edge" situations are the ideal habitats of this species. Coniferous forests are avoided, but aspen groves are used, as are other natural vegetational habitats that offer rich sources of insects and berries.

Northern Mockingbird, *Mimus polyglottos*: rare visitant, reported all months except April); breeding possible L4, suspected L5. About thirty-one records, 1968–1988, but Mockingbirds are generally scarce in this region. They have been reported at Arvada, Ash Creek, Big Horn, Dayton, Goose Creek, Lake DeSmet, Ranchester, Sheridan and Story. There is one regional eBird report from 1990 through 4-25-2013; Bighorn National Forest, 9-15-2009. In the Rocky Mountains, Mockingbirds are associated with windbreaks, shrubs and scattered trees in grasslands. Lowland riparian habitats, with scattered cottonwoods or other isolated trees, represent typical habitat. Breeding records are limited to southern Wyoming, but the species appeared on Breeding Bird Surveys in Bighorn County in 2002 and 2003 (Faulkner, 2010).

Sage Thrasher, *Oreoscoptes montanus*: uncommon spring, summer and fall (Apr.–Oct.) resident; breeding confirmed L4 & 5. Average spring arrival, 5-17. Sage Thrashers have been recorded on Ash Creek–Monarch roads. Beatty Gulch–Prairie Dog Road, Crazy Woman Creek southeast of Buffalo, Kumor Road south of Moore's Reservoir, and Lake DeSmet. This species is closely associated with sage-dominated grasslands and, to a much lesser extent, other shrub lands dominated by shrubs of similar growth-forms such as rabbitbrush and greasewood. Like other sage obligates, this species is declining in Wyoming. Breeding Bird Surveys suggest that national populations are decreasing (1.1% annually, 1966-2011), but not yet at statistically significant levels.

Brown Thrasher, *Toxostoma rufum*: fairly common spring, summer and fall resident, rare winter vagrant; breeding confirmed L4 & L5. Average spring arrival, 5-11. Recorded at Red Grade 6-15-2013. Recorded at Big Horn, Hidden Hills and Dow-Dutch Creek east of Sheridan, Little Piney, and U. S. Hwy. 16 east of Buffalo; highest elevation reported near Story, on North Piney Creek at 5,100'. The species was observed during 19 of 21 years of Spring Bird Counts in Johnson County, 1984–2004, during one of 26 years of Christmas Bird Counts at Buffalo, 1986–2011, and during two of four years of Spring Bird Counts in Sheridan County, 2009–2012. Associated with open, brushy woodlands, scattered clumps of woodland in open environments, shelterbelts, woodlots, and shrubby residential areas. Breeding Bird Surveys indicate that national populations are decreasing significantly (1.0% annually, 1966-2011).

Family Sturnidae: Starlings

European Starling

European Starling, *Sturnus vulgaris*: abundant permanent resident; breeding confirmed L4 & 5. The species was observed during all 21 years of Spring Bird Counts in Johnson County, 1984–2004, during all 26 years of Christmas Bird Counts at Buffalo, 1986–2011, and during all four years of Spring Bird Counts in Sheridan County, 2009–2012. Starlings reached eastern Wyoming in 1937, and by 1941 had expanded west to Jackson. Christmas Counts of 1,000 or more were routine by 1990 (Faulkner, 2010). Largely associated with humans, and most abundant in cities, farms, and suburbs, but also utilizes natural woodlands such as aspen groves, with woodpecker holes or other potential nest sites, where it competes effectively with native hole-nesting birds. Breeding Bird Surveys indicate that national populations are decreasing significantly (1.3% annually, 1966-2011), but the U.S. population still probably numbers in the hundreds of millions.

Family Motacillidae: Pipits

Sprague's Pipit

American Pipit, *Anthus rubescens*: fairly common spring and fall transient, common summer resident (Apr.–Nov.); breeding confirmed L4, presumed L5. Average spring arrival, 4-19. Seen in migration at Healy Reservoir, Lake DeSmet and McClain's Pond; in summer on Battle Park, Black Tooth Mountain, Buckley Creek, Caribou Mesa, Geneva Pass, Half Ounce Creek, Hunt Mountain Road, and Penrose Park; also reported on Elk Mountain to 11,000' elevation. Two birds recorded on Hunt Mountain Road feeding at 9,980' elevation in a snowfield, 6-29-2013. During the breeding season this species is found on alpine tundra and high meadows, while at other seasons it occurs on similar very open terrain, usually with only sparse vegetation, and often a moist substrate. Shorelines, flooded fields, river edges, and similar habitats are commonly used by migrants or wintering birds.

Sprague's Pipit, *Anthus spragueii*: uncommon and limited spring, summer and fall (Apr.–Nov.) resident L4 & 5; breeding confirmed L4 & L5. Average spring arrival, 5-8. They have been seen spring and fall at Kumor Road south of Moore's Reservoir, Lake DeSmet and McClain's Pond. Also reported 5-7-1982 from near Buffalo (Faulkner, 2010). Six were seen on Marcum Creek 9-10-1976, at slightly over 8,000' elevation. The species was observed during one of 21 years of Spring Bird Counts in Johnson County, 1984–2004, but was not observed during 26 years of Christmas Bird Counts at Buffalo, 1986–2011. Associated during the breeding season with native grasslands of short to moderate stature. Breeding also occurs in alkaline meadows and around the edges of alkaline lakes. Outside the breeding season the birds are also associated with grassy habitats. Up to 15 Sprague's Pipits were seen during July and August, 1977, and on 7-5-1978, on Billy Creek. In August of 1978 cattle and sheep were moved into the area, and by 1979 the area was badly overgrazed and the pipits were absent. As is typical of most prairie-dependent species, Breeding Bird Surveys indicate that national populations are decreasing significantly (3.2% annually, 1966-2011).

Family Bombycillidae: Waxwings

Cedar Waxwing

Bohemian Waxwing, *Bombycilla garrulus*: uncommon early spring and late fall, common winter resident (Sept.–May) L4 & 5; erratic in movements and numbers. These birds are found where wild fruit is available at all elevations, usually in winter in the Bighorns, up to the top of Red Grade, the West Fork of Little Bighorn River, and at Park Reservoir, 8,285' elevation. Over 250 birds were seen in Big Horn 12-15-2012. The species was not observed during 21 years of Spring Bird Counts in Johnson County, 1984–2004, but was reported during 18 of 26 years of Christmas Bird Counts at Buffalo, 1986–2011. During the breeding season it is associated with coniferous and mixed forests, often nesting as loosely associated groups in conifer groves. Outside the breeding season the birds move about opportunistically, seeking out sources of berries and small fruits in trees and hedges, such as junipers, mountain ash, crab apples, and pyracantha.

Cedar Waxwing, *Bombycilla cedrorum*: fairly common resident; breeding confirmed L4 & 5. Cedar Waxwings have been found at Big Horn, Buffalo, Clearmont, Dayton, Little Goose Canyon, Little Piney, Sheridan, Story and Tongue River Canyon. One was found dead at 13,000' elevation, near the summit of Cloud Peak, 7-6-1980. These waxwings are one of the most commonly observed birds and can be heard in the trees and shrubs where they feed on berries. The species was observed during seven of 21 years of Spring Bird Counts in Johnson County, 1984–2004, during 16 of 26 years of Christmas Bird Counts at Buffalo, 1986–2011, and during two of four years of Spring Bird Counts in Sheridan County, 2009–2012. Somewhat open woodlands, primarily of broad-leaved species, are used for nesting, including riparian forests, farmsteads, parks, cedar groves, shelterbelts, and brushy edges of forests. Habitats that have abundant growths of berry-bearing bushes or trees are especially favored, although buds, insects, and other foods are also consumed. Some resident Cedar Waxwings join the huge winter flocks of Bohemian Waxwings in search of juniper berries and crab apples.

Family Calcariidae: Longspurs and Snow Buntings

McCown's Longspur

Lapland Longspur, *Calcarius lapponicus*: rare late fall, winter, and early spring (Oct.–April) visitant L4 & 5. Recorded at Ash Creek–Monarch roads, McClain's Pond, Decker, Healy Reservoir, Hidden Hills development east of Sheridan off U. S. Hwy. 14, Lake DeSmet, Prairie Dog Creek, Red Hills, Sheridan Airport, U. S. 87 south of Banner, and Wyarno. The species was not observed during 21 years of Spring Bird Counts in Johnson County, 1984–2004, but was reported during one of 26 years of Christmas Bird Counts at Buffalo, 1986–2011. Not reported regionally on eBird from 1-1-1990 through 4-25-2013. Migrants of this arctic-breeding longspur can be found in eastern grasslands of the region during fall, winter and spring, often foraging with Horned Larks or other longspurs

Chestnut-collared Longspur, *Calcarius ornatus*: rare spring (March–April) and fall (Aug–Nov.) visitant L4 & 5. Average spring arrival, 4-6. Extremely rare in summer, one July record L4; breeding possible but not confirmed. Reported at Big Goose Road, Big Horn, Lake DeSmet, McClain's Pond, and I-90 southbound Scenic Overlook; also at the top of Hesse Mountain, 10,382' elevation, 7-3-1974. There are two regional eBird reports through 11-5-2011: ten were reported at Medicine Lodge State Park, 9-10-2009, and an unstated number were seen near Sheridan, 7-26-2009. Migrant birds often are found in cultivated fields rich in weed seeds, especially of such species as amaranth. Breeding Bird Surveys indicate that national populations are decreasing significantly (4.1% annually, 1966-2011).

McCown's Longspur, *Rhyncophanes mccownii*: rare spring (April) and fall (Aug.–Nov.) transient, and summer visitant L5; breeding presumed, L5. Recorded at Lake DeSmet, McClain's Pond, and on U. S. Hwy. 16, northeast of Buffalo. There is one regional eBird report through 4-25-2013: 42 were seen on the Powder River Road about seven miles north of I-90, 10-12-2008. During the breeding season this species is mostly limited to short-grass prairies and grazed mixed-grass prairies, but also breeds to some degree on stubble fields or newly sprouting grain fields. Elsewhere the birds breed almost exclusively in very sparse grasses, with a large amount of exposed bare soil and a low diversity of other plants. Breeding Bird Surveys indicate that national populations are decreasing significantly (4.0% annually, 1966-2011).

Snow Bunting, *Plectrophenax nivalis*: rare wintering (Oct.-March) visitant, limited occurrence L4 & 5. Found in all areas in open country up to Burgess Junction area at 8,028', extremely rare at feeders in Sheridan. The species was not observed during 21 years of Spring Bird Counts in Johnson County, 1984–2004, but was reported during five of 26 years of Christmas Bird Counts at Buffalo, 1986–2011. There are two regional eBird reports through 4-25-2013: one was seen at Sheridan, 11-29,1996, and nine were seen south of Sister's Hill, eastern Bighorns, 11-22-2008.

Family Parulidae: American Warblers

Yellow-rumped Warbler

Ovenbird, *Seiurus aurocapillus*: fairly common spring and summer (May–Sept.) resident, uncommon in fall; breeding presumed L4, confirmed L5. Average spring arrival, 5-19. Often reported from Little Piney Creek Road and Story. The Ovenbird was observed during five of 21 years of Spring Bird Counts in Johnson County, 1984–2004. It was not observed during 26 years of Christmas Bird Counts at Buffalo, 1986–2011. This species is associated with mature forests, especially deciduous forests, during the breeding season, where its loud and distinctive song provides easy evidence of its presence.

Northern Waterthrush, *Parksia noveboracensis*: uncommon spring transient, rare summer vagrant, rare early fall transient (May–Aug.) L4 & 5; breeding not confirmed. Two were seen 7-30-1978, and 7-15-1979, at the Polo Ranch on Red Grade Road above Bighorn; heard singing at Sourdough Creek, southwest of Buffalo at 80001 elevation, 7-10-1980, and 6-23-1981. They have been found at Acme, Goose Creek Bridge at Wrench Ranch, near Jackson Creek, Little Goose Creek Bridge on Race

Track Road, and McClain's Pond. The species was observed during four of 21 years of Spring Bird Counts in Johnson County, 1984–2004. It was not observed during 26 years of Christmas Bird Counts at Buffalo, 1986–2011. As their name implies, waterthrushes are rarely found far from creeks or other usually small streams.

Blue-winged Warbler, *Vermivora cyanoptera*: probably an extremely rare vagrant or transient (Faulkner, 2010). A bird believed to be a male of this species was seen 6-16-1991, along Wagon Box Road, Johnson County. There are two other Wyoming records recognized by Faulkner. Not reported regionally on eBird from 1-1-1990 through 4-25-2013.

Black-and-White Warbler, *Mniotilta varia*: extremely rare spring (May) and fall (Sept.) transient L4 & 5. Six records to 1990; they include: 5-8 & 9-1970 (location unknown), McClain's Pond 5-29-1975, Barkey Draw near Lake DeSmet 5-15-1983, east of Burgess Junction, about 8,000', 9-7-1984, Clear Creek east of the Buffalo City Park 5-15-1988, Sheridan 4-14-1989, and 5-13-1989, Bradford Brinton Road 5-9-2011. The species was observed during three of 21 years of Spring Bird Counts in Johnson County, 1984–2004. It was not observed during 26 years of Christmas Bird Counts at Buffalo, 1986–2011. Not reported regionally on eBird from 1-1-1990 through 4-25-2013. This species occurs in a wide variety of wooded areas, from second-growth to mature forests, especially deciduous or mixed forests.

Tennessee Warbler, *Oreothlypis peregrina*: uncommon regular spring and fall (May-June, Aug.-Oct.) transient L4 & 5; breeding not confirmed. Average spring arrival, 5-9. One observer reported four Tennessee Warblers on Rapid Creek 8-2-1987 that appeared to be a family group. However, the Bighorns would be well out of the species' known breeding range and habitat. There are records for all four weeks of June and for the second week of July. This species was observed during three of 21 years of Spring Bird Counts in Johnson County, 1984–2004. It was not observed during 26 years of Christmas Bird Counts at Buffalo, 1986–2011. The usual boreal breeding habitat consists of coniferous boggy areas such as those of spruce and tamarack or white cedar, usually where sphagnum mosses are abundant. It also breeds on brushy hillsides, along forest clearings, and deciduous forests, and in Canada favors deciduous or mixed woods that have poplars or aspens present. Foraging is done rather high up in the crown foliage, although nesting is on the ground, usually in sphagnum-covered hummocks.

Orange-crowned Warbler, *Oreothlypis celata*: common spring and fall transient, fairly common summer resident (Apr.–Oct.); breeding presumed L4, confirmed L5. Average spring arrival, 5-5. Found at Big Horn, Johnson Creek northwest of Buffalo, Little Goose Canyon, Little Piney Creek, Sheridan Cemetery Draw, Story, UM Ponds and Wolf Creek. The species was observed during 12 of 21 years of Spring Bird Counts in Johnson County, 1984–2004, and during one of four years of Spring Bird Counts in Sheridan County, 2009–2012. It was not observed during 26 years of Christmas Bird Counts at Buffalo, 1986–2011. Woodland and brushy habitats used by this species for breeding range from riparian woodlands, pinyon–juniper habitats, and aspen groves. In montane areas they favor willow or alder thickets near streams, or willow thickets at tree line. At lower elevations they tend to breed along riverine woods, or in brushy vegetation surrounding beaver ponds.

Nashville Warbler, *Oreothlypis ruficapilla*: rare spring (May) transient, uncommon (Aug.–Oct.) fall transient L4 & 5. Average spring arrival, 5-23. Has been reported at Ash Creek, Big Goose Creek north of Sheridan, Kendrick Park, Little Piney Creek Road, Sheridan Cemetery, Story, Tongue River Canyon and Trail End grounds. Not reported regionally on eBird from 1-1-1990 through 4-25-2013. Moderately open deciduous woods, or the deciduous portions of mixed woods, are the primary summer habitats of this species. On migration a wider array of habitats are used, but riparian woodlands are favored.

Virginia's Warbler, *Oreothlypis virginiae*: extremely rare spring (May) vagrant L5. One observation on Spring Bird Count May 16, 1987, northeast of Buffalo. Not reported regionally on eBird from 1-1-1990 through 4-25-2013. The species was observed during one of 21 years of Spring Bird Counts in Johnson County, 1984–2004. It was not observed during 26 years of Christmas Bird Counts at Buffalo, 1986–2011. Generally, this species is associated with scrubby oak, open pinyon–juniper woodlands, and similar semi-arid and brush-dominated habitats. It breeds north locally in Wyoming to the Laramie Mountains (Faulkner, 2010).

MacGillivray's Warbler, *Oporornis tolmiei*: fairly common spring, summer and fall (May–Sept.) resident; breeding confirmed L4 & 5. Average spring arrival, 5-19. Found at Big Goose Canyon, Crazy Woman Canyon, Little Piney Creek and Little Goose Creek roads, North and South Piney Creek at Story, Tongue River Canyon; also reported at Bighorn Falls C. G. near Bighorn Reservoir, 8,400' elevation. The MacGillivray's Warbler was observed during eight of 21 years of Spring Bird Counts in Johnson County, 1984–2004. It was not observed during 26 years of Christmas Bird Counts at Buffalo, 1986–2011. Generally associated with brushy thickets, especially riparian woodlands. Less often it occurs in dense deciduous woods or mixed woodland on upland slopes, or in mature riverbottom forests.

Common Yellowthroat, *Geothlypis trichas*: common spring, summer and fall (Apr.–Oct.) resident; breeding confirmed L4 & 5. Average spring arrival, 5-9. Easily found Ash Creek, Little Piney Creek, McClain's Pond, Sheridan Cemetery, Story and Tongue River Canyon; up to Seven Brothers Lake at 9,000' elevation. The species was observed during all 21 years of Spring Bird Counts in Johnson County, 1984–2004, and during two of four years of Spring Bird Counts in Sheridan County, 2009–2012. It was not observed during 26 years of Christmas Bird Counts at Buffalo, 1986–2011. Moist to wet ground, with associated vegetation such as tall grasses, shrubs, and small trees, are the primary breeding habitat, although at times the birds extend to upland thickets of shrubbery and low trees. Willow thickets around beaver ponds, the edges of muskegs, and scrub alders are among its favorite nesting areas.

American Redstart, *Setophaga ruticilla*: fairly common spring, summer and fall (May–Oct.) resident; breeding confirmed L4 & 5. Average spring arrival, 5-14. Redstarts are found at Sheridan elevation in nearly all riparian habitats, and are easily seen in Tongue River Canyon and at Story, up to about 5,500' elevation. The species was observed during 17 of 21 years of Spring Bird Counts in Johnson County, 1984–2004. It was not observed during 26 years of Christmas Bird Counts at Buffalo, 1986–2011. Breeding habitats of this species include moist bottomland woodlands, the margins or openings of mature forests, young or second-growth stands of various types of forests, and especially deciduous forests. Nearby water and of a brush layer seem to be important habitat components.

Northern Parula, *Setophaga americana*: extremely rare spring (May) vagrant L5. Apparently the same bird was seen three times 5-10-17-1970, at McClain's Pond, but no details were furnished; one was reported 5-4-1981, on Little Piney Road, with written documentation. One was seen near Sheridan for 11 days, 6-18-28, 1991 (Faulkner 2010). Not reported regionally on eBird from 1-1-1990 through 4-25-2013. On migration these birds are likely to be seen in riverine forests or other deciduous forest areas. Most of the approximately 50 Wyoming records are for spring (Faulkner, 2010).

Magnolia Warbler, *Setophaga magnolia*: extremely rare spring (May) and fall (Aug.–Sept.) vagrant L4 & 5. Seen at McClain's Pond 5-15-1970; on Little Piney Creek Road 5-22-1975; at Little Goose Creek bridge on Race Track Road south of Sheridan 5-28-1975; at Padlock Ranch near Dayton 6-8-1978; on Little Piney Creek 9-22-1980; at Bighorn 8-20-1984; and on Little Piney 5-18-1986. The Magnolia Warbler was observed during one of 21 years of Spring Bird Counts in Johnson County, 1984–2004. It was not observed during 26 years of Christmas Bird Counts at Buffalo, 1986–2011. Most of the approximately 50 Wyoming records are for late May and early June (Faulkner, 2010).

Blackburnian Warbler, *Setophaga fusca*: extremely rare spring (May) vagrant L4 & 5. Two records to 1990: 5-19-1974, in willows along Tongue River on Decker Road with good documentations, and 5-26-1990, in Little Goose Canyon. Not reported regionally on eBird from 1-1-1990 through 4-25-2013. Most of the fewer than 20 Wyoming records are for late May (Faulkner, 2010).

Yellow Warbler, *Setophaga petechia*: common spring, summer, and fall (Apr.–Oct.) resident; breeding confirmed L4 & 5. Average spring arrival, 5-10. Found in all areas from the Powder River at Arvada, Buffalo, Dayton, Ranchester and Sheridan; less common into the foothills. Ash Creek supports a large population. One record on Owen Creek 7-14-1977, elevation 8,500'; one at Hunter Corrals 9-4-1985, elevation 7,184'. The species was observed during all 21 years of Spring Bird Counts in Johnson County, 1984–2004, and during two of four years of Spring Bird Counts in Sheridan County, 2009–2012. It was not observed during 26 years of Christmas Bird Counts at Buffalo, 1986–2011. Generally moist habitats, such as riparian woodlands and brush, the brushy edges of marshes, swamps, or beaver ponds, and also drier areas including roadside thickets, hedgerows, orchards, and forest edges. A combination of open areas and dense shrubbery seem to be important for breeding, although migrant birds are rather more widely distributed.

Chestnut-sided Warbler, *Setophaga pensylvanica*: extremely rare spring (May) and early fall (Sept.) vagrant L4 & 5; one summer record (July), breeding not confirmed. Six records to 1990: Acme 5-23-1966, unknown location 5-29-1970; Sheridan 7-1-1973; and Tongue River Canyon 9-15-1974, 5-31-1976, and 5-31-1979. Most of the approximately 50 Wyoming records are for middle to late May (Faulkner, 2010).

Blackpoll Warbler, *Setophaga striata*: rare spring (April–May) and fall (Aug., Oct.) transient L4 & 5. Average spring arrival, 5-15. About thirteen observations existed to 1990. Reported at Ash Creek, Big Goose Creek near T-T Ranch, Clear Creek at Clearmont, McClain's Pond, Sheridan, Tongue River on Decker Road, and at Black Mountain Lookout at 9,489' elevation. A high count of 13 birds were seen at Sheridan, 5-5-1993 (Faulkner 2010). The species was observed during three of 21 years of Spring Bird Counts in Johnson County, 1984–2004. It was not observed during 26 years of Christmas Bird Counts at Buffalo, 1986–2011. Reported regionally on eBird at Thorn Rider Park, Sheridan, on four occasions between 5-16 and 5-27, 1996 and 1997 from 1-1-1990 to 4-25-2013. Most of the numerous Wyoming records are for May 8–30 (Faulkner, 2010).

Black-throated Blue Warbler, *Setophaga caerulescens*: extremely rare spring (May) and fall (Sept.–Oct.) vagrant L5. Seen in Sheridan 8-8-1975 and 9-1-1983; also at the UM Ponds 5-25-1977; all were females. Not reported regionally on eBird from 1-1-1990 through 4-25-2013. Most of the numerous Wyoming records are for fall (Faulkner, 2010).

Palm Warbler, *Setophaga palmarum*: extremely rare spring (May) vagrant. One was seen at Sheridan 5-8-1996 (Faulkner, 2010). Faulkner noted that about two-thirds of the Wyoming records are for spring. Not reported regionally on eBird from 1-1-1990 through 4-25-2013. Most of the approximately 40 Wyoming records are from 4-29 to 5-30 (Faulkner, 2010).

Yellow-rumped Warbler, *Setophaga coronata*: common spring and fall transient and summer resident, rare winter vagrant L4 & 5. The species is found in all areas at Sheridan and Buffalo elevations, and at Burgess Junction at 8,038'. Observed FR (Forest Service Road) 147 at 9,168 'elevation, Dayton Gulch at 9,168 'elevation. Two easily-recognized races occur in the region, The "Myrtle Warbler" race, *D. c. coronata*, is a fairly common spring and fall (Apr.–June, Aug.–Nov.) transient L4 & 5. Average spring arrival, 4-26. The "Audubon's Warbler" race, *D. c. auduboni*, is a common spring and fall transient and summer resident (Mar.–Dec.); breeding confirmed L4 & L5. Average spring arrival, 4-24. Found in all areas at Sheridan and Buffalo on migration, and in summer from 5,000' at Story to 10,800' between Horseshoe Lake and Dutch Oven Pass. The species was observed during all 21 years of Spring Bird Counts in Johnson County, 1984–2004, during one of 26 years of Christmas Bird Counts at Buffalo, 1986–2011, and during all four years of Spring Bird

Counts in Sheridan County, 2009–2012. The Myrtle race was identified in 16 years of Spring Migration Counts in Johnson County, and the Audubon's race was seen in all 21 years. Reported during all four years of Spring Bird Counts in Sheridan County, 2009–2012. This species breeds in a wide array of coniferous forests, from the ponderosa pine zone upwards, and also breeds in riparian forests with conifers present. Habitats range from open, park-like ponderosa pine communities through dense montane forests to timberline species, foraging from low branches to the highest crown levels.

Townsend's Warbler, *Setophaga townsendi*: extremely rare spring (May) and fall (Aug.–Sept.) transient L4 & 5. Three records to 1990: at Story 9-11-1971; on North Piney road at Story 5-19-1984; and in the Highland Park area at about 10,000' 8-29-1988. An undated report was by a reliable birder on Little Piney Creek Road. There is one regional eBird report through 4-25-2013: single birds were reported on Wolf Creek Ranch on 9-14-2009. The species was observed during four of 21 years of Spring Bird Counts in Johnson County, 1984–2004. It was not observed during 26 years of Christmas Bird Counts at Buffalo, 1986–2011. This is a crown-level forager in tall conifers, favoring dense and mature montane forests. This general habitat preference seems to be true during the non-breeding season as well as when nesting. Most of the Wyoming records are for fall, and from the western parts of the state (Faulkner, 2010).

Wilson's Warbler, *Cardellia pusilla*: common spring, summer and fall (May–Oct.) resident; breeding confirmed L4 & 5. Average spring arrival, 5-21. Found at Circle Park above Buffalo, Hazelton, along North Tongue River west of Burgess Junction, and Sourdough Creek. The species was observed during 12 of 21 years of Spring Bird Counts in Johnson County, 1984–2004. It was not observed during 26 years of Christmas Bird Counts at Buffalo, 1986–2011. On their breeding grounds these birds inhabit willow, alder thickets along rivers or beaver ponds, brushy edges of lakeshores, the edges of mountain meadows, timberline areas of low shrubby vegetation, and sometimes also aspen thickets.

Yellow-breasted Chat, *Icteria virens*: fairly common late spring, summer, and early fall (Apr.–Sept.) resident; breeding confirmed L4 & 5. Average spring arrival, 5-16. Found at Ash Creek, near Big Horn, S–R Buffalo Creek Road and Young's Creek, Tongue River near Acme, Red Grade draw. This bird sings at night, particularly on first arrival from wintering grounds in Central America. The species was observed during five of 21 years of Spring Bird Counts in Johnson County, 1984–2004, and during two of four years of Spring Bird Counts in Sheridan County, 2009–2012. It was not observed during 26 years of Christmas Bird Counts at Buffalo, 1986–2011. During the breeding season this species occurs along the shrubby coulee areas of the plains, oak and mountain mahogany woodlands of the foothills, along alder and willow-lined creeks of prairies, brushy forest edges, and shrubby overgrown pasturelands. Over much of its eastern range this species has been in a serious decline. Breeding Bird Surveys indicate that national populations are decreasing significantly (0.5% annually, 1966-2011).

Family Emberizidae: Towhees & Sparrows

Lark Sparrow

Green-tailed Towhee, *Pipilo chlorurus*: uncommon spring, summer and fall (May–Oct.) resident; breeding confirmed L4, presumed L5. Average spring arrival, 5-16. Green-tailed Towhees have been seen at Big Horn, Johnson Creek northwest of Buffalo, Little Piney Road, Little Goose Canyon, Penrose Trail, Red Grade Road, Rock Creek, UM Ponds and U. S. Hwy. 14 above Dayton. Observed at Hunt Mountain Road at about 10,000' on 8-2-1974. The species was observed during five of 21 years of Spring Bird Counts in Johnson County, 1984–2004, and during two of four years of Spring Bird Counts in Sheridan County, 2009–2012. It was not observed during 26 years of Christmas Bird Counts at Buffalo, 1986–2011. During the breeding season this species occurs in brushy foothills areas dominated by sagebrush, scrub oaks, saltbush and greasewood flats, scrubby riparian woodlands, and similar open and semi-arid habitats. Forested areas are avoided, but scattered trees in brush lands are used as singing posts. Spreading shrubs that allow for easy movement and foraging on the ground surface below are favored vegetation types.

Spotted Towhee, *Pipilo maculatus*: common spring, summer and fall resident, rare winter vagrant; breeding confirmed L4 & 5. Average spring arrival, 4-29. Widespread from the Powder River near Arvada, Buffalo, Clearmont and Sheridan areas; easily found in Ash Creek, SR–Buffalo Creek Road and Tongue River Canyon. The Spotted Towhee was observed during all 21 years of Spring Bird Counts in Johnson County, 1984–2004, during one of 26 years of Christmas Bird Counts at Buffalo, 1986–2011, and during three of four years of Spring Bird Counts in Sheridan County, 2009–2012. Considered from the 1960s until 1995 by the A.O.U. as conspecific with the Eastern Towhee, *P. erythropthalmus*; both then were collectively known as the "Rufous-sided Towhee". Intermediate-plumaged birds are frequent where both plumage phenotypes occur, as is true over much of western Nebraska. Breeding occurs in brushy fields, thickets, woodland openings or edges, second-growth forests, city parks, and well-planted suburbs. Habitats that have a good accumulation of litter and humus, and a protective screen of shrubby foliage above the ground, are highly favored by these birds, which forage by scratching in the litter.

American Tree Sparrow, *Spizella arborea*: common late fall, winter, and early spring (Oct.–May) resident, L4 & 5. Found in all areas to 5,000' elevation. The species was not observed during 21 years of Spring Bird Counts in Johnson County, 1984–2004. It was reported during 24 of 26 years of Christmas Bird Counts at Buffalo, 1986–2011, and during one of four years of Spring Bird Counts in Sheridan County, 2009–2012. This species occupies brushy prairie areas, roadside thickets, farmsteads, old orchards, overgrown and weedy pastures, and similar relatively open habitats. The birds often occur in company with juncos and other gregarious and hardy sparrows, and feed about on the ground or snow surface, searching out small seeds.

Chipping Sparrow, *Spizella passerina*: common spring, summer and fall (Mar.–Oct.) resident; breeding confirmed L4 & 5. Average spring arrival, 4-28; recorded as early as 3-30 at Sheridan (Faulkner, 2010). Recorded in all areas up to 8,000' at Burgess Junction and Twin Buttes; one record at 10,000' on Hunt Mountain Road, 8-13-1981. Also seen at 9,800' at Mirror Lake, 7-21-2012. Juveniles were observed at Mirror Lake, 7-29-2012, 9,800' elevation and at Crystal Creek Ridge at 9,250' elevation. Also seen along the North Tongue River, 6-30-2013, 8,500' elevation. The species was observed during 20 of 21 years of Spring Bird Counts in Johnson County, 1984–2004, and during all four years of Spring Bird Counts in Sheridan County, 2009–2012. It was not reported during 26 years of Christmas Bird Counts at Buffalo, 1986–2011. Breeding in this species is done in open deciduous or mixed forests, the margins of forest clearings, the edges of muskegs, in timberline scrub, riparian woodlands, pinyon–juniper or oak–mountain mahogany woodlands, and similarly transitional habitats. Generally scattered trees, an unshaded forest floor, and a sparse ground covering of herbaceous plants seem to be the kinds of habitat considerations that are important. Breeding Bird Surveys indicate that national populations are decreasing significantly (0.5% annually, 1966-2011).

Clay-colored Sparrow, *Spizella pallida*: fairly common spring and fall transient, uncommonly reported summer resident (Apr.–Oct.); breeding presumed L4 & 5. Average spring arrival, 5-9. Has been seen at Acme, Decker Road, Johnson Creek Road northwest of Buffalo, Prairie Dog Creek Road,, S-R Creek Road, Sheridan, Soldier Creek Road and Wolf Creek Road. The species was observed during seven of 21 years of Spring Bird Counts in Johnson County, 1984–2004. It was not reported during 26 years of Christmas Bird Counts at Buffalo, 1986–2011. Favored breeding habitats consist of brushy thickets in prairies, fence-line shrubbery along pastures or meadows, mixed-grass prairies with scattered shrubs or low trees, brushy woodland margins, early successional stages of forests following logging or fires, and retired croplands. Nesting sometimes also occurs in city parks or residential areas. Breeding Bird Surveys indicate that national populations are decreasing significantly (1.3% annually, 1966-2011).

Brewer's Sparrow, *Spizella breweri*: fairly common spring, summer and fall (Apr.–Oct.) resident; breeding confirmed L4 & L5. Common around Lake DeSmet and Moore's Reservoir; also reported from Ash Creek-Monarch Road, Crazy Woman C. G., Hazelton Road off U. S. Hwy. 16, Healy Reservoir and Young's Creek, up to 8,100' elevation. The species was observed during ten of 21 years of Spring Bird Counts in Johnson County, 1984–2004, and during one of four years of Spring Bird Counts in Sheridan County, 2009–2012, but was not reported during 26 years of these counts at Buffalo, 1986–2011. This sparrow breeds across Wyoming in short-grass prairies with sage or other semi-arid shrubs present in varying densities.

Vesper Sparrow, *Pooecetes gramineus*: abundant spring, summer and fall (Mar.–Nov.) resident; breeding confirmed L4 & 5. Average spring arrival, 4-22. Common on all areas and elevations from the Powder River to Hazelton Road, also Billy Creek, Burgess Junction and Dayton Gulch, up to Hunt Mountain Road at 10,000'. The Vesper Sparrow was observed during 20 of 21 years of Spring Bird Counts in Johnson County, 1984–2004, and during all four years of Spring Bird Counts in Sheridan County, 2009–2012. It was not reported during 26 years of these counts at Buffalo, 1986–2011. During the breeding season this species is found in overgrown fields, prairie edges, grasslands with scattered shrubs and small trees, sagebrush areas where the plants are scattered and stunted, and similar open habitats, but not extending to mountain meadows or tundra zones.

Lark Sparrow, *Chondestes grammacus*: common to abundant spring, summer and fall (Apr.–Oct.) resident; breeding confirmed L4 & 5. Found in all areas from Powder River to Buffalo and Sheridan; also seen on Turkey Creek, 9-6-1976, at 7,000'; and at Paintrock area 7-2-4-1988, at 9,000–9,500' elevation. Five were recorded on Hunt Mountain Road at 9,980' elevation. The species was observed during all 21 years of Spring Bird Counts in Johnson County, 1984–2004, and during all four years of Spring Bird Counts in Sheridan County, 2009–2012. It was not reported during 26 years of these counts at Buffalo, 1986–2011. This species favors grasslands that have scattered trees, shrubs, large forbs, or adjoin such vegetation; thus weedy fencerows near grasslands, open brush land on slopes, sagebrush flats, scrubby and open oak woodlands, orchards, and similar habitats are all suitable. Generally, open views and a variety of plants, including scattered woody vegetation some grasses and herbs, are preferred. Breeding Bird Surveys indicate that national populations are decreasing significantly (0.9% annually, 1966-2011).

Sage Sparrow, *Amphispiza belli*: rare to occasional spring, summer and fall (Mar.–Sept.) resident and/or transient; breeding suspected L4 S 5. Migrants usually begin to arrive in mid-March. Breeding probably occurs locally in Big Horn and Johnson counties (Faulkner, 2010). Thirteen records to 1990: Lake DeSmet, lower part of Little Piney Road, Moore's Reservoir, Powder River, Red Hills Road east of Buffalo and Soldier Creek Road. Recent regional eBird reports, include an unreported number at Red Gulch Road, 8-10-2009, and one at Dinosaur Tracksite, 10-3-2009, four at Sage Flats, 5-31-2010, and two at Greybull 5-27-2011. This species is closely associated with fairly dense to sparse and scrubby sagebrush vegetation during the breeding season, but also breeds at times in similar semi-desert vegetation types, such as in saltbush. Foraging is done on rather bare ground areas of gravel or alkali soil around the bushes, and it escapes by fleeing into shrubbery.

Lark Bunting. *Calamospiza melanocorys*: abundant spring and summer (Apr.–Sept.) resident, common fall resident; breeding confirmed L4 & L5. Average spring arrival, 5-8. Large numbers have been reported at Kumor Road, Lake DeSmet, Powder River near Arvada, SR–Buffalo Creek Road, and Soldier Creek Road. A few males have been seen at high elevations on the Dry Fork, Hay Creek, and a cow camp west of Burgess R. S., all near 8,000'; one was seen at Long Park, 10,000' on 7-20-1988. The species was observed during 16 of 21 years of Spring Bird Counts in Johnson County, 1984–2004, and during three of four years of Spring Bird Counts in Sheridan County, 2009–2012, but not observed during 26 years of these counts at Buffalo, 1986–2011. This species favors mixed-grass prairies for nesting, but also can be found in short-grass and tall-grass prairies, as well as sage grasslands, retired croplands, alfalfa fields, and stubble fields. Areas with abundant shrubs are avoided, but fence posts or scattered trees may be used as song posts. Breeding Bird Surveys indicate that national populations are decreasing significantly (3.5 % annually, 1966-2011).

Savannah Sparrow, *Passerculus sandwichensis*: fairly common spring, summer and fall (Apr.–Oct.) resident, breeding confirmed L4 & 5. Average spring arrival, 4-25. Found at Lake DeSmet, Hunt Mountain Road, Little and Lower Piney Creek roads, Soldier and Wolf Creek roads. Also in the Bighorn Mountains at Circle Park C. G., meadows along the North Tongue River on U. S. Hwy. 14A, and Upper Tensleep Meadows, from 8,000–10,000' elevation. The species was observed during all 21 years of Spring Bird Counts in Johnson County, 1984–2004, and during all four years of Spring Bird Counts in Sheridan County, 2009–2012, but was not reported during 26 years of these counts at Buffalo, 1986–2011. During the breeding season this species is closely associated with moist but low-stature prairies, the wet meadow zones around marshes or other wetlands, and the moist and open areas of mountain meadows, or even alpine grasslands. Growths of dense ground cover, preferably only a few inches tall, with scattered bushes or clumps of taller vegetation for song perches, are typical aspects of nesting habitats. Breeding Bird Surveys indicate that national populations are decreasing significantly (1.2% annually, 1966-2011).

Baird's Sparrow, *Ammodramus bairdii*: extremely rare spring (May) transient, rare fall (Aug.–Oct.) transient L4 & 5. Reported from Fort Phil Kearney (before improvements), Lake DeSmet (before the lake was enlarged), Kern's Elk Pasture, McCain's Pond , and Sheridan Cemetery; also along

Little Piney Creek, Lower Prairie Dog Creek, Soldier Creek and Wolf Creek roads. Not reported regionally on eBird from 1-1-1990 through 4-25-2013. Most Wyoming reports are from fall, and are largely from east of a north-south Sheridan–Laramie line (Faulkner, 2010). Breeding Bird Surveys indicate that national populations of this prairie-dependent species are decreasing significantly (2,8% annually, 1966-2011).

Grasshopper Sparrow, *Ammodramus savannarum*: uncommon spring, summer and fall (Apr.–Oct.) resident L4 & 5; breeding presumed. Average spring arrival, 5-17. May be more abundant than is known due to difficulty of identification. Has been found on Ash Creek–Monarch, Bird Farm and Little Piney roads; also Healy Reservoir, Hidden Hills off U. S. Hwy. 14 east of Sheridan, Lake DeSmet, McClain's Pond, Red Hills Road, SR–Buffalo Creek Road, and old Wyarno road. The species was observed during two of 21 years of Spring Bird Counts in Johnson County, 1984–2004. It was not observed during 26 years of Christmas Bird Counts at Buffalo, 1986–2011. During the breeding season this species is closely associated with moist but low-stature prairies, the wet meadow zones around marshes or other wetlands, and the moist and open areas of mountain meadows. A growth of dense ground cover, preferably only a few inches tall, with scattered bushes or clumps of taller vegetation for song perches, are typical aspects of nesting habitats. The breeding range is probably contiguous from Laramie to Sheridan (Faulkner, 2010). Breeding Bird Surveys indicate that national populations are decreasing significantly (2.4% annually, 1966-2011).

LeConte's Sparrow, *Ammodramus leconteii*: extremely rare spring (Apr.–May) and fall (Sept.) vagrant L5. Found at a Sheridan residence September 25, 1969, and September 18, 1971; Sheridan Cemetery 9-13-1970, and 9-8-1972; Lake DeSmet 4-20-1977, and 5-9-1978, before the lake was enlarged; and south of Story 4-21-1977. Not reported regionally on eBird from 1-1-1990 through 4-25-2013. Many of the very few Wyoming reports of this grassland-adapted species are from the Sheridan–Story area (Faulkner, 2010).

Fox Sparrow, *Passerella iliaca*: uncommon spring and fall (Apr.–May, Aug.–Oct.) transient L4 & 5; breeding not confirmed. Average spring arrival, 5-10. The Fox Sparrow has been recorded in spring and fall at Big Horn, Johnson Creek northwest of Buffalo, Little Goose Canyon, McClain's Pond, Sheridan Cemetery, Story and Wolf Creek. During the breeding season, dense brushy thickets, and the brushy margins of thick forests, are the favored habitats, but no Wyoming breeding has been reported east of the northwestern ranges (Faulkner, 2010). Riparian thickets of willows or alders, alder clumps on mountain slopes, and the twisted and stunted conifers near timberline all serve to attract this species. Thickets that provide sufficient space underneath for ground foraging, and have a carpet of leaves and litter for scratching towhee-like for food, are particularly favored.

Song Sparrow, *Melospiza melodia*: fairly common spring, summer and fall resident, uncommon winter resident; breeding confirmed L4 & 5. Distribution is widespread, the most accessible places to find them are at Story along North and South Piney Creeks, Tongue River Canyon and many of the western slope canyons along the riparian areas, and Bradford Brinton Road. They have been found at various mountain locations: Nickle Creek, the South Tongue River near Arrowhead Lodge, Twin Buttes, Upper Tensleep Meadows and from Horseshoe Lake to Dutch Oven Pass, 8,000–10,000'. The species was observed during all 21 years of Spring Bird Counts in Johnson County, 1984–2004, during 11 of 26 years of Christmas Bird Counts at Buffalo, 1986–2011, and during all four years of Spring Bird Counts in Sheridan County, 2009–2012. Breeding habitats include such woodland edge types as the brushy margins of forest openings, the edges of ponds or lakes, shelterbelts, farmsteads, prairie coulees and aspen groves. Foraging occurs mostly on the ground, both in open areas and leaf-covered ones, where the birds can scratch to expose foods.

Lincoln's Sparrow, *Melospiza lincolnii*: fairly common in spring and fall migration, common in nesting season (Apr.–Oct.); breeding confirmed L4 & L5. Average spring arrival, 4-30. Seen at all elevations in migration from the Powder River at Arvada to Little Piney Creek and Story. They have been found during the nesting season at Sourdough Creek on U. S. Hwy. 16, at Hazelton, in willows along U. S. Hwy. 14 and at Sibley Lake, the North Tongue River on U. S. Hwy. 14A, and up to Bald Mountain C. G. at 9,299' elevation. The species was observed during 12 of 21 years of Spring Bird Counts in Johnson County, 1984–2004. It was reported during three of four years of Spring Bird Counts in Sheridan County, 2009–2012, but was not observed during 26 years of these counts at Buffalo, 1986–2011. This species is mainly associated with slow-moving streams, marshes and bogs having extensive growths of willows and alders. Willow thickets and brushy borders of muskeg pools are also utilized. The birds favor boggy mountain meadows, especially those fringed with willow thickets and supporting a fairly tall growth of grasses, sedges and herbs.

Swamp Sparrow, *Melospiza georgiana*: extremely rare spring (May) and fall (Sept.) vagrant L5. One was reported south of Sheridan 5-16-1969, and one documented near Lake DeSmet at Shell Reservoir 9-29-1989. Not reported regionally on eBird from 1-1-1990 through 4-25-2013. Most of the approximately 15 Wyoming reports are from spring, and east of a north–south Sheridan–Laramie line (Faulkner, 2010).

Harris' Sparrow, *Zonotrichia querula*: uncommon spring, fall and winter visitant (Sept.–May) L4 & 5. Seen on Clear Creek near Loiter but mostly at feeding stations in Buffalo, Big Horn, Dayton, Rochester and Story, but also on Little Goose Canyon, Lower Piney Creek and Rapid Creek. The species was observed during four of 21 years of Spring Bird Counts in Johnson County, 1984–2004, and during 14 of 26 years of Christmas Bird Counts at Buffalo, 1986–2011, and was reported during one of four years of Spring Bird Counts in Sheridan County, 2009–2012. Outside the breeding season this sparrow is much like the other *Zonotrichia* sparrows, foraging on the ground in areas close to thickets, which are used for protection and roosting. At that time, hedgerows, orchards, farmsteads, riparian thickets, woodland edges, and even sagebrush and desert scrub habitats are often utilized.

White-throated Sparrow, *Zonotrichia albicollis*: uncommon vagrant spring, fall and winter (Aug.–May); rarely overwintering. L4 & 5. Average spring arrival, 4-15. Usually seen at feeding stations, but also at Big Goose and Wolf Creek roads, Healy Reservoir, Holly Pond, Sheridan Cemetery, and UM Ponds. The species was observed during two of 21 years of Spring Bird Counts in Johnson County, 1984–2004, and during two of 26 years of Christmas Bird Counts at Buffalo, 1986–2011. Six were seen 12-17-1978 at Sheridan (Faulkner, 2010). Non-breeding birds are often observed foraging on the ground in somewhat brushy habitats.

Golden-crowned Sparrow, *Zonotrichia atricapilla*: probably an extremely rare vagrant. One was reported near Banner, 2-18-1978, and one was reported from Sheridan, 5-10-12-2003. Both records were accepted by Faulkner (2010), though Downing (19900 considered the earlier single sighting inadequate for inclusion of this species in the regional list.

White-crowned Sparrow, *Zonotrichia leucophrys*: common spring, summer and fall resident, rare winter visitant; breeding confirmed L4, presumed L5. Average spring arrival, 4-12. Present at Sheridan and Buffalo elevation in migration, and at nearly all high-elevation sites in summer and fall. Easily seen along the North Tongue River on U. S. Hwy. 14A; common at Woodchuck Pass 7-12-1985, elevation 9,612'; six were seen on Elk Mountain up to 11,000' on 6-6-1989. Observed Hunt Mountain Road, 6-29-2013, 9,601' elevation. The White-crowned Sparrow was observed during 19 of 21 years of Spring Bird Counts in Johnson County, 1984–2004, during two of 26 years of Christmas Bird Counts at Buffalo, 1986–2011, and during all four years of Spring Bird Counts in Sheridan County, 2009–2012. During the breeding season this species occurs in riparian brush, in coniferous forests with well developed wooded undergrowth, in aspen groves with a shrubby understory, willow thickets around beaver ponds or marshes, and on mountain meadows with alders or similar low and thick shrubbery, often to timberline.. On migration and during winter the birds are found in a variety of lower elevation habitats that offer a combination of brushy cover and open ground for foraging.

Dark-eyed Junco, *Junco hyemalis:* the Dark-eyed Junco is common throughout the region, and was observed during all 21 years of Spring Bird Counts in Johnson County, 1984–2004, during all 26 years of Christmas Bird Counts at Buffalo, 1986–2011, and during all four years of Spring Bird Counts in Sheridan County, 2009–2012. Christmas Counts at Buffalo reported the slate-colored race as present in all 26 years, and the Oregon race in 18 years. There seems to be an elevational migration for breeding. Breeding habitats include open coniferous forests, especially pinyon–juniper woodlands, ponderosa pine forests, mixed forests, aspen woods, forest clearings, the edges of muskegs or jackpine-covered ridges at higher elevations. Similar habitats that offer ground-foraging and ground-nesting opportunities as well as tree or brush cover for escape are also used. Winter birds are very common at local feeders. A recent estimate of the species' total population is 260,000,000 (Rich *et al.*, 2004), making this one of America's most abundant land birds.

The following five races of this species have been described as occurring in this region:

The "Slate-colored" Junco, *J. h. hyemalis,* is a fairly common spring, late fall, and winter visitant L4 & 5. Observed 8-18-1976, at Bald Mountain C. G., at 9,200'. Found in all areas, but most common at Story.

The "White-winged Junco, *J. h. aikeni,* is a rare spring, fall and winter vagrant L4 & 5. Most records are from Story, but also reported from Big Horn, Rapid Creek, and Sheridan.

The "Oregon" Junco, *J. h. oreganus*, is a fairly common spring and fall visitant, uncommon winter visitant L4 & 5. Found in all areas but most often reported at Story.

The "Pink-sided" Junco, *J. h. mearnsi*, is a common resident, numbers decreasing in winter depending on the severity of weather; breeding confirmed L4 & 5. It is found in all areas in spring, fall, and winter but most often at Story; nesting from about 6,000' upward as high as suitable habitat is available. Two were seen between 10,000' and 11,000' elevation 7-29 & 30-1989.

The "Gray-headed" Junco, *J. h. caniceps*, is a rare spring and fall vagrant, and extremely rare winter vagrant L4 & 5. It has been recorded most often at Story, but also seen at Acme, Bighorn, Buffalo, Johnson Creek, Little Goose Canyon, Rapid Creek and Wolf Creek.

Family Cardinalidae: Cardinals & Grosbeaks

Lazuli Bunting

Western Tanager, *Piranga ludoviciana*: common spring, summer and fall (Apr.–Oct.) resident; breeding confirmed L4 & 5. Average spring arrival, 5-17. Occurs at Clear Creek west of Buffalo City Park, Little Piney Creek Red Grade Road, and Story. Highest elevations are Sourdough to Lame Deer Lake, behind Meadowlark Ski Area, Pole Creek, and Doyle Creek C. G., above 8,000'. The species was observed during 13 of 21 years of Spring Bird Counts in Johnson County, 1984–2004. It was not observed during 26 years of Christmas Bird Counts at Buffalo, 1986–2011. Breeding occurs in riparian woodlands, aspen groves, ponderosa pine forests, and occasionally in Douglas-fir forests and pinyon–juniper or oak–mountain mahogany woodlands. It is usually found in areas having a predominance of coniferous trees, preferably those that are fairly open, but occasionally extends into fairly dense forests. Breeding Bird Surveys indicate that national populations are increasing significantly (1.2% annually, 1966-2011).

Scarlet Tanager, *Piranga olivacea*: extremely rare spring vagrant. Two sightings: one reported, Meade Creek, 5-26-1974; one, Sheridan, 5-28-1974. Faulkner (2010) mentioned both records, and considered the species a vagrant in Wyoming, although Downing had excluded the species from her main list.

Northern Cardinal, *Cardinalis cardinalis*: extremely rare fall (Oct.) and winter (Dec.–Feb.) vagrant L4. A female was observed on Big Goose Creek west of Sheridan 1-17-1991; it was present into February, 1991. This species also reported earlier, 10-15-1979, at a ranch on Rock Creek, lati-long 5, but without details. Not reported regionally on eBird from 1-1-1990 through 4-25-2013. It is a fairly recent arrival in Wyoming (1983), and is likely to increase gradually, as it has both expanded in range and increased in the western edges of its Great Plains range. Breeding Bird Surveys indicate that national populations are increasing significantly (0.3% annually, 1966-2011).

Rose-breasted Grosbeak, *Pheucticus ludovicianus*: rare to uncommon spring to fall (Apr.–Sept.) visitant, L4 & 5; breeding not confirmed. This species appears to be expanding its range westward. It has been found in Big Horn, Buffalo, Dayton, Johnson Creek northwest of Buffalo, Lake DeSmet, Lower Piney Creek, Rapid Creek, Sheridan and Story. A single male was observed at a bird feeder in Red Grade 6-15-2013. Hybrids with Black-headed Grosbeaks might also be present. Not reported regionally on eBird from 1-1-1990 through 4-25-2013. The species was observed during seven of 21 years of Spring Bird Counts in Johnson County, 1984–2004, but was not observed during 26 years of Christmas Bird Counts at Buffalo, 1986–2011. During the breeding season this species is found in deciduous woodlands or the deciduous portions of mixed forests on floodplains, slopes, and bluffs. Forests where the undergrowth is tall but not too dense are apparently preferred, although a variety of undergrowth conditions are utilized.

Black-headed Grosbeak, *Pheucticus melanocephalus*: fairly common spring, and summer, uncommon fall resident (Apr.–Oct.), and extremely rare winter vagrant; breeding presumed L4, confirmed L5. Average spring arrival, 5-17. This species has been found at Acme, Ash Creek, Buffalo, Little Goose Canyon, Little Piney Creek, Lower Piney Creek, Rapid Creek, Sheridan, and Story (to about 5,500'). A breeding pair was observed at Big Horn 5-15-2013. The species was observed during 15 of 21 years of Spring Bird Counts in Johnson County, 1984–2004, during one of 26 years of Christmas Bird Counts at Buffalo, 1986–2011, and during two of four years of Spring Bird Counts in Sheridan County, 2009–2012. In the breeding season this species is associated with open deciduous woodlands having fairly well developed shrubby understories, and usually on floodplains or upland areas. It extends into wooded coulees and riparian forests of cottonwoods and similar vegetation in the plains, and sometimes also nests in orchards, oak–mountain mahogany woodlands, and aspen groves. Breeding Bird Surveys indicate that national populations are increasing significantly (1.0% annually, 1966-2011).

Blue Grosbeak, *Passerina caerulea*: extremely rare spring and summer (May-June) vagrant L5. One detailed report of three males in Sheridan Kendrick Park 5-5-1977. A male and female were seen 6-30-1986, east of Shell on U. S. Hwy. 14, barely outside the Bighorn National Forest, and just beyond the longitudinal limits of this book. Not reported regionally on eBird from 1-1-1990 through 4-25-2013. Breeding Bird Surveys indicate that national populations are increasing significantly (0.9% annually, 1966-2011).

Lazuli Bunting, *Passerina amoena*: fairly common spring, summer and fall (Apr.–Oct.) resident; breeding confirmed, L4 & 5. Average spring arrival, 5-10. Recorded at Ash Creek, Big Horn, Buffalo, Dayton, Little Piney Creek, Lower Piney Creek, Ranchester, Sheridan, Story and Tongue River Canyon. Rare at elevations 8,000–9,300', Lower Paintrock C. G. 7-2-1988, Meadow Lark Lake 6-5-1988, and Twin Buttes 7-4-1978. Hybrid male Lazuli x Indigo Buntings have been seen at UM Ponds, in Sheridan, and on Ash Creek. The Lazuli Bunting was observed during 16 of 21 years of Spring Bird Counts in Johnson County, 1984–2004, and during two of four years of Spring Bird Counts in Sheridan County, 2009–2012. It was not reported during 26 years of Christmas Bird Counts at Buffalo, 1986–2011. In mountainous areas these birds breed along the edges of deciduous forests on gentle valley slopes, such as aspen groves, or thickets of willow or alder. On the foothills and plains the birds are usually found in riparian woodlands supporting a mixture of shrubs, low trees, and herbaceous vegetation.

Indigo Bunting, *Passerina cyanea*: uncommon spring, summer and fall (Apr.–Oct.) vagrant, L4 & 5; breeding confirmed L4. They have been reported at Ash Creek, Big Horn, Buffalo, Dayton, Little Piney Creek, Rapid Creek, Sheridan, Story, Wolf Creek, and as high as near Sheep Mountain Lookout southwest of Buffalo, elevation 9,000'. A hybrid Indigo × Lazuli Bunting was found at Sheridan, 4-5-1980 (Faulkner 2010), and a probable hybrid male were seen on Johnson Creek northwest of Buffalo 5-22-26-1986. Many breeding birds in Wyoming are mixed-species pairs, although assortative mating occurs (Faulkner, 2010). This species typically breeds in relatively open hardwood forests on floodplains or uplands. Open woodlands, with a high density of shrubs and an open canopy, are favored, and thus forest edges, second-growth areas, orchards, overgrown pastures, and similar habitats are typically utilized. Breeding Bird Surveys indicate that national populations are decreasing significantly (0.6% annually, 1966-2011).

Dickcissel, *Spiza americana*: uncommon spring, summer and fall resident (May–Sept.), absent some years; breeding confirmed L4 & 5. A female was carrying food to alfalfa field south of Sheridan. 8-14-1975. This is a prairie-adapted species that breeds in grasslands having a combination of tall forbs, grasses, and shrubs, or in grassy meadows having nearby hedges or brushy fencerows. Nests are impacted by early haying, so declines have been significant.

Family Icteridae: Blackbirds & Relatives

Red-winged Blackbird

Bobolink, *Dolichonyx oryzivorus*: fairly common spring and summer and early fall (Apr.–Sept.) resident; breeding confirmed L4 & 5. Average spring arrival, 5-16. Found on Big Goose Creek Road, Little Piney Road near Fort Phil Kearney, McClain's Pond area, Rapid Creek and Soldier Creek roads; highest elevation recorded was near Meadowlark Lake, 8,817', 8-7-1984. A high count of 162 were seen at Sheridan, 8-5-1981 (Faulkner, 2010). The species was observed during 11 of 21 years of Spring Bird Counts in Johnson County, 1984–2004. It was not observed during 26 years of Christmas Bird Counts at Buffalo, 1986–2011, but was reported during two of four years during Spring Bird Counts in Sheridan County, 2009–2012. Breeding occurs in tallgrass prairies, ungrazed or lightly grazed mid-grass prairies, wet meadows, hayfields, retired croplands, and similar habitats. Scattered bushes or other singing posts in the territory add to a breeding area's attractiveness. Breeding Bird Surveys indicate that national populations are decreasing significantly (2.1% annually, 1966-2011).

Red-winged Blackbird, *Agelaius phoeniceus*: abundant spring, summer and fall, uncommon winter resident; breeding confirmed L4 & 5. Average spring arrival, 3-12. Found in all areas (uncommon above 5,000'), and is one of the most common species on local counts. The species was observed during all 21 years of Spring Bird Counts in Johnson County, 1984–2004, during 18 of 26 years of Christmas Bird Counts at Buffalo, 1986–2011, and during all four years of Spring Bird Counts in Sheridan County, 2009–2012. Fall roosts of as many as 20,000+ birds have seen at Sheridan, and Big Horn consistently has had the highest Christmas Counts (Faulkner, 2010). Typical breeding habitats are wetlands ranging from deep marshes or the emergent vegetation zones of lakes and reservoirs through variably drier habitats including wet meadows, ditches, brushy patches in prairies, hayfields, and weedy croplands or roadsides. Wetlands with bulrushes or cattails are especially favored for nesting, but sometimes shrubs or other woody vegetation are used for nest sites. Outside the breeding season the birds often seek grain fields, city parks, pasturelands, and other habitats offering food sources. This is one of the most widespread and abundant land birds in North America, that adapts well to human presence. Breeding Bird Surveys indicate that national populations are decreasing significantly (0.7% annually, 1966-2011). A recent estimate of the species' total population is 210,000,000 (Rich *et al.*, 2004), making it one of the most common of American land birds.

Western Meadowlark, *Sturnella neglecta*: abundant spring, summer and fall resident below 5,000' (uncommon 5,000 –8,000'), rare winter visitant; breeding confirmed L4 & 5. Average spring arrival, 3-16. The species was observed during all 21 years of Spring Bird Counts in Johnson County, 1984–2004, during one of 26 years of Christmas Bird Counts at Buffalo, 1986–2011, and during all four years of Spring Bird Counts in Sheridan County, 2009–2012. A very common species on breeding bird counts. As many as 200+ birds have seen during fall near Sheridan (Faulkner, 2010). During the breeding season this species occupies mixed-grass to tallgrass prairies, wet meadows, hayfields, the weedy borders of croplands and retired croplands. To some extent short-grass prairies, sage prairies and mountain meadows are also used by this grassland-adapted species. Breeding Bird Surveys indicate that national populations are decreasing significantly (1.3% annually, 1966-2011).

Yellow-headed Blackbird, *Xanthocephalus xanthocephalus*: common spring, summer and fall resident (Apr.–Oct.), breeding confirmed L4 & 5. Average spring arrival, 4-18. Found in many areas spring and fall. Nesting reported at Healy's and Moore's reservoirs, McClain's Ponds, and South Dam Pond. The species was observed during all 21 years of Spring Bird Counts in Johnson County, 1984-2004, and during three of four years of Spring Bird Counts in Sheridan County, 2009-2012. It was not reported during 26 years of these counts at Buffalo, 1986-2011. Restricted during the breeding seasons to relatively permanent marshes, the marshy zones of lakes, and the shallows of river impoundments where there are good stands of cattails, bulrushes, or phragmites. Although sometimes breeding in the same areas as Red-winged Blackbirds, Yellow-headed Blackbirds occupy the deeper areas adjacent to open water.

Rusty Blackbird, *Euphagus carolinus*: rare fall, winter and spring (Oct.–June) vagrant L4 & 5. Eight records without details, 10-3-1966 to 6-9-1972. Eight birds were reported on Big Goose Road 12-18-1972, and two were seen on Kumor Road 8-25-1977. Not reported regionally on eBird from 1-1-1990 through 4-25-2013. On migration and during winter these birds use a wider variety of habitats, but typically roost in marshy or swampy areas. Breeding Bird Surveys indicate that national populations are decreasing significantly (3.6% annually, 1966-2011).

Brewer's Blackbird, *Euphagus cyanocephalus*: common spring, summer and fall resident, rare winter visitant; breeding confirmed L4 & 5. Average spring arrival, 4-8. Found in all areas spring and fall; nesting from 4,000' at Sheridan to 9,300' at Paintrock Creek. Often found at Burgess Junction. Healy Reservoir, and Lake DeSmet. The species was observed during 20 of 21 years of Spring Bird Counts in Johnson County, 1984-2004, during eight of 26 years of Christmas Bird Counts at Buffalo, 1986-2011, and during all four years of Spring Bird Counts in Sheridan County, 2009-2012. Roosts of as many as 15,000 birds in two locations have seen near Sheridan (Faulkner, 2010). Low-stature grasslands are the primary breeding habitats of this species, including mowed or burned areas, farmsteads and residential areas, the edges of marshes, especially where scattered shrubs are present, such as aspen groves and the brushy banks of prairie creeks. Nesting occurs on the ground or in low shrubs such as sage and shrubs or fence posts also serve as singing posts where they are available. Outside the breeding season a wider array of open habitats are used, including grain fields, orchards, and similar agricultural lands. Breeding Bird Surveys indicate that national populations are decreasing significantly (2.1% annually, 1966-2011).

Common Grackle, *Quiscalus quiscula*: abundant spring, summer and fall resident, rare in winter; breeding confirmed L4 & 5. Average spring arrival, 4-6. A few individuals linger into winter at feeders, and have been found frozen. Recorded in all areas to 5000', less common to 8,000' elevation. The species was observed during all 21 years of Spring Bird Counts in Johnson County, 1984–2004, during 12 of 26 years of Christmas Bird Counts at Buffalo, 1986–2011, and during all four years of Spring Bird Counts in Sheridan County, 2009–2012. Breeding habitats consist of woodland edges, areas partially planted to trees such as residential areas, farmsteads, shelterbelts, coniferous or deciduous woodlands of an open nature, woody shorelines around lakes, and riparian woodlands. Junipers, spruces, and other small and dense conifers are preferred nesting sites, although hardwoods, shrubs, buildings, birdhouses, and even cattails are sometimes also used. Breeding Bird Surveys indicate that national populations are decreasing significantly (1.6% annually, 1966-2011).

Brown-headed Cowbird, *Molothrus ater*: common spring, summer and early fall (Apr.–Sept.) resident; breeding confirmed L4 & 5. Found in nearly all fairly open habitats up to about 8,000'. Average spring arrival, 5-4. Females are brood parasites, and have been known to deposit eggs in the nests of almost 150 other North American "host" species. Hosts are often ground-nesting or shrub-nesting passerines, whose reproductive success is then often greatly reduced by their own young being ignored and starved to death while the cowbird young are being preferentially fed. Each female is likely to lay nearly 50 eggs in a single season, typically placing one egg per host nest. Unusually high incidences of parasitism (more than 300 total reported cases) are known for such regional breeders as the Red-eyed Vireo, Yellow Warbler, Spotted/Eastern towhees, Chipping Sparrow, Song Sparrow, Indigo Bunting and Red-winged Blackbird (Johnsgard, 1997). Parasitic egg-laying occurs in a variety of often woodland edge habitats, including brushy thickets, forest clearings, brushy creek-bottoms in prairies, aspen groves, sagebrush, desert scrub, agricultural lands, and open coniferous forests at lower altitudes. Breeding Bird Surveys indicate that national populations are decreasing significantly (0.6% annually, 1966-2011). A recent estimate of the species' total population is 56.000,000 (Rich et al., 2004).

Orchard Oriole, *Icterus spurius*: extremely rare spring (May) and summer (July) resident; breeding confirmed L5. First found in the Powder River area near Arvada July 8, 1986, and May 31, 1987. Adults seen feeding three fledglings 7-8-1987. Orchard Orioles may be more common along the Powder River than is now known, owing to a lack of observers. Not reported regionally on eBird from 1-1-1990 through 4-25-2013. Associated with lightly wooded riverbottoms, scattered trees in open country, shelterbelts, farmsteads, residential areas, and orchards during the breeding season, and extending into sagebrush and juniper woodlands during the non-breeding season. Breeding Bird Surveys indicate that national populations are decreasing significantly (0.8% annually, 1966-2011).

Bullock's Oriole, *Icterus bullockii*: fairly common spring, summer and early fall (May–Sept.) resident; extremely rare winter straggler (Nov.–Jan.); breeding confirmed L4 & 5. Average spring arrival, 5-13. Widely distributed from Powder River to Buffalo, Sheridan, and Story, to near Bear Lodge, 8,028' elevation. The species was observed during all 21 years of Spring Bird Counts in Johnson County, 1984–2004, and during all four years of Spring Bird Counts in Sheridan County, 2009–2012, but was not reported during 26 years of these counts at Buffalo, 1986–2011. Previously (1973–1998) classified collectively (as the "Northern Oriole") by the A.O.U. with the eastern-oriented Baltimore Oriole, with which it sometimes hybridizes. During the breeding season males of the Bullock's Oriole especially favor riverbottom forests of willows and cottonwoods, but also occur in city parks, and on plains or foothill slopes and valleys with aspen, poplars, birches, and similar vegetation. Breeding Bird Surveys indicate that national populations are decreasing significantly (0.6% annually, 1966-2011).

Baltimore Oriole, *Icterus galbula*: rare spring and summer (May–July) vagrant L5; breeding not confirmed. Thirteen observations to 1990; three have written details. They have been recorded at Lake DeSmet, Powder River near Arvada, Prairie Dog and Dow Prong roads, Sheridan, and Wrench Ranch pasture along Decker Road. Reported in Sheridan, 5-28-1997 (Faulkner, 2010). Not reported regionally on eBird from 1-1-1990 through 4-25-2013. Hybrids with Bullock's Orioles have not been found in Wyoming, but they sometimes occur farther east in areas of breeding overlap.

Family Fringillidae: Northern Finches

Red Crossbill (drawing by Jeanne Konkel)

Brambling, *Fringilla montifringilla*: extremely rare (accidental) Eurasian vagrant L5. Seen & photographed at a Sheridan feeding station from November (no date) to 12-1-1985. Not reported regionally on eBird from 1-1-1990 through 4-25-2013.

Gray-crowned Rosy-Finch, *Leucosticte tephrocotis*: common resident; breeding confirmed L4 presumed L5 (Orabona et al., 2010), but questionable. Five immature Gray-crowned Rosy-Finches were seen on the east face of Black Tooth Mountain at 12,000' elevation, 8-29-1979. Downing (1990) judged this to be evidence of local breeding, but Faulkner (2010) considered that to be an invalid conclusion. Altitudinal and latitudinal migrations takes place in spring and fall. There are six subspecies, sorted into two phenotypically distinct groups of three subspecies each: gray-cheeked and brown-cheeked birds. Representatives of both groups occur in Wyoming. The gray-cheeked race, *littoralis*, makes up about one percent of the Wyoming birds (Faulkner, 2012). This race breeds from south-central Alaska to northern California. The nominate race, *tephrocotis*, breeds from interior Alaska to northwestern Montana. In winter rosy-finches appear at lower elevations in large flocks at Big Horn, Buffalo, Dayton, Lower Piney Creek, Ranchester, Red Grade, Sheridan and Story. Vistara Parham has a home off Red Grade Road (elevation 5,200 feet) and has had up to 12 bird feeders up since 1983. Rosy-finches are present there from October to April, averaging about 500–1,000 Gray-crowned and 100–150 Black Rosy-finches, plus up to about 50 Evening Grosbeaks. In the winter of 2012-2013 as many as 1,500 birds were recorded in mid-February. Nearly all of the birds in that flock are brown-cheeked, which corresponds to Faulkner's estimated ratio of brown-cheeked to gray-cheeked plumage types. The Gray-crowned Rosy-Finch was observed during two of 21 years of Spring Bird Counts in Johnson County, 1984–2004, and during 22 of 26 years of Christmas Bird Counts at Buffalo, 1986–2011. During the breeding season these birds inhabit cirques, talus slopes, alpine meadows with nearby cliffs, and adjacent snow and glacial surfaces, where foraging for frozen insects is common. Nesting is done in cliff crevices or among talus rocks. During fall and winter the birds move to lower elevations, and to habitats that include mountain meadows, grasslands, sagebrush, and agricultural lands. A recent estimate of the species' total population is 200,000 (Rich et al., 2004).

Black Rosy-Finch, *Leucosticte atrata*: fairly common resident; breeding presumed L4 (Orabona et al., 2012). Altitudinal and latitudinal migrations occurs spring and fall. A pair was at Cloud Peak, 13,175', the highest point in the Bighorns, 7-6-1980, and 50 were there 7-4-1986. Three females and five males were collected at 11,300' near Cloud Peak (French, 1959), indicating that it is the Black Rosy-finch that breeds in the Bighorns, Faulkner (2010) also concluded that the Black Rosy-Finch, not the Gray-crowned Rosy-Finch, that very probably breeds in the Bighorns (Mengel and Mengel, 1952; French, 1959; Johnson, 2002). The Black Rosy-Finch was observed during one of 21 years of Spring Bird Counts in Johnson County, 1984–2004. It was not observed during 26 years of Christmas Bird Counts at Buffalo, 1986–2011. However, there are peak numbers of 100-150 birds at Red Grade feeders near Sheridan in March; lower numbers in December and January. These finches disperse widely during winter over the lowlands and plains of Wyoming. They are not seen at plains and foothills in winter as often or in such large numbers as the Gray-crowned. A recent estimate of the species' total population is 20,000 (Rich *et al.*, 2004), making it one of Wyoming's rarest birds.

Pine Grosbeak, *Pinicola enucleator*: fairly common if erratic resident; breeding confirmed L4, presumed L5. Widely recorded in the mountains all year, often at Story. An estimated eighty birds were seen at Granite Pass 2-28-1983; Dayton Gulch Road is an accessible place to search for them in summer. A male and a female were seen at Burgess R. S. 9-1-1982. Their appearance at Buffalo and Sheridan elevations is erratic. The Pine Grosbeak was observed during one of 21 years of Spring Bird Counts in Johnson County, 1984–2004, and during one of 26 years of Christmas Bird Counts at Buffalo, 1986–2011. Breeding occurs in the subalpine levels of the coniferous forest, primarily the alpine fir–Engelmann spruce zone. Nesting usually occurs in conifers, especially in open or scattered woods near meadows or streams.

Cassin's Finch, *Carpodacus cassinii*: fairly common spring, summer and fall resident, uncommon to rare in winter; breeding confirmed L4 & 5. There is an altitudinal migration spring and fall. Nesting occurs rarely at 4,000' at Sheridan, ordinarily from 5,000' at Story to 9,500' at Lily Lake area. Nearly 1,000 Cassin's Finches were west of Big Goose Canyon, 10-30-1981. The Cassin's Finch was also reported during 11 of 26 years of Christmas Bird Counts at Buffalo, 1986–2011, during all four years of Spring Bird Counts in Sheridan County, 2009–2012, and during three of four years of Spring Bird Counts in Sheridan County, 2009–2012. Breeding typically occurs in open, rather dry coniferous forests, including ponderosa pine forests, with the nests placed at considerable heights in large conifers. Generally it occurs at rather higher altitudes than do either the House Finch or the Purple Finch, sometimes almost to timberline. Breeding Bird Surveys indicate that national populations are decreasing significantly (2.6% annually, 1966-2011).

Purple Finch, *Haemorhous purpureus*: rare spring, fall and winter (Sept.–April) vagrant L4 & 5. Commonly reported, but extremely difficult to separate from the Cassin's Finch. Only one male-female pair has been reported, Big Goose Road 3- 23-1984; the rest were females or immature males at Little Goose Canyon, Sheridan and Story feeding stations. Not reported regionally on eBird from 1-1-1990 through 4-25-2013. Buds and blossoms of a variety of broad-leaved trees are favored by migrants in spring. During the winter period they eat a variety of weed and grass seeds, and thus have a broad winter habitat distribution. Breeding Bird Surveys indicate that national populations are decreasing significantly (1.5% annually, 1966-2011).

House Finch, *Haemorhous mexicanus*: abundant resident; breeding confirmed L4 & 5. The species was observed during all 26 years of Christmas Bird Counts at Buffalo, 1986–2011, and reported during all four years of Spring Bird Counts in Sheridan County, 2009–2012. Now generally associated with human habitations over most of its range, nesting on buildings in many areas. Otherwise it nests in open woods, riverbottom woodlands, scrubby desert or semi-desert vegetation such as sagebrush, and tree plantings. Many variably albino and plumage variations from yellow to orange have been noted, the latter probably reflecting differences in carotene consumption.

Red Crossbill, *Loxia curvirostra*: common resident but highly erratic in location and numbers; breeding confirmed L4, presumed L5. Most often reported at Story but also in Amsden Creek, near Arrowhead Lodge on U. S. Hwy. 14 (adults feeding young 7-25-1987), Ash Creek (female carrying nesting material 1-28-1984), Sheridan, Wolf Creek, and as high as Hunt Mountain Road at about 10,000'. Juveniles were seen on Bull Elk Trail 7-14-2012, There was an eruption of Red Crossbills the winter of 2013 that increased the numbers seen at local bird feeders in Big Horn and at Red Grade. Crossbills are appearing at feeders due to reduced cone crops in the north. The Red Crossbill was not observed during 21 years of Spring Bird Counts in Johnson County, 1984–2004, but was reported during nine of 26 years of Christmas Bird Counts at Buffalo, 1986–2011. Breeding is associated with coniferous forest habitats, especially those of pines, including ponderosa, lodgepole, and pinyon, but nesting in the Rocky Mountain region has also been observed in Engelmann spruces and subalpine firs, at elevations from 4,000–10,000 feet or more.

White-winged Crossbill, *Loxia leucoptera*: rare and erratic vagrant all seasons L4 & 5; breeding not confirmed, but two singing males were reported at 9,000' to 9,200', 7-9-1977. Has been found in the Big Goose Creek west of Sheridan, Black Mountain, Dayton, Dayton Gulch, Elgin Park southwest of Buffalo off U. S. Hwy. 16, Red Grade above the spring, Sheep Mountain Road, Sheridan Cemetery, Story, and a mountain east of She-Bear Mountain. An estimated 200 were seen in Dayton Gulch 7-12-1984. Not reported regionally on eBird from 1-1-1990 through 4-25-2013. Although nesting occurs most commonly during spring and summer or early fall, like the Red Crossbill, this species can occur almost any time a rich seed source becomes available. In spring, catkins of aspens and poplars are sometimes eaten, and large weed seeds may be eaten during fall and winter. Spruces and tamaracks seem to be their prime food sources, as their beaks are too weak to handle the larger cones of pines.

Common Redpoll, *Acanthus flammea*: uncommon late fall, winter and spring (Oct.–May) visitant L4 & 5. They have been found at Acme, Big Goose Road, Big Horn, Buffalo, Decker Road, Lake DeSmet, Little Goose Canyon, Lower Piney Road, Prairie Dog Road, Sheridan, UM Ponds and Wyarno Road. Redpolls also visit cities during winter, eating the seed cones of birches, visit bird feeders, and seek out weedy patches. There was an eruption of redpolls in winter of 2013 causing a dramatic increase in the number of people reporting redpolls at their feeder. The species was not observed during 21 years of Spring Bird Counts in Johnson County, 1984–2004, but was reported during nine of 26 years of Christmas Bird Counts at Buffalo, 1986–2011.

Hoary Redpoll, *Acanthus hornemanni*: extremely rare winter (Dec.–Jan.) visitant L5. This species is difficult to distinguish from some races of the Common Redpoll. Reported during one week in December and three weeks in January. Not reported regionally on eBird from 1-1-1990 through 4-25-2013.

Pine Siskin, *Spinus pinus*: common resident, erratic in locations and numbers; breeding confirmed L4 & L5. Common at feeders at 4,000'. It has nested in Sheridan and on Little Piney Road, and occurs widely in the mountains up to Geneva Pass, 10,250' elevation. The species was observed during 22 of 26 years of Christmas Bird Counts at Buffalo, 1986–2011, and during all four years of Spring Bird Counts in Sheridan

County, 2009–2012. Breeding occurs in coniferous or mixed forests, and rarely in deciduous woodlands. Nesting preferentially occurs in conifers of almost any type, but has also been observed in cottonwoods, lilacs, and willows in the Rocky Mountain region. Breeding Bird Surveys indicate that national populations are decreasing significantly (3.4% annually, 1966-2011).

Lesser Goldfinch, *Spinus psaltria*: extremely rare fall (Sept.) vagrant L5; breeding not confirmed. Two records to 1990: a male in Sheridan 9-18-1969, and a male in Buffalo 9-10-1990. In addition, at least four females were repeatedly seen one summer at Buffalo. There are two regional eBird reports through 4-25-2013: five reported on 9-10-2009 at Medicine Lodge State Park. Breeding occurs in sagebrush and riparian thicket areas, as well as where scrub oaks merge with ponderosa pines.

American Goldfinch, *Spinus tristis*: common resident; breeding confirmed L4 & 5. They are widespread from the Powder River near Arvada to Story, where most easily seen; two were present at Upper Tensleep Meadows, about 8,500', 7-24-1984. The species was observed during 23 of 26 years of Christmas Bird Counts at Buffalo, 1986–2011, and during all four years of Spring Bird Counts in Sheridan County, 2009–2012. Breeding occurs in open grazing country, especially where thistles are abundant, or where cattails are to be found. The downy seeds of both are used for nest-building and, at least in the case of thistles, feeding nestlings.

Evening Grosbeak, *Coccothraustes vespertinus*: common resident; breeding confirmed L4 & 5. This species appears to be uncommon during the breeding season: known nesting sites are at Buffalo, Dayton, Sheridan, and Tongue River Canyon, 3,745' to 4,675' elevation. They have been seen at feeders from Sheridan to Dome Lake, at 8,800'. As many as 50 birds can be regularly seen at feeders on Red Grade from October through May. This species was observed during 13 of 26 years of Christmas Bird Counts at Buffalo, 1986–2011. During the breeding season it is primarily associated with mature coniferous forests, although nesting has been observed in riparian willow thickets and even in city parks and orchards. Breeding Bird Surveys indicate that national populations are decreasing significantly (1.4% annually, 1966-2011).

Family Passeridae: Old World Sparrows

House Sparrow

House Sparrow, *Passer domesticus*: abundant resident; breeding confirmed L4 & 5. Widespread throughout the area from the Powder River to about 4,500'; seldom seen at Story at 5,000'. The House Sparrow was observed during all 26 years of Christmas Bird Counts at Buffalo, 1986–2011, and during all four years of Spring Bird Counts in Sheridan County, 2009–2012. Associated throughout the year with humans, and breeding occurs in cities, suburbs, farmsteads, ranches, developed campgrounds, and the like. Nesting is usually done on artificial structures such as buildings that offer cavities or crevices, such as vine-covered buildings, billboard braces, birdhouses, or old nests of other species. Nesting also occurs in tree cavities and birdhouses. Breeding Bird Surveys indicate that national populations are decreasing significantly (3.8% annually, 1966-2011).

Hypothetical and Questionable Species

The following is a list of 16 species having questionable reports; reported only once by reliable observers but without documentation or details, or with incomplete documentation or details.

Northern Bobwhite *Colinus virginianus:* possibly a very rare vagrant. A record of occurrence in L5, with no information, was listed by Orabona et al. (2010). This was possibly an escaped captive, since Bobwhites are highly sedentary, and the nearest resident population is located far to the south in the Platte & Laramie valleys (Faulkner, 2010).

White-tailed Ptarmigan, *Lagopus leucurus*: during August, 1977, the entire Bighorn Mountain range was surveyed aerially and on foot. No ptarmigan or their signs were found; habitats appeared to be average to marginal (Dr. Clait E. Braun, November 30, 1990 interview). There is no recent evidence of this species' occurrence in the Bighorn region (Faulkner, 2010).

White-tailed Kite, *Elanus leucurus caeruleus*: one reported, Lower Piney Creek, 7-12–16, 1971. Previously considered a distinct species and known and listed as "Black-shouldered Kite (*Elanus caeruleus)*" by Downing. This record was not mentioned by Faulkner (2010), who considered the species a vagrant in Wyoming. Downing excluded this species, with only a single regional report, from her list.

Whooping Crane, *Grus americana*: one reported, north of Buffalo 3-25-1987; one, Lake DeSmet, 11-4-1988. These observations were accepted by Faulkner (2010) and probably represented birds hatched from eggs experimentally transplanted into Sandhill Crane nests in Idaho. This population has now died out. Downing excluded this species, with only a single regional report, from her list.

Short-billed Dowitcher, *Limnodromus griseus*: seven tentatively identified by voice, Healy Reservoir, 11-18-1984. Not mentioned by Faulkner (2010). Downing excluded this species, with only a single regional report, from her list.

Black Swift, *Cypseloides niger*: one reported, Medicine Wheel, 7-3-1981. Downing excluded this species, with only a single regional report, from her list. Not yet accepted for the state list (Faulkner, 2010).

Yellow-bellied Sapsucker, *Sphyrapicus varius*: one reported, Tongue River Canyon, 7-17-1988. This eastern sapsucker was reported regionally a few times before the Red-naped Sapsucker was recognized by the A.O.U. as a separate species in 1983. See Red-naped Sapsucker account.

Boreal Chickadee, *Poecile hudsonicus*: reported near Shell, 6-25-1977 (*American Birds* 32:1192). Downing excluded this species, with only a single regional report, from her list. Not accepted by Faulkner (2010).

Bushtit, *Psaltriparus minimus*: probably an extremely rare vagrant; 4 reported, Sheridan, 5-20-1968. This single extralimital sighting was rejected by Downing (1990) but was accepted by Faulkner (2010), who noted that the nearest probable breeding area is near Casper, but regular state breeding occurs only in southwestern Wyoming.

Bewick's Wren, *Thryomanes bewickii*: one reported, Sheridan, 5-30-1966. Southwestern Wyoming is the nearest known breeding area. Downing excluded this species, with only a single regional report, from her list.

Cape May Warbler, *Setophaga tigrina*: one reported, Story, 11-26-1980. Not accepted by Faulkner (2010). Downing excluded this species, with only a single regional report, from her list.

Pine Warbler, *Setophaga pinus*: a single regional record was not accepted by the Wyoming Bird Records Committee. Downing excluded this species, with only a single regional report, from her list.

Black-throated Green Warbler, *Setophaga virens*: one reported, location unknown, 5-15-1983. This sighting was not mentioned by Faulkner (2010). Downing excluded this species, having only a single regional report, from her list.

Canyon Towhee, *Pipilo fuscus*: one reported, Tongue River Canyon, 7-7-1988. Not accepted by Faulkner (2010) as a documented Wyoming species. Downing excluded this species, having only a single regional report, from her list.

Nelson's Sparrow, *Ammodramus nelsoni*: one reported, City Dump Road, Sheridan. No date given. Downing excluded this species, with only a single undocumented report, from her list. This record was not mentioned by Faulkner (2010). Previously (until 1995) known as Sharp-tailed Sparrow, *Ammodramus caudacutus*.

Appendix

Table 1. North American Breeding Bird Survey (BBS) results for Tensleep and Worland Wyoming, with the mean number of birds observed per survey route from 1966 to 2009, arranged by descending averages.

Tensleep	No./rt.	Worland	No./rt.
Western Meadowlark	163.25	Western Meadowlark	88.29
Red-winged Blackbird	71	Lark Bunting	60
Lark Bunting	37.75	Horned Lark	28.57
Brewer's Blackbird	32.25	Mourning Dove	14.29
American Robin	28.25	Red-winged Blackbird	14
Common Grackle	26.75	Ring-necked Pheasant	10.57
European Starling	26.5	Lark Sparrow	7.14
Lark Sparrow	25.75	Common Grackle	5.43
Vesper Sparrow	18.5	Rock Wren	5.14
Sage Thrasher	11.75	Barn Swallow	5
Mourning Dove	11	Brewer's Sparrow	4.29
Brewer's Sparrow	11	American Robin	3.57
Rock Wren	10.5	Killdeer	3.43
Yellow Warbler	8.75	Say's Phoebe	3.14
House Sparrow	8.25	Sage Sparrow	3.14
Cliff Swallow	8	Grasshopper Sparrow	3.14
Barn Swallow	7.25	Common Nighthawk	2.71
Brown-headed Cowbird	6.75	Vesper Sparrow	2.43
American Goldfinch	6.5	Western Kingbird	2.29
Killdeer	4.5	Black-billed Magpie	1.86
Rock Pigeon	4	Mallard	1.71
Violet-green Swallow	4	Brewer's Blackbird	1.71
Black-billed Magpie	3.25	Clay-colored Sparrow	1.57
Common Nighthawk	3	Sage Thrasher	1.43
Tree Swallow	2.75	Brown-headed Cowbird	1.43
American Kestrel	2.5	House Sparrow	1.43
Say's Phoebe	2.5	Loggerhead Shrike	1.14
Mallard	2.25	American Crow	1
Western Wood-Pewee	2.25	Rock Pigeon	0.86
Eastern Kingbird	2.25	Greater Sage-Grouse	0.57
Sage Sparrow	2.25	Cliff Swallow	0.57
Yellow-head. Blackbird	2	Savannah Sparrow	0.57
Ring-necked Pheasant	1.75	Golden Eagle	0.43
Common Snipe	1.75	Common Snipe	0.43
Common Yellowthroat	1.75	Blue-winged Teal	0.29
Song Sparrow	1.75	Red-tailed Hawk	0.29

Table 1. (continued) BBS results for Tensleep and Worland

Tensleep	No./rt.	Worland	No./rt.
Western/Clark's Grebe	1.5	Eastern Kingbird	0.29
N. Rough-w. Swallow	1.25	Western Tanager	0.29
Gray Catbird	1.25	Lazuli Bunting	0.29
Cinnamon Teal	1	Green-winged Teal	0.14
Bullock's Oriole	1	Northern Harrier	0.14
House Finch	1	American Kestrel	0.14
Great Blue Heron	0.75	Prairie Falcon	0.14
Red-tailed Hawk	0.75	Sandhill Crane	0.14
Golden Eagle	0.75	Wilson's Phalarope	0.14
Lazuli Bunting	0.75	Northern Flicker	0.14
Northern Flicker	0.5	Bank Swallow	0.14
Common Raven	0.5	Canyon Wren	0.14
Turkey Vulture	0.25	Marsh Wren	0.14
Gadwall	0.25	Chipping Sparrow	0.14
Northern Shoveler	0.25		
Northern Harrier	0.25		
Spotted Sandpiper	0.25		
Wilson's Phalarope	0.25		
Belted Kingfisher	0.25		
Loggerhead Shrike	0.25		
House Wren	0.25		
Savannah Sparrow	0.25		
Black-headed Grosbeak	0.25		
Pine Siskin	0.25		

Table 2. North American Breeding Bird Survey (BBS) results for Dayton and Crazy Woman Canyon, Wyoming, with the mean number of birds observed per survey route from 1966 to 2009, arranged by descending averages.

Dayton	No./rt.	Crazy Woman	No./rt.
Red-winged Blackbird	230	American Robin	51.38
Western Meadowlark	171.18	Pine Siskin	45.29
European Starling	59	Brewer's Blackbird	39.62
American Robin	53.29	Ruby-crowned Kinglet	25.9
Brewer's Blackbird	27.88	Dark-eyed Junco	22.05
Common Grackle	27.12	Horned Lark	20.86
Common Snipe	23.71	Mountain Bluebird	16.62
Yellow Warbler	22.59	Chipping Sparrow	13.19
Savannah Sparrow	21	Red-winged Blackbird	10.95
Ring-necked Pheasant	20.82	Savannah Sparrow	10.14
Bobolink	20.59	Western Wood-Pewee	9.33
Vesper Sparrow	20.24	Vesper Sparrow	9
Brown-head. Cowbird	18.65	Yellow-rmpd. Warbler	8.71
Mourning Dove	16.29	Lincoln's Sparrow	7.24
Barn Swallow	16.29	Mountain Chickadee	7.19
Com. Yellowthroat	15.76	Cassin's Finch	7.14
House Sparrow	13.47	Western Meadowlark	7.14
Eastern Kingbird	11.29	Warbling Vireo	6.76
Killdeer	11.12	Brown-head. Cowbird	6.48
Cliff Swallow	10.82	White-crownd Sparrow	6.24
Western Wood-Pewee	7	Tree Swallow	6.05
American Goldfinch	6.53	Common Snipe	5.62
Yellow-hd. Blackbird	6.47	Wilson's Warbler	5.33
Northern Flicker	4.76	Red Crossbill	5.1
Mallard	4.53	Common Raven	3.76
American Kestrel	4.24	Song Sparrow	3.62
House Wren	4.18	Swainson's Thrush	3.14
Tree Swallow	3.94	Common Yellowthroat	3.1
Black-billed Magpie	3.65	Townsend's Solitaire	3
Willow Flycatcher	3.47	Dusky Flycatcher	2.57
"Traill's" Flycatcher	3.47	Hermit Thrush	2.43
Rock Pigeon	3.41	Black-capd. Chickadee	2.29
Canada Goose	2.65	Common Nighthawk	2.19
Gray Catbird	2.53	Mallard	2.1
Lazuli Bunting	2.53	Willow Flycatcher	2
N. Rough-wd Swallow	2.24	"Traill's" Flycatcher	2
Spotted Towhee	2.12	Brewer's Sparrow	1.71
Lark Sparrow	2.12	Orange-crd. Warbler	1.71
Warbling Vireo	2	Spotted Towhee	1.71
American Redstart	2	House Wren	1.62

Table 2. (continued) BBS results for Dayton and Crazy Woman Canyon

Dayton	No./rt.	Crazy Woman	No./rt.
Great Blue Heron	1.88	Least Flycatcher	1.52
Lark Bunting	1.88	Red-breasted Nuthatch	1.48
Bullock's Oriole	1.53	Violet-green Swallow	1.43
Common Nighthawk	1.35	Rock Wren	1.38
American Crow	1.35	Yellow Warbler	1.33
Red Crossbill	1.35	MacGillivray's Warbler	1.24
Least Flycatcher	1.24	Killdeer	1.1
Black-billed Cuckoo	1.18	Northern Flicker	1
Brewer's Sparrow	1.12	Cordilleran Flycatcher	1
Pine Siskin	1.12	Western Tanager	0.9
Song Sparrow	0.94	Barn Swallow	0.86
Black-capd Chickadee	0.82	Spotted Sandpiper	0.86
Northern Harrier	0.76	Clark's Nutcracker	0.71
Wild Turkey	0.76	Gray Jay	0.71
Say's Phoebe	0.76	Grasshopper Sparrow	0.67
Black-head. Grosbeak	0.76	Hairy Woodpecker	0.62
Grasshopper Sparrow	0.71	Plumbeous Vireo	0.57
Red-tailed Hawk	0.59	American Goldfinch	0.52
Yellow-breasted Chat	0.47	American Crow	0.48
Wilson's Phalarope	0.41	Veery	0.48
American Coot	0.35	American Kestrel	0.43
Western Kingbird	0.35	Lazuli Bunting	0.43
Cedar Waxwing	0.35	Olive-sided Flycatcher	0.43
Golden Eagle	0.29	Wilson's Phalarope	0.43
Veery	0.29	Downy Woodpecker	0.38
Chipping Sparrow	0.29	Golden Eagle	0.38
American Wigeon	0.24	Green-tailed Towhee	0.33
Spotted Sandpiper	0.24	Lark Sparrow	0.33
Belted Kingfisher	0.24	Sora	0.33
Downy Woodpecker	0.18	Cinnamon Teal	0.29
Common Raven	0.18	Cliff Swallow	0.29
Bank Swallow	0.18	Lesser Scaup	0.29
Pied-billed Grebe	0.12	Golden-crownd Kinglet	0.24
Western/Clark's Grebe	0.12	Red-naped Sapsucker	0.24
Cinnamon Teal	0.12	Red-tailed Hawk	0.24
Gray Partridge	0.12	Ring-necked Duck	0.24
Sharp-tailed Grouse	0.12	Sapsucker sp.	0.24
Sandhill Crane	0.12	Western/Clark's Grebe	0.24
Loggerhead Shrike	0.12	Green-winged Teal	0.19
Horned Lark	0.12	Hammond's Flycatcher	0.19
Lincoln's Sparrow	0.12	Northern Pintail	0.19
House Finch	0.12	Red-eyed Vireo	0.19

Table 2. (continued) BBS results for Dayton and Crazy Woman Canyon

Dayton	No./rt.	Crazy Woman	No./rt.
Turkey Vulture	0.06	American Coot	0.14
Wood Duck	0.06	House Finch	0.14
Green-winged Teal	0.06	Mourning Dove	0.14
Common Mergansr	0.06	White-brstd Nuthatch	0.14
Sharp-shinned Hawk	0.06	Black-head. Grosbeak	0.1
Sora	0.06	Clay-colored Sparrow	0.1
Upland Sandpiper	0.06	Common Grackle	0.1
Common Poorwill	0.06	Gray Catbird	0.1
Red-eyed Vireo	0.06	Great Horned Owl	0.1
Red-breasted Nuthatch	0.06	Northern Goshawk	0.1
Rock Wren	0.06	Sharp-shinned Hawk	0.1
Mountain Bluebird	0.06	White-throated Swift	0.1
Brown Thrasher	0.06	Black-billed Magpie	0.05
Ovenbird	0.06	Blue-winged Teal	0.05
MacGillvry's. Warbler	0.06	Brown Creeper	0.05
Clay-colored Sparrow	0.06	European Starling	0.05
Cassin's Finch	0.06	N. Rough-wd Swallow	0.05
		Northern Harrier	0.05
		Peregrine Falcon	0.05
		Pygmy Nuthatch	0.05
		3-toed Woodpecker	0.05
		Turkey Vulture	0.05

Table 3. North American Breeding Bird Survey (BBS) results for Arvada and Wyarno, Wyoming, with the mean number of birds observed per survey route from 1966 to 2009, arranged by descending averages.

Arvada	No./rt.	Wyarno	No./rt.
Western Meadowlark	230.47	Western Meadowlark	389.26
Mourning Dove	74.82	Red-winged Blackbird	135.9
European Starling	60.41	Lark Bunting	124.39
Western Kingbird	42.76	Mourning Dove	37.13
Cliff Swallow	42.65	Brown-headed Cowbird	37.1
Lark Bunting	34.94	American Robin	35.29
Red-winged Blackbird	20.12	Vesper Sparrow	33.16
Common Grackle	16.76	Cliff Swallow	26.32
Lark Sparrow	15.12	Spotted Towhee	24.1
Eastern Kingbird	14.94	Yellow Warbler	23.26
American Robin	14.53	Ring-necked Pheasant	23.13
Brewer's Blackbird	13.82	Eastern Kingbird	20.16
Northern Flicker	12.88	Lark Sparrow	18.19
House Wren	9.82	House Wren	17.58
Bullock's Oriole	9.24	Bullock's Oriole	17.52
American Kestrel	8.82	Common Grackle	15.55
Barn Swallow	8.65	Rock Wren	13.84
Killdeer	8.12	Brewer's Sparrow	13.42
N. Rough-wgd. Swallow	8.12	Barn Swallow	13.16
Yellow Warbler	7.59	Brewer's Blackbird	9.29
Tree Swallow	7.35	Yellow-head. Blackbird	9
Brown-headed Cowbird	7	Killdeer	8.55
Rock Wren	4.88	European Starling	7.94
Say's Phoebe	3.59	Say's Phoebe	5.58
Red-tailed Hawk	3.24	Black-headed Grosbeak	5.52
House Sparrow	2.94	Black-billed Magpie	5.48
Vesper Sparrow	2.71	Mallard	5.26
Loggerhead Shrike	2.65	American Goldfinch	4.55
Wild Turkey	2.47	Common Yellowthroat	4.48
Western Wood-Pewee	2.24	Western Kingbird	4.42
American Goldfinch	1.82	Northern Flicker	3.87
Common Nighthawk	1.76	Common Nighthawk	3.55
Mountain Bluebird	1.76	Red-tailed Hawk	3.23
Mallard	1.53	Loggerhead Shrike	3.1
Grasshopper Sparrow	1.41	Common Snipe	2.9
Greater Sage-Grouse	1.29	Western Wood-Pewee	2.48
Horned Lark	1.29	Gray Catbird	2.45
Bank Swallow	1.29	Wild Turkey	1.9
Chipping Sparrow	1.24	American Kestrel	1.87

Table 3. (continued) BBS results for Arvada and Wyarno, Wyoming

Arvada	No./rt.	Wyarno	No./rt.
Red-head. Woodpecker	1.18	Yellow-breasted Chat	1.84
Great Blue Heron	1.06	Brown Thrasher	1.45
Spotted Towhee	0.88	Blue-winged Teal	1.32
Ring-necked Pheasant	0.82	Mountain Bluebird	1.23
Brewer's Sparrow	0.82	Wilson's Phalarope	1.19
Northern Harrier	0.71	Northern Harrier	1.1
Cassin's Kingbird	0.71	Upland Sandpiper	1.06
Turkey Vulture	0.65	Black-billed Cuckoo	0.87
Least Flycatcher	0.65	Sage Thrasher	0.87
Canada Goose	0.59	Horned Lark	0.77
Brown Thrasher	0.53	Chipping Sparrow	0.77
Black-headed Grosbeak	0.53	Grasshopper Sparrow	0.68
Short-eared Owl	0.47	Gadwall	0.58
Upland Sandpiper	0.41	Greater Sage-Grouse	0.55
House Finch	0.35	Canada Goose	0.52
Golden Eagle	0.29	American Coot	0.45
Black-billed Magpie	0.29	Short-eared Owl	0.45
Black-capped Chickadee	0.29	Lazuli Bunting	0.45
Savannah Sparrow	0.29	Golden Eagle	0.42
Song Sparrow	0.29	Pied-billed Grebe	0.35
Gray Catbird	0.24	Great Horned Owl	0.35
Clay-colored Sparrow	0.24	Black-capped Chickadee	0.35
Blue-winged Teal	0.18	Savannah Sparrow	0.35
Gray Partridge	0.18	American Wigeon	0.32
Black-billed Cuckoo	0.18	Spotted Sandpiper	0.26
Great Horne Owl	0.18	N. Rough-wgd. Swallow	0.26
American Crow	0.18	Northern Shoveler	0.19
Common Yellowthroat	0.18	Cedar Waxwing	0.19
Field Sparrow	0.18	Song Sparrow	0.16
Swainson's Hawk	0.12	Sharp-tailed Grouse	0.13
Sharp-tailed Grouse	0.12	Ferruginous Hawk	0.1
American Avocet	0.12	Tree Swallow	0.1
Eastern Bluebird	0.12	Great Blue Heron	0.06
Yellow-head. Blackbird	0.12	Cinnamon Teal	0.06
Orchard Oriole	0.12	Northern Pintail	0.06
Hooded Merganser	0.06	Green-winged Teal	0.06
Ferruginous Hawk	0.06	Redhead	0.06
Hairy Woodpecker	0.06	Bald Eagle	0.06
Willow Flycatcher	0.06	Prairie Falcon	0.06
Willow/Alder Flycatcher	0.06	Yellow-billed Cuckoo	0.06
Eastern Phoebe	0.06	Yellow-rumped Warbler	0.06

Table 3. (continued) BBS results for Arvada and Wyarno, Wyoming

Arvada	No./rt.	Wyarno	No./rt.
Northern Mockingbird	0.06	Clay-colored Sparrow	0.06
Yellow-breasted Chat	0.06	Cooper's Hawk	0.03
Baltimore Oriole	0.06	Downy Woodpecker	0.03
		Dusky Flycatcher	0.03
		American Crow	0.03
		Swainson's Thrush	0.03
		American Redstart	0.03
		Indigo Bunting	0.03
		Bobolink	0.03

Table 4. Christmas Bird Count (CBC) results for Story/Big Horn, Sheridan, and Buffalo, with the total number of birds observed from 1990-1991 to 2009-2012 arranged in descending numerical totals among the 43 most abundant species.

Story/Big Horn	Total	Sheridan	Total	Buffalo	Total
Bohemian Waxwing	17666	Bohemian Waxwing	13190	European Starling	8129
Mallard	10531	European Starling	12886	Bohemian Waxwing	7112
American Crow	5633	Mallard	10624	Gray-cr. Rosy-Finch	4160
European Starling	4545	House Finch	8753	Mallard	3177
Black-capped Chick.	4100	House Sparrow	4072	House Finch	2484
Gray-cr. Rosy-Finch	3145	Canada Goose	2946	House Sparrow	2454
Pine Siskin	2401	Black-billed Magpie	2086	Black-billed Magpie	2402
Ring-necked Ph.	2093	Ring-necked Ph.	2083	American Tree Sp.	1848
House Finch	1779	Black-capped Chick.	1858	American Crow	1786
Evening Grosbeak	1407	American Robin	1710	Black-capped Chick.	1629
Rock Pigeon	1355	American Tree Sp.	1354	Canada Goose	1232
House Sparrow	1258	Sharp-tailed Grouse	1335	Common Raven	1103
Cedar Waxwing	840	Cedar Waxwing	1141	Rock Pigeon	945
Sharp-tailed Grouse	821	American Crow	980	Pine Siskin	748
American Tree Sp.	800	Northern Flicker	664	Evening Grosbeak	747
American Goldfinch	688	Gray Partridge	656	Common Goldeneye	733
Rough-legged Hawk	586	Common Goldeneye	569	Horned Lark	722
Dark-eyed Junco	567	Rough-legged Hawk	562	American Robin	716
Bald Eagle	462	Pine Siskin	558	Red-shafted Flicker	586
Black-billed Magpie	462	Gray-cr. Rosy-Finch	342	Gray Partridge	564
Junco/Pink-sided	459	Evening Grosbeak	294	Red-winged Black.	532
Cassin's Finch	438	American Goldfinch	292	Cedar Waxwing	448
American Robin	404	Bald Eagle	287	Rough-legged Hawk	385
Mountain Chick.	380	Red-tailed Hawk	270	Eurasian Coll.-dove	364
Gray Partridge	337	Horned Lark	236	Cassin's Finch	357
Common Redpoll	326	Golden Eagle	221	Junco/Slate-colored	351
White-breasted Nut.	323	Cassin's Finch	164	Sharp-tailed Grouse	346
Junco/Slate-colored	316	Eurasian Coll.-dove	163	Bald Eagle	288
Red-breasted Nut.	312	Junco/Slate-colored	141	American Goldfinch	279
Golden Eagle	282	Rock Pigeon	135	Ring-necked Pheasant	255
Common Raven	278	Downy Woodpecker	129	Golden Eagle	242
Downy Woodpecker	273	Common Raven	106	Greater Sage-Grouse	221
Red-shafted Flicker	260	Blue Jay	88	Mountain Chickadee	214
Hairy Woodpecker	183	Northern Shrike	80	Common Redpoll	180
Oregon Junco	171	Red-winged Blackbird	69	Clark's Nutcracker	173
Red-tailed Hawk	130	American Kestrel	66	Gadwall	168
Pygmy Nuthatch	104	Oregon Junco	60	Red Crossbill	151
Northern Flicker	93	Ring-necked Duck	58	Red-breasted Nuthatch	137
Red Crossbill	87	Townsend's Solitaire	57	Downy Woodpecker	130
Eurasian Coll.-dove	85	Dark-eyed Junco	55	American Coot	129
American Dipper	78	Brewer's Blackbird	52	White-breasted Nut.	122
Canada Goose	77	Mountain Chickadee	50	Pygmy Nuthatch	121
Greater Sage-Grouse	46	White-breasted Nuthatch	44	Oregon Junco	115

References

American Ornithologists' Union (A.O.U.). 1998. *The A.O.U. Checklist of North American Birds*. 7th ed. Washington, D.C. American Ornithologists' Union (Supplements in *Auk*, 117:847-856; 119:923–932; 120:923–931; 121:985–995; 122:1026–1031; 123:926–936; 124:1109–1115; 125:758–768; 126:705–714; 127:726–744; 128: 600–613; 129:573-588).

Anderson, D. 2013. Bighorn National Forest 2005 Plan Inventoried Roadless Area. Data provided by the office of the Bighorn National Forest.

Beauvais, G. 2001. Insular populations of vertebrates in Wyoming. Unpublished report, Wyoming Natural Diversity Database, Laramie, WY.

Bonham, D. M. and B. A. Cooper. 1986. *Birds of West-Central Montana*. Missoula, MT: Five Valleys Audubon Society.

Braun, C. E. 1980. Alpine bird communities of western North America: Implications for management and research. Pp. 280–291, in *Management of Western Forests and Grasslands for Nongame Birds* (R. M. DeGraaf and N. G. Tilghman, eds.). Ogden, UT: USDA Forest Service Gen. Tech. Report INT– 86.

Burkart, M. R. 1976. Pollen biogeography and late Quaternary vegetation history of the Bighorn Mountains, Wyoming. Ph.D. diss., Univ. of Iowa, Iowa City.

Chalfaun, A., K. Gerow, J. Carlisle, and L. Sanders. 2013. *Analysis of Temporal and Spacial Patterns of Raptor Nest Occupancy in Areas of Coal-bed Methane Development in the Powder River Basin, Wyoming*: Final Report to the BLM, Buffalo Field Office, Buffalo, Wyoming. 33 pp.

Clark, T. and M. R. Stromberg, 1987. *Mammals of Wyoming*. Lawrence, KS: Univ. of Kansas Museum of Natural History.

Dalton, N. H. 1906. *Geology of the Bighorn Mountains*. Washington, D.C.: U. S. Geol. Survey, Professional Paper 51.

Daubenmire, R. D. 1943. Vegetational zonation in the Rocky Mountains. *Bot. Rev.* 9:325–393.

DeGraaf, R. M. (Technical Coordinator). 1978. *Proceedings of the workshop on nongame bird habitat management in the coniferous forests of the western United States*. Portland, OR: USDA Forest Service Gen. Tech. Rep. PNW-65.

DeSante, D. and P. Pyle. 1986. *Distributional Checklist of North American Birds*. Lee Vining, CA: Artemisia Press.

Diem, K. and S. L. Zeveloff. 1980. Ponderosa pine bird communities. Pp. 170–197, in *Management of Western Forests and Grasslands for Nongame Birds* (R. M. DeGraaf and N. G. Tilghman, eds.), Ogden, UT: USDA Forest Service Gen. Tech. Report INT– 86.

Dorn, J. L. 1978. Wyoming Ornithology: A History and Bibliography with Species and Wyoming Area Indexes. Bureau of Land Management and Wyoming Game and Fish Department. 369pp.

Dorn, J. L., and R. D. Dorn. 1990. *Wyoming Birds*. Cheyenne, WY: Mountain West Publishing Co.

Dorn, R. D. 1977a. *Manual of the Vascular Plants of Wyoming.* 2 vol. New York, NY: Garland Pub. Co. 1,498 pp.

Dorn, R. D. 1977b. *Flora of the Black Hills.* Cheyenne, WY: Published by the author, 377 pp.

Dorn, R. D. 1986. *The Wyoming Landscape.* Cheyenne, WY: Mountain West Publishing.

Dorn, R. D. 2010. Landforms and vegetation. Pp. 25-27. In *Birds of Wyoming* (D. W. Faulkner) 2010. Greenwood Village, CO: Roberts & Co.

Downing, H. (ed.). 1990. Sheridan area birds, 1966-present. Sheridan, WY: Unpublished document.

Downing, H. (ed.). 1990. *Birds of North-Central Wyoming and the Bighorn National Forest.* Sheridan, WY: Published by the author. 98 pp.

Erlich, G. 1986. *The Solace of Open Spaces.* New York, N.Y: Penguin Books.

Faulkner, D. W. 2010. *Birds of Wyoming.* Greenwood Village, CO: Roberts & Co.

Fenneman, N. M. 1931. *Physiography of Western United States.* New York: McGraw Hill.

Flack, J. A. D. 1976. *Bird Populations of Aspen Forests in Western North America.* American Ornithologists' Union: *Ornithological Monographs* No. 19.

French, N. R. 1959. Distribution and migration of the Black Rosy Finch. *Condor* 61:18–29.

Froiland, S. G. 1990. *Natural History of the Black Hills and Badlands.* Sioux Falls, SD: Augustana College Center for Western Studies.

Hanni, D. J., J. Birek, C. White, R. Sparks and J. Blakesley. 2009. *Monitoring Wyoming's Birds: 2008 Field Report.* Brighton, CO: Rocky Mt. Bird Observatory. 91 pp.

Heidel, B. 2011. Endemic plants of the Bighorn Mountains. *Publ. Wyo. Native Plant Soc.* 30(2):1, 9.

Hein, D. 1980. Management of lodgepole pine for birds. Pp. 238–246, in *Workshop Proceedings: Management of Western Forests and Grasslands for Nongame Birds* (R. M. DeGraaf and N. G. Tilghman, eds.). Ogden, UT: USDA Forest Service Gen. Tech. Rep. INT-86.

Hurd, R. M. 1961. Grassland vegetation in the Bighorn Mountains. *Ecol.* 42:459–467.

Johnsgard, P. A. 1997. *The Avian Brood Parasites: Deception at the Nest*. New York: Oxford Univ. Press. 409 pp.

Johnsgard, P. A. 2002. *Grassland Grouse and their Conservation*. Washington, D.C.: Smithsonian Inst. Press.

Johnsgard, P. A. 2009a. *Birds of the Rocky Mountains*. Boulder, CO: Colorado Associated Univ. Press. Revised ed, Lincoln, NE: U. of Nebraska Digital Commons and Zea Press. http://digitalcommons.unl.edu/bioscibirdsrockymtns/1/, and Supplement: http://digitalcommons.unl.edu/bioscibirdsrockymtns/3/

Johnsgard, P. A. 2009b. *Birds of the Great Plains: Breeding Species and their Distribution*. Lincoln: Univ. of Nebraska Press. Revised edition, with a 2009 supplement. http://digitalcommons.unl.edu/bioscibirdsgreatplains/1/

Johnsgard, P. A. 2011. *Rocky Mountain Birds: Birding in the Central and Northern Rockies*. Lincoln, NE: U. of Nebraska Digital Commons and Zea Press. http://digitalcommons.unl.edu/zeabook/7/; hardcopy version: Raleigh, NC: Lulu Enterprises.

Johnsgard, P. A. 2013a. *Wings over the Great Plains: The Central Flyway*. Lincoln, NE: Digital Commons, Univ. of Nebraska-Lincoln Libraries, and Zea Press; hardcopy version: Raleigh, NC: Lulu Enterprises. 249 pp. http://digitalcommons.unl.edu/zeabook/13/

Johnsgard, P. A. 2013b. *Yellowstone Wildlife: Ecology and Natural History of the Greater Yellowstone Ecosystem*. Boulder: Colorado Univ. Press. 250 pp.

Johnson, J. R, and G. E. Larson. 1999. *Grassland Plants of South Dakota and the Northern Great* Plains. Brookings, SD: South Dakota State Univ., Agric. Ext. Station Publ. B566 (rev.).

Johnson, R. E. 2002. Black Rosy-Finch (*Leucosticte atrata*). In *The Birds of North America,* No. 78(A. Poole and F. Gill, eds.). The Birds of North America, Inc. Philadelphia: The Academy of Natural Sciences, and Washington, DC: the American Ornithologists' Union. 28 pp.

Johnson, R. R., L. T. Haight, M. F. Riffey, and J. M. Simpson. 1980. Steppe-steppe bird populations. Pp. 98–112, in *Workshop Proceedings: Management of Western Forests and Grasslands for Nongame Birds* (R. M. DeGraaf and N. G. Tilghman, eds.). Ogden, UT: USDA Forest Service Gen. Tech. Rep. INT-86.

Kessinger, J. T. 1972. Bird checklist, Sheridan, 1966 to 1972. Sheridan, WY: Unpublished manuscript.

Knick, S. T., and J.W. Connelly. 2011. *Greater Sage-Grouse: Ecology and Conservation of a Landscape Species and Its Habitats*. Berkeley, CA: University of California Press.

Knight, D. 1994. *Mountains and Plains: The Ecology of Wyoming Landscapes.* New Haven, CT: Yale Univ. Press.

Knopf, F. L., R. R. Johnson, T. Rich, F. B. Sampson, and R. C. Szaro. 1988. Conservation of riparian ecosystems in the United States. *Wilson Bulletin* 100:272–284.

Lageson, D. R., and D. R. Spearing. 1988. *Roadside Geology of Wyoming.* Missoula, MT: Mountain Press Publishing Company.

Larson, G. E., and J. R. Johnson. 1999. *Plants of the Black Hills and Bear Lodge Mountains.* Brookings, SD: South Dakota State Univ., Agric. Ext. Station Publ. B-732.

Mathews, D. 2003. *Rocky Mountain Natural History: Grand Teton to Jasper.* Portland, OR: Raven Editions.

Meyer, C. B., D. H. Knight, G. C. Dillon, and K. Gregory. 2005. Historic range of variability for upland vegetation in the Bighorn National Forest, Wyoming. Gen Tech. Rpt. RMRS-GTR-140, Fort Collins, CO: Department of Agriculture, Forest Service, Rocky Mountain Research Station.

McCreary, O. 1937. *Wyoming Bird Life.* Minneapolis: Burgess Publishing Company

Mengel, R. M., and J. S. Mengel. 1952. Sprague Pipit and Black Rosy Finch in north-central Wyoming in summer. *Condor* 54:61–62.

Montgomery, G. L. 1996. *Riparian Areas: Reservoirs of Diversity.* U.S. Natural Resources Conservation Service Working Paper No. 13. Lincoln, NE. Northern Plains Regional Office.

Molvar, E. 1999. *Hiking Wyoming's Cloud Peak Wilderness.* Helena, MT: The Globe Pequot Press.

Nicholoff, S. H. (compiler). 2003. *Wyoming Bird Conservation Plan, Version 2.0.* Lander, WY: Wyoming Partners in Flight & Wyoming Game and Fish Department.

Orabona, A., S. Patla, L. Van Fleet, M. Grenier, B. Oakleaf & Z. Walker. 2009. *Atlas of Birds, Mammals, Amphibians and Reptiles in Wyoming.* Lander, WY: Wyoming Game and Fish Department. 227 pp. http://wgfd.wyo.gov/web2011/Departments/Wildlife/pdfs/WILDLIFE_ANIMALATLAS0000328.pdf

Palmer, R. S. (ed.). 1978. *Handbook of North American Birds,* Vol.1. Loons through Flamingos. New Haven and London: Yale University Press.

Paulin, K. M., J. J. Cook, and S. R. Dewey. 1999. *Pinyon-Juniper Woodlands as Sources of Avian Diversity.* Denver, CO: USDA Forest Service Proceedings RMRS-P-9.

Peterson, R. A. 1995. *The South Dakota Breeding Bird Atlas.* Aberdeen, SD: South Dakota Ornithologists' Union.

Porter, C. L. 1962. Vegetation zones in Wyoming. *Univ. Wyo. Publ.* 27:6–12.

Reed, R. M. 1976. Coniferous forest habitat types of the Wind River Mountains, Wyoming. *Am. Midl. Nat.* 95:159–175.

Rich, T. D., C. J. Beardmore, H. Berlanga, P. J. Blancher, M. S. W. Bradstreet, G. S. Butcher, D. W. Demarest, E. H. Dunn, W. C. Hunter, E. E. Iñigo-Elias, J. A. Kennedy, A. M. Martell, A. O. Panjabi, D. N. Pashley, K. V. and C. Rosenberg. 2004. *North American Landbird Conservation Plan.* Ithaca, NY: Partners in Flight and Cornell Univ. Laboratory of Ornithology.

Rosenberg, K. 2004. *Partners in Flight Continental Priorities and Objectives Defined at the State and Bird Conservation Region Levels.* Ithaca, NY. Partners in Flight and Cornell Univ. Laboratory of Ornithology. 33 pp.

Scott, V. F., J. A. Whelan and P. L. Svoboda. 1980. Cavity-nesting birds and forest management. Pp. 31–324, in *Workshop Proceedings: Management of Western Forests and Grasslands for Nongame Birds* (R. M. DeGraaf and N. G. Tilghman, eds.). Ogden, UT: USDA Forest Service Gen. Tech. Rep. INT-86.

Scott, O. K. 1993. *A Birder's Guide to Wyoming.* Colorado Springs, CO: American Birding Association.

Snoke, A. W. 1995. *Geology of Wyoming.* Memoir #5. Cheyenne, WY: Geological Society of Wyoming.

Tallman, D. A., D. L. Swanson, and J. S. Palmer. 2002. *Birds of South Dakota.* Aberdeen: So. Dakota Ornithologists' Union.

Urbanek, M. 1988. *Wyoming Place Names.* Missoula, MT: Mountain Press.

Whitney, N. R. 1971. Bird species observed Bighorn National Forest Primitive Area, 1967, 1968, 1970, 1971. Rapid City, SD: Unpublished manuscript.

Winters, D. S. 2004. Aquatic, Riparian, and Wetland Ecosystem Assessment: Denver, CO. Bighorn National Forest, Wyoming.

Wyoming Game and Fish Department. 2008. *Wyoming Bird Checklist.* Lander, WY: Wyoming Game and Fish Department. 15 pp.

Index to Species

Obsolete names and names given distinctive subspecies are indicated with parentheses, Pages containing illustrations are identified by *italics*. The Appendix is not indexed.

American (Water) Pipit, 21
American Avocet, *109*, **110**,
American Bittern, **86**
American Coot, 29, 55, 56, **103**
American Crow, **161**
American Dipper, 21, 26, 38, 59, ***179***
American Goldfinch, **229**
American Golden-Plover, **107**
American Kestrel, 34, 42, 44, **146**
American Pipit, 32, 35, **191**
American Redstart, 33, 49, 50, **200**
American Robin, 24, **187**
American Three-toed Woodpecker, 63, **144**
American Tree Sparrow, **206**
American White Pelican, **85**
American Wigeon, 56, **67**
Anna's Hummingbird, **139**
Ash-throated Flycatcher, 25, **152**
Audubon's (=Yellow-rumped) Warbler, 24, **202**

Baird's Sandpiper, 115, **116**
Baird's Sparrow, **209**
Bald Eagle, 34, 38, 63, **97**
Baltimore (Northern) Oriole, **223**
Band-tailed Pigeon, **125**
Bank Swallow, **166**
Barn Owl, 34, *129*
Barn Swallow, 45, 62, **166**
Barred Owl, **132**
Barrow's Goldeneye, **73**
Belted Kingfisher, 38, ***140***
Bewick's Wren, **232**
Black Scoter, **71**
Black Rosy-Finch, 21, 23, 26, 32, 35, **225**
Black Swift, **231**
Black Tern, **121**
Black-and-White Warbler, **198**
Black-bellied Plover, **107**
Black-billed Cuckoo, **127**
Black-billed Magpie, **160**
Blackburnian Warbler, **201**

Black-backed Woodpecker, 63
Black-capped Chickadee, **168**
Black-chinned Hummingbird, **138**
Black-crowned Night-Heron, *86*, **88**
Black-headed Grosbeak, **217**
Black-necked Stilt, **109**
Blackpoll Warbler, **202**
Black-shouldered Kite,
Black-throated Blue Warbler, **202**
Black-throated Green Warbler, **232**
Blue Grosbeak, **217**
Blue Jay, *158*, **159**
Blue-gray Gnatcatcher, ***177***
Blue-winged Teal, **68**
Blue-winged Warbler, **198**
Bobolink, **219**
Bohemian Waxwing, **193**
Bonaparte's Gull, **120**
Boreal Chickadee, **232**
Boreal Owl, **133**
Brambling, **224**
Brewer's Blackbird, **221**
Brewer's Sparrow, **207**
Broad-tailed Hummingbird, **139**
Broad-winged Hawk, 99
Brown Creeper, 24, 38, *172*. **173**
Brown Thrasher, 33, *188*, **189**
Brown-headed Cowbird, **222**
Buff-breasted Sandpiper, **117**
Bufflehead, **72**
Bullock's (Northern) Oriole, 26, 44, 45, **223**
Burrowing Owl, 34, **131**
Bushtit, **232**

Calliope Hummingbird, 26, 32, 38, 49, 50, 61, *138*, **139**
Cackling Goose, 65
California Gull, **120**
Canada Goose, 27, 40, 44, 55, 63, **65**
Canvasback, **69**
Canyon (Brown) Towhee, **232**
Canyon Wren, 33, 34, 48, 60, **175**

247

Cape May Warbler, **232**
Caspian Tern, **121**
Cassin's Finch, 24, 38, **226**
Cassin's Kingbird, **153**
Cattle Egret, **87**
Cedar Waxwing, 38, *193*, **194**
Chestnut-collared Longspur, **196**
Chestnut-sided Warbler, 48, **201**
Chimney Swift, **136**
Chukar, **76**
Chipping Sparrow, 25, 46, 62, **206**
Cinnamon Teal, **68**
Clark's Grebe, **83**
Clark's Nutcracker, 24, 33, 47, 48, 63, **160**
Clay-colored Sparrow, **207**
Cliff Swallow, 62, **166**
Common Goldeneye, **72**
Common Grackle, **222**
Common Loon, *79*, **80**
Common Merganser, **73**
Common Nighthawk, *134*
Common Poorwill, **135**
Common Raven, 33, **161**
Common Redpoll, **228**
Common Tern, **121**
Common Yellowthroat, 37, 55, 200
Cooper's Hawk, 24, 25, 34, 38, **98**
Cordilleran Flycatcher, 26, *149*, **151**

Dark-eyed Junco, 24, 32, 35, 62, **213**
Dickcissel, 25, **217**
Double-crested Cormorant, 54, *84*
Downy Woodpecker, **143**
Dunlin, **117**
Dusky (Blue) Grouse, 25, 32, 59, *75*, **77**
Dusky Flycatcher, 150, **151**

Eared Grebe, **82**
Eastern Bluebird, 33, **184**
Eastern Kingbird, 45, **153**
Eastern Phoebe, **152**
Eastern Screech-Owl, 25, 130
Eurasian Collared-Dove, **126**
Eurasian Wigeon, 56, **67**
European Starling, *190*
Evening Grosbeak, 33, 63, **229**

Ferruginous Hawk, 34, **100**
Forster's Tern, *119*,
Fox Sparrow, **210**
Franklin's Gull, **120**

Gadwall, 44, 56, **67**
Golden Eagle, 34, 35, 44, 55, 60, *96*, **101**
Golden-crowned Kinglet, 33, *181*
Golden-crowned Sparrow, **212**
Grasshopper Sparrow, 44, **210**
Gray Catbird, **188**
Gray Jay, 33, **159**
Gray Partridge, **75**
Gray-cheeked Thrush, **185**
Gray-crowned Rosy-Finch, 23, 38, **225**
Gray-headed (Dark-eyed) Junco, **214**
Great Blue Heron, 38, 42, 45, **87**
Great Egret, **87**
Great Gray Owl, **132**
Great Horned Owl, 34, 48, **131**
Greater Sage-Grouse, 26, 33, **77**
Greater Scaup, **70**
Greater White-fronted Goose, **64**
Greater Yellowlegs, **112**
Green Heron, **88**
Green-tailed Towhee, 25, **205**
Green-winged Teal, **69**
Gyrfalcon, **147**

Hairy Woodpecker, **143**
Hammond's flycatcher, 32
Harlan's (= Red-tailed) Hawk, **99**
Harlequin Duck, 59, **71**
Harris's Sparrow, **212**
Hermit Thrush, 24, **186**
Herring Gull, 54, **121**
Hoary Redpoll, **228**
Hooded Merganser, 55, *64*, **73**
Horned Grebe, **82**
Horned Lark, 21, 25, 26, 44, *162*, **163**
House Finch, 226, **227**
House Sparrow, ***230***
House Wren, **175**
Hudsonian Godwit, **114**

Indigo Bunting, 26, 33, **217**

Killdeer, **108**
Krider's (= Red-tailed) Hawk, **100**

Lapland Longspur, **195**
Lark Bunting, **209**
Lark Sparrow, *205*, **208**
Lazuli Bunting, *215*, **217**
Least Flycatcher, 38, 150, **151**
Least Sandpiper, **116**

Index to Species

Least Tern, **121**
LeConte's Sparrow, **210**
Lesser Golden-Plover,
Lesser Goldfinch, **229**
Lesser Scaup, **70**
Lesser Yellowlegs, **113**
Lewis' Woodpecker, 24, 63, *141*
Lincoln's Sparrow, 33, **211**
Loggerhead Shrike, *154*, **155**
Long-billed Curlew, 25, **114**
Long-billed Dowitcher, **117**
Long-eared Owl, 34, **132**
Long-tailed Duck, **72**

MacGillivray's Warbler, 25, 33, 48, 50, **199**
Magnolia Warbler, **201**
Mallard, 40, 44, 56, **67**
Marbled Godwit, **114**
Marsh Wren, *174*. **176**
McCown's Longspur, *195,* **196**
Merlin, **147**
Mississippi Kite, **97**
Mountain Bluebird, 24, 25, 35, 38, 41, 48, 60, 62, *183,* **184**
Mountain Chickadee, 24, 32, 49, 50, 60, 62, **169**
Mourning Dove, *125,* **126**
Myrtle (= Yellow-rumped) Warbler) **202**

Nashville Warbler, **199**
Nelson's Sparrow, **232**
Northern Bobwhite, **231**
Northern Cardinal, **216**
Northern Flicker, 38, **144**
Northern Goshawk, *98*
Northern Harrier, 34, 42, 46, 55, **97**
Northern Mockingbird, **189**
Northern Parula, **200**
Northern Pintail, 56, **68**
Northern Pygmy-Owl, 25, **131**
Northern Rough-winged Swallow, 62, **165**
Northern Saw-whet Owl, 25, *130,* **133**
Northern Shoveler, 56, **69**
Northern Shrike, **155**
Northern Waterthrush, **197**

Olive-sided Flycatcher, 32, **149**
Orange-crowned Warbler, 33, **199**
Orchard Oriole, **223**
Oregon (= Dark-eyed) Junco, **214**
Osprey, 45, 56, 63, *94,* **95**

Ovenbird, 24, 33, 50, 51, **197**

Pacific Loon, **80**
Palm Warbler, 202
Parasitic Jaeger, *122*
Pectoral Sandpiper, **116**
Peregrine Falcon, 32, 34, *146,* **148**
Philadelphia Vireo, **157**
Pied-billed Grebe, 27, 29, 55, **81**
Pine Grosbeak, 32, **226**
Pine Siskin, 25, 33, 62, **228**
Pine Warbler, **232**
Pink-sided (= Dark-eyed) Junco, **213**
Pinyon Jay, **159**
Piping Plover, **107**
Plumbeous Vireo, 33, **156**
Prairie Falcon, 34, 44, 60, **148**
Purple Finch, 226, **227**
Purple Martin. **165**
Pygmy Nuthatch, 24, 33, **172**

Red Crossbill, 23, 24, 33, 63, *224,* **227,** 228
Red Knot, **115**
Red Phalarope, **118**
Red-breasted Merganser, **74**
Red-breasted Nuthatch, 24, 33, 50, **170**
Red-eyed Vireo, 33, *156,* **157**
Redhead, **69**
Red-headed Woodpecker, 24, 26, **142**
Red-naped Sapsucker, 25, 38, **143**
Red-necked Grebe, **82**
Red-necked Phalarope, **118**
Red-tailed Hawk, 34, 45, 55, **99**
Red-throated Loon, 54, 79
Red-winged Blackbird, 37, 53, *219,* **220,** 221
Ring-billed Gull, 54, **120**
Ring-necked Duck, **70**
Ring-necked Pheasant, 37, **76**
Rock Pigeon (Rock Dove), **125**
Rock Wren, 34, 48, **174**
Rose-breasted Grosbeak, **216**
Ross's Goose, **65**
Rough-legged Hawk, 38, 55, **100**
Ruby-crowned Kinglet, 24, 33, 38, 50, 62, **182**
Ruby-throated Hummingbird, **138**
Ruddy Duck, **74**
Ruddy Turnstone, **115**
Ruffed Grouse, 25, 59, **76**
Rufous Hummingbird, 61, **139**
Rusty Blackbird, **221**

Sabine's Gull, **119**
Sage Sparrow, 26, 62, **208**
Sage Thrasher, 26, **189**
Sanderling, *111*,
Sandhill Crane, 26, 32, 42, 44, 45, 46, ***104***
Savannah Sparrow, **209**
Say's Phoebe, 44. **152**
Scarlet Tanager, **216**
Semipalmated Plover, *106, 107*
Semipalmated Sandpiper, **115**
Sharp-shinned Hawk, 24, 25, **98**
Sharp-tailed Grouse, 41, 50, **78**
Short-billed Dowitcher, **231**
Short-eared Owl, 34, **132**
Slate-colored (= Dark-eyed) Junco, **213**
Snow Bunting, **196**
Snow Goose, 63, **65**
Snowy Egret, **87**
Snowy Owl, 131
Solitary Sandpiper, **112**
Solitary Vireo,
Song Sparrow, 26, 60, **211**
Sooty Grouse, 78
Sora, 27, 55, **103**
Spotted Sandpiper, **111**
Spotted Towhee, **206**
Sprague's Pipit, *191*, *192*
Steller's Jay, **159**
Stilt Sandpiper, **117**
Surf Scoter, 54, **71**
Swainson's Hawk, 34, **99**
Swainson's Thrush, 24, 33, 48, **186**
Swamp Sparrow, **212**

Tennessee Warbler, 48, **198**
Townsend's Solitaire, 33, 48, 60, 61, 62, **185**
Townsend's Warbler, **203**
Tree Swallow, 26, 40, *164*, **165**
Trumpeter Swan, **65**
Tundra Swan, 54, 56, **66**
Turkey Vulture, 34, 50, *92*, **93**

Upland Sandpiper, 25, 44, 55, **113**

Varied Thrush, **187**
Veery, **185**
Vesper Sparrow, 44, 46, 55, **207**
Violet-green Swallow, 25, 33, 59, 61, 62, **165**
Virginia Rail, 27, 55, ***102***
Virginia's Warbler, **199**

Warbling Vireo, 25, 26, 44, 60, **167**
Western Bluebird, **184**
Western Flycatcher,
Western Grebe, 54, *81,* **82**
Western Kingbird, 45, **153**
Western Meadowlark, 25, 44, 45, 61, **220**
Western Sandpiper, 115
Western Screech-Owl, 131
Western Scrub-Jay, 25, **160**
Western Tanager, 33, 49 50, 60, **215**
Western Wood-Pewee, 25, 49, 61, **150**
Whimbrel, **113**
White Ibis, **91**
White-breasted Nuthatch, 24, 38, *170*, **172**
White-crowned Sparrow, 21, 33, **212**
White-faced Ibis, *90,* **91**
White-rumped Sandpiper,
White-tailed Kite, **231**
White-tailed Ptarmigan, 32, **231**
White-throated Sparrow, **212**
White-throated Swift, 48, *136,* **137**
White-winged (= Dark-eyed) Junco, **213**
White-winged Crossbill, 23, 32, 63, **228**
White-winged Scoter, 54, **72**
Whooping Crane, **105**
Wild Turkey, 48, **78**
Willet, **112**
Williamson's Sapsucker, 32, **142**
Willow Flycatcher, 26, **150**
Wilson's (Common) Snipe, **117**
Wilson's Phalarope, 118
Wilson's Warbler, **203**
Winter Wren, **175**
Wood Duck, 40, **66**
Wood Thrush, **187**

Yellow Rail, **102**
Yellow Warbler, 26, 37, 40, 42, 45, 60, **201**
Yellow-bellied Sapsucker, **232**
Yellow-billed Cuckoo, 26, ***127***
Yellow-billed Loon, **80**
Yellow-breasted Chat, 26, **203**
Yellow-breasted Sapsucker, 143
Yellow-crowned Night-Heron, **88**
Yellow-headed Blackbird, 37, **221**
Yellow-rumped Warbler, 24, 49, 50, 62, *197,* **202**

About the Authors

Jacqueline Canterbury earned her Bachelor degrees at the University of Washington and The Evergreen College, and Masters and Ph.D. degrees from the University of Nebraska-Lincoln with emphasis in physiology and neuroscience. Dr. Canterbury acquired a passion for birds in college and subsequently developed a conservation strategy for non-game birds for the state of Nebraska, and worked as a biologist studying birds on the Tongass National Forest in southeast Alaska. She has always been actively involved in conservation. Jackie is currently teaching in the Biology Department at Sheridan College in Sheridan Wyoming.

Paul A. Johnsgard is Foundation Professor Emeritus at the University of Nebraska–Lincoln. Paul is the author of more than 60 books, including two additional books on Rocky Mountain birds that are available from the University of Nebraska's Digital Commons library (see Johnsgard citations 2009a & 2011).

The University of Nebraska–Lincoln does not discriminate
based on gender, age, disability, race, color,
religion, marital status, veteran's status,
national or ethnic origin,
or sexual orientation.